RECOVERING TOGETHER

A STEP-BY-STEP PROGRAM

RECOVERING TOGETHER

*How to Help an Alcoholic
Without Hurting Yourself*

Arthur Wassmer, Ph.D.

An Owl Book

Henry Holt and Company · New York

Published by Henry Holt and Company, Inc., 115 West 18th Street
New York, New York 10011.
Published in Canada by Fitzhenry & Whiteside Limited
195 Allstate Parkway, Markham, Ontario L3R 4T8.

Library of Congress Cataloging-in-Publication Data
Wassmer, Arthur C.
Recovering together : how to help an alcholic without hurting
yourself / Arthur Wassmer.—1st Owl book ed.
p. cm.
"An Owl book." Originally published: New York : St. Martin's
Press, 1989.
Includes bibliographical references (p. 308).
ISBN 0-8050-1328-8 (alk. paper)
1. Alcholics—Rehabilitation. 2. Co-dependence (Psychology)
I. Title.
HV5275.W37 1990
362.29'28—dc20 90-4481
CIP

Henry Holt books are available at special discounts
for bulk purchases for sales promotions, premiums,
fund-raising, or educational use. Special editions
or book excerpts can also be created to specification.
For details contact:
Special Sales Director, Henry Holt and Company, Inc.,
115 West 18th Street, New York, New York 10011.

First published in hardcover by St. Martin's Press in 1989.

First Owl Book Edition—1990

Printed in the United States of America
Recognizing the importance of preserving the written word,
Henry Holt and Company, Inc., by policy, prints all of its
first editions on acid-free paper. ∞

1 3 5 7 9 10 8 6 4 2

For Holly

CONTENTS

ACKNOWLEDGMENTS

I want to express my gratitude to the following people, who are just some of those who are responsible for this book.

To Joy Howard, my "mom," and to Bobbi St. John, my "favorite aunt," for their love and support through the years.

To Walter Wassmer, my father, for being the man that he is.

To Marcy Ofrancia, whose patient tolerance and quiet support have almost made me believe it's possible to have a relationship and write a book at the same time.

To my friends and partners in practice, Reba Baudino, Susan Perry, Lynn Garvey, Theresa Nuccio, and Kim Pickett, for keeping my consciousness about addiction and codependence raised every day.

To Dr. Angelina Di Fazio, clinical director of the Charter Nightingale Hospital in London, for providing the emotional and intellectual stimulation that generated the energy to write.

To Dr. James R. Milam, for being my friend and mentor over the years, and for his work, which has saved so many thousands of lives.

To my friends and colleagues in the alcoholism and addictions field, especially Val Roney, Susan Palmer, Jan Chiles, Jacque Wallace, Chandra Frederickson Smith, George Wolfe, Jim McClure, David Dixon, Ginny Gustafson, Rebecca McLeish, and the dozens of other addictions professionals who have been so willing to teach me and share their work.

To my patients, who have trusted me to share in their lives. They have been my greatest teachers.

INTRODUCTION:

A Personal Story

I met her in the fall of 1972. She was beautiful, brilliant, talented, and perhaps the shiest person I had ever encountered. I was drawn to her with a power and urgency that I had never experienced. I stepped into her office at about 11:00 A.M. to introduce myself, and by 2:00 that afternoon I, who am normally somewhat reserved and conservative, was telling her that I loved her.

So began ten of the most passionate, agonizing, and ultimately tragic years of my life.

I had begun graduate studies in psychology the previous year, and I was thrilled with the sophisticated, intellectual world of the university. We worked hard, studied hard, and played hard. And when we played hard, we drank hard (or at least those of us who didn't use marijuana did!).

She was a perfect companion and lover for me. Her great intelligence stimulated my mind and her great beauty stimulated my body. On one of our first dates, we went skiing. At the top of the mountain, she drew a hip flask from her parka and offered it to me, and I thought, "What a woman!" Later I was to brag to my friends that not only was my girl bright and beautiful, but she could "drink like a man!"

Our love deepened and grew, and in the course of time we moved in together. In the fashion of the times, we were firmly convinced that marriage was a dead institution and that our commitment to each other would be meaningless if it were not free.

We found, as most young couples do, that we had differences in values, standards, and life-style preferences that led to frequent disagreements. But one issue over which we never disagreed was the role of drinking in our lives. It was pleasurable, fostered quiet times of intense intellectual and emotional conversation, was often the prelude to lovemaking, and generally fit with our image of ourselves as chic, sophisticated, upwardly mobile young professionals.

It seems ironic in retrospect that two graduate students in the field of psychology should have had such a cavalier attitude toward a potentially dangerous drug that has since been recognized as causing the nation's gravest medical problem. But those times, just a few short years ago, were very different from now in awareness of the dangers of alcohol. Never, in seven years of graduate training in psychology, did I hear a single lecture, read a single research study, or glean a single thought about alcoholism that made a whit of sense. We were warned that alcoholic patients were difficult to treat, that they suffered from some kind of "underlying personality disorder" that made them "self-destructive" and "psychopathic," but generally we preferred not to talk about alcoholism, because the real fact was that none of us even knew what it was, let alone how to treat it.

The only real exposure to alcoholism we had was from our professors, some of whom, in retrospect, I see were actively alcoholic. Every Friday afternoon saw the convening of our "Departmental Symposium" in the hallowed halls of our local pub, where we would drink late into the evening and debate the "Pressing Questions Facing Psychology Today" (Alcoholics Anonymous members will recognize the less academic version of this kind of discussion as "Solving the Problems of the World"). Several of the faculty could be relied upon to become drunk, and it fell to loyal students to get those who passed out safely home and into bed. The chairman of my doctoral committee took me to lunch prior to my oral examination and treated me to three double martinis to "conquer my nerves" before appearing for the examination. It was a miracle that I didn't conquer seven years of study!

Fortunately, my own drinking moderated significantly when

I left the university to enter clinical practice. I say fortunately, because I believe that had I been unlucky enough to have inherited the metabolic and genetic predisposition to alcoholism, I would surely have become alcoholic during this phase of my life. Dr. James R. Milam, author of *Under the Influence* (New York: Bantam, 1983) and now professional consultant to the Viewpoint Recovery Center in Seattle, cites examples of subcultural groups (for example, soldiers in combat) in which everyone drinks in alcoholic fashion, but many of whom revert to more moderate drinking habits when the circumstances become more normal, less stressful, and less encouraging to drinking.

In retrospect, I see that this change in my drinking habits was the beginning of real troubles between my lover and me. We moved to a nice new home in the suburbs, where I had gone into practice. Two years behind me in her educational career, my lover was still immersed in the university world by day, a world full of excitement, challenge, stimulation, and alcohol. But she returned each evening to the more staid and pedestrian life of the middle-class suburbs. She began to express resentment toward me because I was unwilling to drink large amounts of alcohol with her, or go to drinking parties with her fellow university students, or sit up late into the night solving the problems of the world. Increasingly, the "high times" of student life held more appeal for her than our more pharmacologically normal workaday life. Our arguing increased, she began to stay later and later at the university, and to come home drunk more often.

I see now that at this point in the development of her illness, much of the appeal that the student environment held for my lover lay in its encouragement of heavy drinking. Her drinking, which was continuing to increase in both quantity and frequency, still did not seem abnormal in the context of graduate-student life. In the context of our home and community, however, it was becoming increasingly apparent that she had a developing problem. Nevertheless, we seldom argued over her drinking itself.

Nothing in my experience or training would have led me to recognize a drinking problem, and she had been a drinking woman as long as I had known her. The increase in both the quantity and frequency of her drinking was gradual, and it simply did not occur to me that a growing addiction to alcohol could be the cause of her restless dissatisfaction with our life, and the real reason for her attraction to the "fast lane."

The tensions between us continued to grow. I had changed from a drinking buddy to a disapproving parental figure, full of judgments and opinions about her life. I was threatened by her attraction to the "party life," and by her involvement with university friends and social life, of which I was no longer a part. She experienced me as increasingly stuffy, boring, and disapproving. Our conflicts and disagreements became more frequent and more intense, and finally we parted after four years together.

It did not take long for us both to realize that although we did not seem able to live together, our love for each other just would not go away. Each of us became involved in several short, serial relationships and even, for each of us, a longer-term more involved relationship. During our separation we saw each other often and simply demanded that our respective partners accept our presence in each other's life. When she graduated from her doctoral program, it seemed natural for me to take her into my clinical practice as a partner.

She was an extremely talented "natural" therapist, whose patients quickly came to love her with an intensity that amazed me. She impressed local physicians, who referred patients to her in droves. She still liked to drink as much as ever, and several times a week pressed to "stop off for a pop" after leaving work. She had become romantically involved during this time with a man who was both a heavy drinker and a cocaine user, and I became increasingly concerned as her personal life became consumed with nightly drinking-and-drugging parties.

Over the course of time, cracks began to appear in the polish of her professional life. Sometimes she was late for morning office hours. Her clinical notes became vague and sloppy. On those occasions when we would meet for pre-office breakfasts, she often seemed ill and out of sorts. I was shocked and disapproving when she began at these breakfast meetings to have a Bloody Mary or a screwdriver, but the drink seemed to improve her mood, and she never seemed to be affected, so I dismissed my concern as fuddy-duddyism.

She came to me in tears one day to tell me that she had to end her relationship with the man she had been living with. Neither her body nor her mind, she feared, could stand much longer the life-style of constant alcohol and drug consumption, the all-night parties, and the fear and paranoia of illegal substances. She was not yet addicted to cocaine but felt she would become addicted if she continued to live with him.

I was overwhelmed with feelings of compassion, and with them came all the feelings of love and attraction I had held so long in suspension. I had, a half year earlier, ended my "interim" relationship, and I immediately proposed that she collect her things and move in with me, at least until she made other arrangements.

I was shocked by her condition. She was physically rundown by the marathon of professional responsibilities during the day and drugs and alcohol by night. She had developed anemia and had stopped menstruating. She was shaky and had nausea much of the time. Emotionally, she was depressed and anxious. Though her career showed great promise, she seemed to have little hope or joy about her life. Looking back, I see that she was suffering from alcohol toxicity, which has profound mental and emotional symptoms as well as physical symptoms, but I had no way of understanding that at the time.

Outsiders are often amazed that the spouse and family of the alcoholic cannot seem to see what is going on in front of their very eyes. Alcoholism counselors attribute this blindness to "denial" (I just don't want to believe it), and certainly denial does play an important role. But other factors also play a role. Simple ignorance is a major factor. Here I was with a Ph.D. in psychology living with a person whom I loved and who was clearly and obviously suffering from severe symptoms of alcoholism, but I had so little information that it simply did not occur to me that alcohol, which I drank myself on a fairly regular basis, could be the cause of my lover's physical and emotional suffering. Everyone knew, even then, that drugs were dangerous, and I simply attributed her condition to her exposure to "drugs," never seeing that she was continuing to use her drug of choice in a highly addicted way right under my nose.

The gradual and insidious way that alcoholism progresses is yet another factor in the blindness of codependents (the spouse, family, friends, and often the employer of the alcoholic). Our relationship with our alcoholic began, usually, before drinking was a problem in any way. We came to know him or her as a person we admired, respected, and loved. The slow development of alcoholic symptoms, which in some cases may not appear for five, ten, or sometimes even twenty years after drinking begins, is so subtle that in our day-to-day relationship with the alcoholic we simply do not notice the changes. Others who have only infrequent contact with our alcoholic may be startled by his or her deterioration, but our perceptions adapt easily to the very gradual changes that take place. For the codependent, as for the alcoholic himself, it is often only a shocking, traumatic, or horribly embarrassing event that blasts us out of our fixed perception of normality, and it finally dawns on us that something is very, very wrong.

It is but one example of my own codependent illness (we'll look more closely at codependency in chapter 7, "The Codependent Syndrome,") that I began to see myself as my lover's savior. It's embarrassing to admit, but I really came to believe that the sheer strength of my love for her would rehabilitate her and restore her to wellness. I imagined myself nursing her back to physical and emotional wellness, and pictured us as a husband-and-wife (or cohabitant-and-cohabitant, if you prefer) psychologist team, helping hundreds of patients with their problems while nurturing each other with our love.

The only problem was that she wasn't getting well. Even with the drugs absent from her life, her physical and emotional condition continued to deteriorate. Her professional performance began to worry me, not only for her but because my name was on the office door, and I could be held responsible for her potential acts of malpractice. The first real red flag went up for me (finally!) when, in the process of balancing our checkbook (a distasteful task that I usually get around to every six months or so) some three months after we had resumed living together, I found that our liquor expenditures had gone up more than tenfold! My own drinking pattern was to enjoy a drink, and sometimes two, on most evenings after work, accounting for perhaps a bottle of Scotch per month. I found, however, that since we had resumed living together, an average of twelve to fifteen bottles of hard liquor had been purchased each month! This did not account for beer and wine, which I do not commonly drink but which she did, and which would have been included in our grocery expenses. I remember to this day the chilling feeling as the realization dawned upon me that not only was my lover drinking to an excess that I could barely imagine, but that she was somehow doing it under my nose and I hadn't seen it. How could I have imagined I would "love her to wellness" when I was so stupid I couldn't even see the problem?

Guilt and self-recrimination plague many spouses of alcoholics whose perception of the real problem comes long after it "should" have. We wonder often if only . . . If only I hadn't drunk with him. . . . If only I hadn't bought the rationalizations about stress on the job and his rotten boss. . . . If only I hadn't secretly supported her drinking because after she'd had a few she was so much more sexy. . . . We heap guilt and blame on ourselves just the same way we took responsibility for whether our spouse drank or whether he or she got drunk on any given occasion. It's just another way in which we become sick with the disease of alcoholism along with our alcoholic.

I resolved, in my typically academic way, to learn as much about alcoholism as I could. I still couldn't accept the idea that my lover was an alcoholic, exactly. After all, she still functioned, albeit poorly by now, at her work. She wasn't pawning our possessions to buy booze, or selling her body in our local red-light district. In those days I still had the typical picture of the alcoholic as a skid-row bum, and anyone short of that who drank too much was to me simply a person with problems. I did not know, as most people still do not, that skid-row alcoholics represent only an estimated 3 percent of the total alcoholic population, and it never occurred to me to wonder how they got to skid row in the first place.

I contacted a local psychologist whom I had vaguely heard knew "something" about alcoholism and arranged to have lunch with him. It turned out to be a lunch that changed both my personal and professional life. Dr. James R. Milam had been doing radical pioneering work in the field of alcoholism treatment and had founded his own recovery hospital, which had gained considerable fame in the Northwest. Yet so complete in those days was the separation between the fields of mental health and addiction treatment that I had only the dimmest awareness of the importance of his work, despite the fact that Alcenas Hospital was located right in our very small suburban community of Kirkland, Washington. Little did I know that Milam's work, which he summarized in a later book called *Under the Influence* (New York: Bantam, 1983), would have tremendous impact on the entire field of alcoholism and addiction treatment. Dr. Milam graciously accepted my near-total ignorance of the disease and began to patiently separate out my closely held myths about alcoholism and to educate me from the ground up.

I left that lunch both enlightened and shaken. It seemed beyond question, based upon what I had learned, that my lover was not only an alcoholic but that she was advancing at an alarming rate into the late and potentially terminal stages of the disease. Armed with my new knowledge I renewed my determination to save my lover from the jaws of this frightening demon, which had possessed her body and mind.

Many adult children of alcoholics find themselves, to their surprise and dismay, married to an alcoholic. There was no alcoholism in my family, but I was the child of an emotionally disturbed parent whose problems behaviorally mimicked many of the behaviors of a drinking alcoholic. I learned early and well not only to rely on myself but also to take undue degrees of responsibility for the needs and problems of others around me, particularly if I cared for them in any way. I suppose this mothering streak in me contributed to my choice of psychology as a profession, where I put it to good use. But for every way the tendency to take care of others has enhanced my professional life, where it is well controlled by the ethical constraints of my profession, it has detracted consistently from the quality of my personal life. I find, to my chagrin, that I have "s-mothered" my friends, my associates, and most particularly my relationship partners by trying to take responsibility for their well-being, sometimes to the point of driving them away.

My lover was no exception. I embarked on a campaign to get her to stop drinking, to acknowledge her drinking problem, and to accept help (at least I had reached a point in my learning about the disease to recognize that I was not going to be able to "cure" her myself). I stopped drinking entirely, and became self-righteously pointed about my abstinence in her presence. I tried to eliminate liquor from the house, though it persistently kept showing up. I don't know how many dollars worth of booze I poured down the drains of our home. I left books and pamphlets about alcoholism lying about in prominent places, which were, of course, studiously ignored. I was silently reproachful when she drank, which was constantly, and morally outraged when she was drunk, which was often.

The campaign was wonderfully successful in driving her underground with her addiction. She began to drink in a desperate isolation, withdrawing emotionally and physically into an alcoholic cocoon. She began to find other places to do her drinking, and other people who would drink with her and not judge her behavior. If she became too drunk, she would often not come home. Although infidelity was never a problem with us, I literally worried myself sick over her physical safety, often driving for hours in the night hoping to at least locate her car.

We codependents become sick with the disease of alcoholism, too, although our livers may remain in better condition. We are usually the last to recognize our condition. The total preoccupation with our alcoholic, the crazy things we do to keep them from drinking, the suppressed rage that sometimes inappropriately erupts on our kids, our bosses, our customers, or our friends, the depression and despair that falls upon us as we realize that things are not getting any better, are all symptoms of our progressive emotional sickness.

Our friends and relatives are of little help. They either tell us to "leave the bum," little realizing how tied we are by the heartstrings to this person we love, or they tell us what saints we are to put up with it all. Gradually we withdraw from them, as our alcoholic has withdrawn from us, suffering an isolated martyrdom that promises never to end.

My lover began to experience the predictable difficulties associated with the late stage of the disease. She was cited while driving under the influence. Her professional clientele fell off as she became increasingly unable to render effective counseling.

She wrecked her car in another drunken-driving episode. At home the gap between us widened as I was unable to talk about anything except her alcoholism and she was unable to communicate from within her alcoholic fog.

Finally, the court succeeded where I had failed by ordering her to accept inpatient alcoholism treatment as a consequence of her DWI (Driving While Intoxicated) citation. She had continued to deny the fact that she was alcoholic, but she had no choice but to accept treatment or face the revocation of her driver's license.

When she emerged from treatment, we greeted the miracle of her new sobriety with a mixture of fear and hope. Could it really be? Was it possible that we might be free of the raging beast that had been tearing our lives to shreds for the past nine years? I was terrified that I would say or do the wrong thing and "drive her to drink." She felt the tremendous pressure of being on the spot to remain abstinent. We were like strangers with each other, constantly walking on eggshells. Several times we attempted to resume our sexual relationship, which years before had been the most passionate of either of our lives, but which had long since fallen casualty to alcoholism and codependency. Our attempts were awkward and uncomfortable; we were barely able to converse comfortably, much less make love!

One of the problems was that I needed help, too. At that time, codependency was at best a poorly understood concept, and many in the alcohol-treatment field flatly rejected it in their focus on the alcoholic. Consequently, when my lover came home from treatment, she was considerably improved after a month of intensive counseling, abstinence, and a healthy introduction to AA (Alcoholics Anonymous). I, however, was no better off than before, except for having had a month's rest from aggravation and worry. Sure, there had been a few family meetings in connection with her treatment program, but they had been mainly concerned with how to treat your alcoholic once he or she comes home. Little if any emphasis was placed on the process of recovery for the codependent spouse.

I continued with my self-righteous smugness. Things had come out right, after all! Instead of checking to see where she had hidden the booze, I now turned my solicitous attention to seeing that she attended all her required AA meetings. I expected that now that drinking was a thing of the past, she would immediately set her life in order, adopt my behavioral standard of perfection in all things, and in her spare time to love me so well and truly as to make up for all my years of hurt and suffering. I had been running everything—the housecleaning, the cooking, the shopping, the office, the checkbook—for so long that it was difficult to let go of some of the controls and adopt a more sharing style.

My lover was having difficulties also. She found it difficult to accept that with all her intelligence and education she could still be an alcoholic, and still need to pursue recovery in the ways that had been suggested to her. She claimed to detest AA, though she seemed to derive real support when she allowed herself to participate. She insisted, based on some well-intended but misguided research (some of which she herself had carried out while in graduate school), that she as an alcoholic would be able to learn to drink "normally" and responsibly once she had completed a long-enough period of abstinence to give her a clean start.

The first relapse came about three months after she completed her inpatient treatment. It was not a "slip" (an accidental or impulsive drink that is usually followed by a renewed intensity in the pursuit of sobriety). It was an intentional embarkation on a program to resume "normal" drinking that involved a self-imposed two-drink limit. The program ended a week later in a massive weekend-long binge.

She felt humiliated and remorseful. After making amends to several people she had called while drinking, she renewed her AA attendance and, with it, abstinence.

An impossible bind had arisen for us, which in retrospect I can see we were never able to solve. Even from the days before her alcoholism had emerged as a problem, I was the power figure in our relationship. I was two years ahead in graduate school. I was the more socially outgoing and (apparently) confident. I was the breadwinner while she finished her doctoral studies. When she finished school, I was the senior member of the practice she joined. I played a role in the confrontation that resulted in her receiving treatment. It must have often seemed to her that I controlled her entire life, though I felt for years that her illness had controlled mine.

Now I was strenuously advocating abstinence and AA as the only lasting and effective program for her recovery. If I was right, how could she do the things she needed to do to recover without appearing to be saying, "Yes, Art, I was wrong and you were right again, you wonderful man!"?

Codependents do not necessarily come to their marriages with a controlling, manipulative, and self-righteous personality style (though many grew up in alcohol- or drug-affected families and learned to be overly responsible caretakers), any more than alcoholics come into adult life with personality styles that are sneaky, irresponsible, and "flaky." The symptoms of codependency develop along with, and perhaps in response to, the developing symptoms of addiction in the spouse. What does a "normal" spouse do when his or her partner seems out of control ' and needs help? It seems to me that the "normal" spouse takes control and renders help. The fact that this control soon becomes controlling, and that the help soon becomes enabling (a concept we'll explore in chapter 7, "The Codependent Syndrome,"), has little to do with the fact that the early behaviors and reactions of codependency spring from essentially normal and decent human emotions.

Many codependents find that they have given over their lives, as I did, to the project of helping their addicted spouses to wellness, creating the illusion that the spouse's recovery depends

on their efforts. In fact, one of the best-known (and very valuable) forerunners of this book is Toby Rice Drews's *Getting Them
Sober* (Plainfield, N.J.: Bridge, 1980), a title that implies in itself
that it is the work of the codependent spouse, child, friend, or
employer that is responsible for the addict's recovery. We engage in this work for selfish reasons as well as loving ones, for
who wants to live a short and horrid married life to a practicing
addict? On the other hand, who wants to leave the wonderful
person one has loved above all others? The only alternative, it
sometimes seems, is to work to "get them sober."

But the delicate power dynamics of relationships often con-
spire to make the controlling and helping codependent spouse
an actual obstacle to the addict's recovery. Women addicts, who
often feel dominated and powerless in their marriages anyway,
may feel that the only way left to them to be an individual is to
resist their partner's efforts to "get them sober." Male alcoholics
may feel compelled to resist the spouse's work on them in a
misguided effort to preserve their masculinity and autonomy
against the demands of "that nagging bitch." It is often terribly
difficult for both the chemically dependent partner and the codependent partner to separate the path of recovery from the dynamics of power within the relationship. This applies not only to
spouses but to children, friends, employers, and other codependents as well.

It certainly would have helped if my attention had been
directed to my own recovery, rather than remaining focused on
my lover's. I needed to recover from my chronic depression,
which had developed during the course of her illness. I needed
a safe place in which to vent my rage over the experiences we
had suffered through. I needed to unlearn my controlling behavior and learn to trust her with her own recovery. But the plight
of the codependent was as yet poorly understood, and I, like
most codependents, was fairly oblivious to the problematic aspects of my own behavior.

Program for controlled drinking followed program. There was the One Drink Per Hour Program. There was the Drink Only Before Dinner Program (which often ended in no dinner). There was the Tumbler of Water Between Each Drink Program. There was the Drink Only On Weekends Program. Each ended, after a short time, in a terrible relapse binge, to be followed by a month or two of abstinence. Finally we decided together to separate, on the theory that she needed to work through the process of recovery in a setting more protected from my watchful and anxious eye. Neither of us contemplated the end of our relationship, but we both needed a breather from the pressure of trying to be together and to pursue recovery at the same time.

She found a small apartment, and we sadly but hopefully moved her in on a Friday in November 1982. We agreed not to be in contact over the weekend so that we could rest and get used to the idea of not living together for a time. We kissed a brief farewell. It was the last time we ever spoke. Three days later I entered her apartment and found her body lying beside an empty bottle.

The temptation is strong, even now after five years, for me to play the torturous game of "What if . . ." on myself. What if a different treatment program had been selected for her? What if the field of addiction treatment had been as well developed then as it is today? What if there had been more help available for me? What if I had been less controlling, more loving? In the quiet moments an accusing voice asks whether in all my attempts to help I did not in fact play a role in her death.

Thankfully, most codependents are not required to confront these questions with the finality with which I must face them. A large proportion of addicts are divorced or separated from their families long before the final tragedy occurs. And more and more suffering addicts and codependents join the ranks of the recovering each year.

The past five years of my professional life have been devoted almost exclusively to helping people whose lives have been touched by alcohol or other drugs. Some come to me not even suspecting that addiction may be the source of their difficulty. Others come after seeing that their lives are being ruined by addiction and seeking guidance about what to do about it. Still others are well on the road to recovery and are seeking help to correct the damage that addiction has caused in their lives.

This book is written for those alcoholics, addicts, and codependents who have reached the point in the process of addictive disease when they have begun to realize that something is very wrong in their lives, and that whatever is wrong is somehow connected to alcohol or drugs. It is written with the hope that the information it contains may help to shorten the period of suffering and hasten the beginning of genuine healing and recovery for the addict and those whose lives he touches. I believe that my lover would have given her blessing to the personal disclosures that are made, and that she would be pleased that her death might indirectly contribute to the enhancement of the lives of others.

I

YOUR

HEARTBREAKING

PREDICAMENT

The person you fell in love with is changing, and you are changing, too, in ways that you don't like. The changes have been slow and subtle, and perhaps it has only occurred to you recently that your lives are turning out very differently from the life you had hoped for together. You have been doing your best, but your best just doesn't seem good enough to overcome the series of bad breaks and unfortunate occurrences that have prevented you from realizing your hopes for success and happiness.

You fell in love with a wonderful person. Where has he gone? The person you live with today is angry, depressed, unreliable. There is a sneakiness about him that didn't used to be there. You argue often, and perhaps the arguments sometimes become physical. Your bills are a burden, and you can't for the life of you figure out why, since you earn enough together for what should be an adequate life-style. The kids are showing the strain, too. Johnny's teacher says his progress is not satisfactory, and little Sarah is wetting the bed. You know it's because of what's going on at home, but what's the problem really, and what to do about it?

John's been drinking more and more, and it's begun to concern you. He always drank, even back in college when you met him, but never so much or so often. Last week alone you and the kids ate dinner without him twice, and John came home after midnight, drunk, saying one night that he had to entertain an important client, and the other that the fellows from work "stopped off" for a drink and one thing led to another. You understand that his work is demanding, but you worry when he has too much, is out too late, and drives home after drinking. You've tried to talk to him about your concern, but he always seems to argue you out of your point of view. It's natural, he says, to drink more when you're facing the stresses and strains of the career world. "You just try and go out there and face the dragons for your wife and family every day, and see how you feel," he says. Besides, he points out, you wouldn't be so uptight and neurotic about it if your father hadn't been an alcoholic bum who beat up his wife and then deserted his family. Besides, he says, he doesn't drink any more, and maybe less, than the other guys he works with. Maybe if he'd attended more of the after-work drinking sessions with the guys, he wouldn't have been passed over for those last two promotions. Somehow, whenever you try to talk to John about his drinking, you end up feeling you're being silly.

• • •

Sandy's beginning to scare you with this cocaine thing. Two years ago, when you met her at the T. J. Pringle's singles bar, you couldn't believe you lucked into meeting such a terrific girl. Now you're not so sure. She was pretty, sexy, and a ton of fun. You began to go out together, and the first time you slept together it was like a beautiful dream. You admired her, respected her, and it didn't take long for your liking and attraction to turn to love. You moved in together six months ago, planning to get married as soon as she finishes her schooling.

It's ironic that her first experience with cocaine happened indirectly because of you.* It was at that party the regional sales

*Throughout this book, the terms alcoholic and addict are used virtually interchangeably. Although alcoholics often do not think of themselves as addicts, in alcoholism the process of addiction appears to be identical to that of addiction to other drugs of abuse. Alcoholism is certainly the best researched and studied of the addictions, and for that reason alcoholism is treated as the model for all drug addictions throughout this book.

manager threw at his house last year. The drinking got pretty heavy later in the evening, and after most of the straight-arrows had left, Joe had tapped you on the shoulder and whispered that there was a toot for you in the back bedroom as a kind of special reward for your outstanding sales record that quarter. You had never used cocaine, but all the guys who ought to know said it was great, and besides you couldn't very well turn down Joe's recognition. You didn't much like it, and really couldn't see the point of spending that kind of money to get yourself jittery, but Sandy took to it like a duck takes to water. In a weird way, you were actually kind of proud of her, tooting up like one of the guys. None of them dared even to tell their wives about the cocaine, much less invite them to participate!

Your first shock came a few weeks later, when Joe slyly asked how you liked your birthday present. Your birthday wasn't for six months yet, but you found out that Sandy had called him to ask where she could buy a gram of cocaine as a special present for you. When you confronted her she laughed it off, saying that she'd planned to surprise you but then decided you wouldn't approve so she'd used it all herself.

When she borrowed five hundred dollars from you to pay a student loan she said had come due, you didn't question it. After all, you were going to be married, and her debts were going to be yours, so who's counting? But when you found the two five-hundred-dollar cash draws on your MasterCard that you didn't make, you really flipped. You and Sandy had the biggest fight of your relationship, and she cried and said she'd pay it back, that she intended the cocaine for a big party for your friends, just like the one that Joe threw, but somehow it just didn't come to pass. Even though you were angry, her misguided devotion to you and your career touched you, and you forgave her.

But now she's pushing you to go to these parties she keeps getting invited to. Where she meets these people, you can't imagine. The parties are good for business, full of young doctors and lawyers and business people who are all potential customers. But you're getting tired of the parties, the late nights, and the tremendous amount of drinking and coking. Sandy just loves it, though. The last few times you've only gone because she's said if you won't go she'll go without you, and you don't want to turn her loose among all those drinks and drugs and slick dudes.

Now you find yourself wondering what you've gotten yourself into. The wedding is planned for June, and her parents are already making the arrangements. But it feels as if the two of you are further apart than you've ever been. It's not as if you argue a lot (in fact, the only times you argue are over your growing distaste for the "high" life she seems to like so much). It's just that you don't feel as if you can reach the real Sandy anymore. All she ever seems to want to talk about is what so-and-so was wearing at last night's party, or how much cocaine that person used, and how drunk this person got. She's always broke and you suspect that she's buying cocaine secretly.

You're feeling really torn. On the one hand, you really and truly love her. On the other hand, every shred of common sense in you is telling you that something is very much wrong with her, and that to tie your life to hers is a sure formula for disaster. The idea of ending the relationship has occurred to you, but it makes you sick every time you think of it, and besides, what would become of her if she didn't have your stabilizing influence in her life?

· · ·

Daddy's mad at you and Mommy again. You used to love Daddy a lot, but now you're mostly scared of him. He acts so funny! Sometimes he's real nice, like the time he gave you ten whole dollars just because, he said, you were so cute. But other times he scares you so much it makes you cry, like the time he threw the saltshaker and just missed your head just because you said you didn't like your lima beans.

Mommy says Daddy's sick, and he only acts bad when he's not feeling well. It seems as if he feels sick most of the time these days. Sometimes you wonder if he's going to die. It's your bad secret that sometimes, mostly when he hits Mommy, you wish he would die. But you know you're being bad when you think that, so you try even harder to be good.

Last night you had supper at Sherri's house. You wish sometimes that you lived in a family just like Sherri's. Her daddy is so smart and funny, and her mom is so cheerful, they just make you feel good to be around them. Sherri says that sometimes they have arguments, but then they make up. In another way it makes you feel bad when you go over to Sherri's, because you can't ask Sherri to come to your house. You just never know when Daddy's going to not feel well, and Mommy says we shouldn't let the neighbors or my teachers know that Daddy is sick. Maybe it would be better to not be really good friends with anybody.

Mommy says if we both try really hard to be good, someday Daddy will get well. The problem is that you just don't know how to try hard to be good. It seems as if no matter how hard you try, you always make some kind of mistake. Maybe if you try to get all A's in second grade, keep your room just as neat as a pin all the time, never get dirty, and never say anything bad, then you can get Daddy to be happy and well.

.   .   .

Something's gotta give here! Bill used to be a hell of a business partner, but now, for the most part, he's a pain in the ass! Back when you were both thirty years old and full of piss and vinegar, the two of you formed the construction company on a shoestring and worked your butts off making a go of it. Now, fifteen years later, you're both fat and happy, drawing a hundred and fifty thou a year and working half as hard, but you're worried. Bill just isn't the guy he used to be.

To be fair, he's had some tough breaks in his life. Two wives have divorced him. His kids treat him like dirt unless they want money. Then there was the car accident two years ago that cost him a hundred thousand dollars because he had let his insurance lapse. You figure that if you had Bill's bad luck, you might drink as heavily as he does. But it's becoming a problem, and you don't know what to do.

Bill used to be the company slave driver, in the office every morning by six-thirty, never out before seven in the evening. Now it's rare to see him before 10:00 A.M., he takes a two-hour lunch with his buddies, and he's gone by 4:30. His disposition's changed, too. He was always hard-nosed, but lately he's become downright disagreeable. Two secretaries and a job foreman have quit in the last two years because of his temper outbursts. You never really thought about the drinking maybe having something to do with it, but now that you think of it, all the really nasty episodes have happened in the morning.

You've done your best to keep the damage to a minimum, but it hasn't been easy and it's getting tougher. Not only is his behavior becoming worrisome, but it's starting to hit you in the wallet. He blew the contract to build that big Mormon church by ordering drinks at the lunch with the elders. He bought that big computer system that you can't use from one of his drinking buddies without even checking with you. The corporate tax return sat on his desk for four months and ended up costing the company sixteen hundred dollars in late fines and was probably the reason for the IRS audit, which cost another eight thousand dollars.

It's happened so slowly you've hardly noticed it, but now you realize that Bill's and your relationship as partners has really gone to hell. You used to be best buddies, but now it's rare that you spend much off-work time together, and when you do, you don't enjoy it very much. You've never been much of a drinker, and you began several years ago to find Bill pretty tiresome after he's had a few. Now you feel you can't rely on him, and you lie awake some nights worrying that some detail he was supposed to take care of might not have gotten done.

The real shocker came the other day when you smelled liquor on his breath first thing in the morning. You've always heard that only alcoholics drink in the morning. Bill's been a heavy drinker as long as you've known him, but an alcoholic? If that were true, you know you'd be in big trouble. You've heard that alcoholics always go downhill eventually, and if Bill goes downhill, he'll take the company and you with him.

You tried to talk with him about it when you smelled the booze on his breath. At first he denied it, saying that he was using a new brand of mouthwash that had alcohol in it. Then he got mad and said his personal habits were no business of yours. You decided to back off before it got nasty, but you know that isn't going to solve the problem.

·   ·   ·

Not one of these people set out to become involved with a chemically dependent person, and neither did you. You formed your relationship, whether it is a business partnership, a friendship, or a love relationship, because you liked and respected the person and felt that a relationship with him or her would add to your happiness. If you are the child of an addict, you certainly had no choice about the matter. If you are reading this book because you suspect that you may be developing a drinking problem, it is certain that it was never among your ambitions to become an addict to alcohol or other drugs.

No medical or psychological tests as yet exist to reliably predict whether a given person will develop alcoholism or another addictive disease, though researchers are coming closer all the time. Even experts in the field can only make predictive guesses about whether a person is developing an addiction in the early stages, and their guesses are often based on very subtle indications in the person's attitudes and behavior.

The development of addiction is a gradual and intricate process, sometimes taking many years to become clearly diagnosable. The use of alcohol and other drugs is extremely common in our culture, and depending on the drug, most people do not develop a problem. Of those who do, few have any reason in advance to suspect that they will become addicted. You are not responsible for making a conscious choice to become addicted or to become involved with an addict.

Yet here you are. Your friend, wife, husband, employee, father, mother, or child is involved with alcohol or other drugs, and your life is being affected for the worse by it. You're angry. You're depressed. You're ashamed. You're disgusted. Your heart and mind are becoming a cesspool of negative feelings.

And you're behaving badly. You get angry often and at inappropriate times. Your attention is occupied with your addict's behavior, and you are constantly trying to head off disasters before they occur. The stress and depression may be causing you to become physically ill with ulcers or headaches or high blood pressure or other stress-related disorders. You feel isolated and alone, and in fact you are, because you don't talk about the problem because of your shame about it. Perhaps you've thought about suicide.

You feel stuck with this problem you can't solve. Just getting out of the relationship would be a solution, but it would mean abandoning the person you care for. For many, dissolving the relationship would also create many other problems affecting life-style and economics. The wife who has three children to care for and few marketable job skills may feel that she cannot leave. Young children of addicts certainly cannot leave. The business partner who has spent years developing the business and now depends on it for his livelihood cannot casually dissolve the partnership. Many others, though otherwise able to leave the relationship, feel bound by a commitment of the heart which they feel unable to revoke.

The other option, to just live with the problem, seems both unthinkable and inevitable at the same time. Nearly every night you lie awake thinking that you don't know how you can stand another day of this. Yet each new day arrives on schedule, and somehow you cope. As your depression increases and your self-esteem decreases, you experience yourself as less and less able to either leave the relationship or to correct the problem.

Your alcoholic or addict is experiencing a similar heart-breaking dilemma, though perhaps you cannot see it because of his defensiveness and your anger. He never stood up in the first grade and said, "When I grow up I want to be a drunk." She never decided as a girl that she wanted to be a Valium or Xanax addict. In fact, your addict had dreams and hopes and aspirations that were similar to your own. Your addict simply has had the misfortune to fall victim to a disease, and he suffers its effects as acutely as you do.

As the illness began to progress through its early stages, your alcoholic couldn't see it happening any more than you could. It seemed normal (or at least not unusual) that drinking became more and more a part of his life. Sure, he drank too much from time to time, but doesn't everyone? As his body accommodated to its relationship with the drug, it seemed natural that he would drink more as the stress of his life increased. As your and his social life centered more on alcohol and you both began to spend more time in drinking situations, there was no comparative basis for you or him to see that his drinking was becoming heavier and more frequent than is considered normal. Your alcoholic is no more responsible for his addiction than you are for ending up in a relationship with him.

Since the primary action of alcohol and other addictive substances is on the brain, and the brain coincidentally is the organ through which we perceive ourselves and the world around us, the addiction begins to gradually shape and dictate the way in which an addict leads his life. He couldn't see this happening because the addict's brain is affected by its addictive relationship to the substance (tolerance), and you couldn't see it because the changes were so gradual. He began to make tiny adjustments in his attitudes and behavior to allow for the presence of his addiction. Can you remember when he went from three evenings of drinking per week to four? Can you remember the first time she called in sick to work because of a "sick headache" that followed a night of partying? Did you notice at the time the process by which restaurants that did not serve alcohol gradually fell off your list of places to go? Did you see any connection between his drinking and the first time he was passed over for a promotion? Did you even notice the point at which she began to become so negative and depressed, let alone connect it to the drugs her doctor prescribed?

Of course you didn't, and neither did your addict. Chances are that only a sudden and shocking event could have brought you and your addict to the point where you see that his or her use of a substance, and/or your distress because of it, has become a major problem in your lives. The DWI citation, the incidents of family violence, the job loss, the impending bankruptcy, the major medical problem, or any number of other traumatic events hits like a bucket of cold water to shock us awake to the fact that the drinking or the drug use is in fact the real problem. You are probably only now realizing that the person you care for is an addict, that you feel powerless to do anything about it, and that both your lives have become unmanageable because of it.

Your addict or alcoholic is living with a similar dawning of realization, although his or her fierce denials may prevent you from knowing it. In his heart of hearts he knows that he is on a path of personal destruction, although this awareness is often only briefly glimpsed in the most private of moments. Whenever the window opens in his mind and allows him to see himself and his behavior as it really is, the addiction steps in with its primary means of psychological defense, denial, and closes it quickly.

Your addict is increasingly caught in her own awful dilemma, just as you are. She is aware of the impact on her health, her emotions, her behavior, her relationships with loved ones, and her career that her addiction is creating. But to end her relationship with her drug seems unthinkable. Drinking has become her only way of coping with life. It's the only thing that makes life fun. It has become the center of her social life. It's the only thing that makes her feel good. In fact, when she is *not* drinking or using drugs, she is anxious, depressed, and often in great physical discomfort. To your addict, the alternatives seem to be either to continue in the addiction with the inevitable consequences of, ultimately, death, or to try to deal with the addiction, probably fail, and, if successful, to live a life that seems painful, boring, and empty.

It seems so cruel, and so unfair. Addiction crept into your lives without either of you suspecting or noticing it. It has driven a wedge between you who were once so close. It has caused you to lose respect and even feel shame for the person whom you once so admired and enjoyed. It has turned you into a worried, self-righteous, nagging, depressed neurotic whom your addict more often than not regards as his enemy. And now it has condemned each of you to your own private hell in which you must daily choose between personal destruction and death or the terrible pain and life disruption of separation, he from alcohol or you from him.

There is good news for you and your addict, and it's called recovery. For most of human history, there has been almost no alternative for the addict to alcohol or other drugs and for those connected to him but to suffer through the agonizing progression of the disease to death. But fortunately for both of you, the past twenty years have seen an explosion of new knowledge about alcoholism and other drug addiction—what it is, how to treat it, how to arrest it, and how to recover from it. Pioneering researchers and theorists, many of them themselves recovering from addiction, have cut through many of our culture's long-held myths about alcoholism, identified ways of getting the addict to help, refined the techniques for effective treatment, and mapped out the path to ultimate recovery from this insidious disease. There is no longer any need for thousands of suffering addicts to die each year, for tens of thousands of addiction-impacted families to be torn apart, for hundreds of thousands of children of alcoholics to be marked for life by their experience of addiction in the family, for millions upon untold millions of dollars to be leached from our personal and national economy due to addiction.

Sadly, the vast majority of alcoholics and addicts still go untreated, although effective treatment technology exists. Even in the face of the wonderful increases in public awareness of the nature of addiction over the past few years, ignorance, both in the general public (the spouses, children, friends, and employers of addicts) and in the professional-health-care community (doctors, psychiatrists, psychologists, and counselors) still prevents the majority of addicts and their families from receiving the help they need. Addicts are still dying needlessly, not only on skid row, but in fine homes and in the finest of families. Codependents still suffer in silence, lapsing deeper by the day into depression and despair. Children continue to experience the psychological and physical abuse resulting from living in an addiction-affected family. Many of these victims are under the well-meaning but incompetent "care" of ignorant professionals who continue to prescribe inappropriate medications or to psychologize away the agony of the suffering addict and his family in terms of spurious emotional or mental conflict.

This book is intended as a guidebook to help addicts and those who love them to find their way through the maze of myth and misinformation and locate the path toward recovery. It is addressed primarily to the spouse, adult child, friend, or business associate of the addict, only because it is assumed that it is the non–chemically dependent person in the relationship, though himself sickened and dysfunctional because of his involvement with the addiction, who is more capable of taking the first steps toward recovery. If you are the chemically dependent partner in the relationship and have taken the initiative to read this book, please forgive the implied underestimation of your ability to reach out for help. The fact is that in most cases, it is the codependent spouse or partner who initiates the recovery process, either by pressuring the alcoholic or addict to seek help, or by beginning his or her own recovery and creating changes in the relationship that cause the alcoholic or addict to seek help.

First of all, we'll try to understand what addiction is and what it is not. For someone like myself, whose friends and professional associates thoroughly understand the nature of addictive disease, it still comes as a shock to hear people at parties and other social gatherings firmly and certainly making statements about alcoholism that I know not only to be false but also very destructive. In spite of the great amount of attention that has been given to addiction in recent years, not only in professional circles but also in the media, most people are still unfamiliar with the facts concerning this country's number-one health problem. Even physicians and psychologists are still largely unacquainted with the current body of knowledge about addiction, and sometimes members of these groups are the most difficult to educate, because they have formed fixed beliefs that are often hard to change. It seems obvious that you're not going to be able to do much about the presence of addiction in your life until you have a clear understanding of what you're dealing with, so we'll start there.

Next, we'll try to take a long, hard look at you, the codependent. It is absolutely imperative throughout this process that you maintain the view that both you and your alcoholic are in desperate need of help. The part of you that rebels against statements like this is your denial, which is the exact counterpart of your alcoholic's instinct to deny that he or she has a drinking problem. It is not true that you "have things under control." In fact, you have gone out of control with trying to control things over which you have no control. When you say, "I'd be just fine if only *she'd* straighten up," you're kidding yourself. Your depression, anxiety, anger, and resentment are not going to go away just because your alcoholic stops drinking. Her addiction has shaped your behavior over a period of many years, just as it has hers. If you do not begin to understand the nature of your codependency and commit to your own recovery, you will remain miserable no matter what your addict does, and you may well create a situation in which she will have to separate herself from you in order to get well. If you propose to be instrumental in starting the process of recovery for your family, you must learn about the addiction-created defects in the instrument itself.

Then we'll examine the various sources of help, both for you and your addict. Finding effective help is not always easy, and sometimes getting the wrong kind of help can be worse than receiving no help at all. Unfortunately, there are still many individuals and organizations, both lay and professional, who purport to offer help to the alcoholic and his family but who in fact do not help and sometimes hurt. Individuals and organizations whose "treatment" is based on myths and pet theories rather than scientific fact almost invariably fail to arrest the addiction and often convince the alcoholic that he or she cannot recover under any treatment. Effective treatment does exist within reach of nearly every major city in this country, but you'll need to know what to look for and what to avoid.

Finally, we'll try to give you some ideas about how to pursue your recovery after treatment, and what kind of life you can reasonably look forward to in recovery. It's important to remember that treatment is not recovery—it's only the first step. Treatment doesn't cure addiction or codependency. There is no cure. Addiction treatment establishes in the alcoholic a condition known as *abstinence,* in which the alcoholic or addict has had the opportunity to withdraw under medical supervision from his or her body's relationship with the drug (we'll talk more about the phenomenon of withdrawal in chapter 11, "Treatment for Addictions"). In treatment, the addict learns about her illness and about the absolute necessity for complete abstinence in order for recovery to take place. In a good treatment program, the alcoholic is started on the first baby steps toward recovery by attending Alcoholics Anonymous or Narcotics Anonymous meetings. True recovery is, however, a lengthy process of emotional learning and spiritual growth that requires commitment and discipline over a period of years.

Most treatment programs for alcoholics and addicts are still, unfortunately, doing far too little by way of addressing the need for treatment and recovery for the codependent, although this situation is rapidly changing. We'll try to give you as the codependent some ideas and resources for your own process of recovery. Remember, if you and your addict don't pursue recovery together, chances are that either your alcoholic will return to drinking or your relationship will eventually end, or both. Addiction has distorted your relationship so badly that recovery on the part of one but not the other would throw it all out of balance. (Warning: This principle cuts both ways; you should know that as you begin to recover, refusal on the part of your addict to pursue recovery may well result either in the end of your relationship, or relapse into codependency on your part.)

Congratulations. As you read and act upon the information contained in these pages, you will be moving toward a turning point from the hopelessness, despair, and unmanageability that has come to dominate your life. As you turn from the isolated suffering of addiction, it's important for you to know that the fellowship of tens of thousands of your brothers and sisters in recovery awaits you. In that fellowship you will find comfort, support, growth, and maturity. May you enjoy it and prosper from it. Life is too short and too sweet to spend it suffering.

I I

UNDERSTANDING

ALCOHOLISM

AND ADDICTION

Once you've discovered that the real problem with your life is the presence of addiction, trying to figure out how to solve the problem can be as frustrating as trying to solve Rubik's cube while standing on the deck of a sailboat in a gale-force wind. New crises and problems come faster than you can solve the old ones. You're running out of thumbs to put in the dike.

The fact is that you won't be able to do much of a constructive nature until you have some sound information to work with. If you are an average person with no special training in addiction, then probably just about everything you think you know about alcoholism is wrong. If that sounds insulting, remember that I had a Ph.D. in psychology and five years of clinical experience in the field before I was luckily able to learn the first thing about addiction. We are all the beneficiaries of several thousand years of ignorant and erroneous prejudices, opinions, moralisms, and guesses that masquerade as "facts" about addiction.

In these next chapters I'm going to try to share with you some of what is now *known* about addiction. The information is not mine. It is the fruit of the labors of thousands of medical researchers, alcoholism workers, and the combined wisdom of hundreds of thousands of recovering alcoholics and addicts.

In chapter 1, "Alcoholism: Misunderstood, Mistreated," you will learn that addiction is a *disease,* not a psychological problem. You will understand that people don't become alcoholics because of a divorce or a death or other life tragedy. People don't become alcoholics because of "deep underlying psychological conflicts" or "personality disorders." You will see, perhaps for the first time, that your alcoholic is not a "flake" or crazy or a moral reprobate or even irresponsible. He or she is sick.

In chapter 3, "The Progression of Addiction," you will learn about the progression, or course, of addictive disease. You will see the way that the subtle, almost unnoticeable signs and symptoms of the early stage take over and distort the course of an entire life in the middle stage and ultimately reduce that life to rubble before it finally kills in the late stage. As you read chapter 3 you may wonder if I have visited your home and spied on you. Be assured that while you and your alcoholic are wonderful and unique individuals, the disease that is ruining your lives is very, very predictable. In most cases it unfolds by stages, and the life events that accompany those stages are the logical and natural consequences of the disease process.

Until now I have tried to use the terms alcoholism and addiction more or less interchangeably, to help you to understand that alcoholism is a drug addiction and to include those readers whose problem or whose loved one's problem is addiction to cocaine, marijuana, heroin, amphetamines, or prescription drugs. From now on we will be focusing on alcoholism, because alcoholism is the best understood, most researched, and most widely experienced of the addictions. Chapter 5, "Addiction to Drugs other than Alcohol," will provide specific information on some of the other addictions. If you or your loved one is suffering from addiction to a drug other than alcohol, this book will be most useful to you if you understand that while addictive drugs vary in their chemical structure, availability, cost, and intoxicating effects, and therefore the experience of addiction differs slightly because of these characteristics, *the physical nature and the process of addiction is very similar.* If you can perform the mental trick of substituting the term addiction for the term alcoholism, and the specific substance in your life for alcohol, you will find that most of the information applies equally to your situation.

Perhaps it will help to adopt the definition of alcoholism supplied by Dr. Stanley E. Gitlow of the Mount Sinai School of Medicine, Mount Sinai Hospital, New York City:

> *Alcoholism is a disease characterized by the repetitive and compulsive ingestion of any sedative drug,* * *ethanol being just one of these, in such a way as to cause interference in some aspect of the subject's life, be it in the area of interpersonal relationships, job, marriage, or physical health. It is absolutely critical to appreciate that this definition does not in any way specify which sedative agent is used, the frequency of its use, or the amount ingested.*

If you try to balance your checkbook believing that $2+2=5$, you can work at it for the rest of your life and never come up with the same balance that the bank does. If you try to rid your life of the destructive effects of addiction with information based on prejudice and myth, you'll never get it right. But with accurate information and proper identification of effective help, alcoholics and their codependents can and do get well and live productive, sane, and happy lives.

---

*According to the author, alcoholism is a disease characterized also by the compulsive ingestion of many nonsedating drugs, such as cocaine, amphetamine, and nicotine. The fact that alcohol is classed as a sedative agent should not confuse us into thinking that people who are chemically dependent are so because they crave a sedative effect.

1

ALCOHOLISM:
MISUNDERSTOOD,
MISTREATED

No one knows exactly when it was in the dim reaches of prehistory that a vagrant airborne yeast spore landed in a pot of honeyed fruit juice, or the name of the hapless clansman who first tasted the potent brew. We can imagine his shock and dismay to feel his consciousness changing. He must have been filled with awe and even fear at the powerful effects of the potion. Did he share his discovery with the rest of his tribe, or did he hoard the secret as a source of power and become the first medicine man? Whoever he was, he pioneered the relationship between mankind and drugs that for millennia to come would be characterized by attraction and fear, ritual and chaos, exhilaration and despair, the wreaking of havoc and the struggle for control.

I recently saw an article that described alcoholism as "the twentieth-century disease," which is a little bit like saying that America came into being in 1492. Humankind has noted the negative effects of alcohol's attraction and tried to control it since the earliest of times. We know that beverage alcohol was being commercially produced in Mesopotamia at least six thousand years ago. Restrictions on the sale and consumption of alcohol that read like modern liquor-control laws are found in the code of laws of Hammurabi, dating from 1700 B.C. The Bible, written over a period of about a thousand years from around 900 B.C. to A.D. 60, contains more than 150 references to alcoholic drink, most of them warning about the dangers of too much consumption. Alcoholism became such a problem in the Roman Empire that the Roman Senate found it necessary to impose radical controls on the production of wine grapes.

The liquor industry became big business as the Roman legions educated the "barbarian" populations of northern Europe about how to drink. Roman and Greek cargo ships have been found on the floor of the Mediterranean carrying huge shipments of amphorae, earthenware wine jugs.

The Middle Ages saw the planting of the valleys of France and Germany with wine grapes imported from the Near East during the Crusades. In the eighth century A.D., an alchemist named Geber discovered the process by which wines could be distilled, adding dramatically to the alcohol content of the beverage and thus heightening its addictive potential.* Normal fermentation allows a maximum concentration of alcohol of 14 percent. Distillation involves the boiling off of the spirit alcohol from the fermented solution and isolating it, allowing a theoretical concentration up to 100 percent. Most distilled, or "hard," liquor commercially available contains between 40 and 50 percent alcohol by volume, though some varieties contain 75 percent alcohol or higher.

*Recent years have witnessed a similar technological advance in the production of marijuana. The high-tech efforts of underground botanists have succeeded in producing strains of the plant with up to *twelve times* the THC—tetrahydrocannabinol, the active agent in marijuana—of that available just ten years ago. Consequently, workers in the addiction field now regularly see people who have developed a true physical dependency on marijuana, which was quite rare until a few years ago.

By the late Middle Ages, most of the newly "alcoholized" areas of northern Europe had their specific and characteristic distilled beverages. France had developed its brandies. Eastern Europe made vodka by distilling fermented potato mash. Scandinavia had its aquavit, or *aqua vitae,* "the water of life," in Latin, and Scotland and Ireland each had their own versions of *uisge beatha* (also meaning "water of life"), from which we get the word whiskey. A Dutchman learned to flavor aquavit with juniper berries to cover its raw taste, and by the year 1700, gin had practically become the English national beverage. Throughout the 1700s the English government, which previously had encouraged the liquor industry, began to impose stiff taxes to try to prevent England from being washed into the sea by a flood of gin. Even today the English policy of trying to control alcohol abuse through taxation makes the price of a bottle of Scotch more expensive in Inverness than it is in most countries to which it is imported.

Drinking was an important feature in the life of Colonial America, in Puritan New England as well as in Dutch New York and the more easygoing southern colonies. Rum, an original American beverage, was distilled from fermented molasses. Molasses, rum, and slaves were the commodities traded in the triangular route from the West Indies to New England to West Africa. Drinking was an around-the-clock activity for the colonists, and we may assume from recent historical evidence that much of the conception, discussion, and actual writing of the documents fundamental to the American Experiment took place in taverns and alehouses. The Declaration of Independence and the U.S. Constitution may be the most constructive result of "Solving the Problems of the World" in history! So important was the freedom to drink to the citizens of the new country that in 1794, Pennsylvania farmers rose up in the Whiskey Rebellion when the government tried to tax their home brew.

It was in the birthplace of the new republic that a Philadelphia physician, Dr. Benjamin Rush, first began to study the medical problems related to excessive alcohol consumption and to regard the insane compulsion to drink alcohol as a disease. In an article published in 1785, Rush applied the concepts then used to define and describe diseases to the patterns exhibited by problem drinkers and found that these cases showed similarities in inception, course, and outcome. He saw that while alcohol was used "normally" (that is, in conformity with normal and usual social standards for when and where it was appropriate to drink) by most drinkers, a sizable minority seemed to develop an apparently insane compulsion to drink more and more alcohol more and more frequently, to the point where it destroyed their ability to function and ultimately killed them.

Rush's scientific voice was drowned out in the moral outcry of the "temperance movements," which began as a plea for moderation in the use of alcohol but soon came to represent total abstinence as a moral and religious issue. The marriage of the temperance movements and various (mainly Protestant) religious denominations resulted in the preaching of abstinence as a unique feature of American religion. The temperance movement, though it undoubtedly saved many from becoming alcoholic by persuading them not to start drinking at all, missed the point entirely by reducing alcoholism to a moral and religious issue. By doing so, it short-circuited what might have been the expansion and development of Rush's earlier work on alcoholism as a disease and set back the clock on effective treatment for at least a hundred years. In 1919, the culmination of more than one hundred years of growing temperance influence resulted in the enactment of the Eighteenth Amendment to the Constitution and the Volstead Act, prohibiting the manufacture, distribution, sale, and consumption of alcoholic beverages in the United States. Never before in history had an entire country attempted to eliminate the drinking of alcohol.

Prohibition, or rather many people's insistence on drinking in spite of alcohol's illegality, ushered in a period of folklore and legend in America. Most Americans have never really made the connection that the whole romanticized but bloody period of speakeasies, Capone, the Mafia, and the Untouchables is really the story of the desire to drink no matter what the consequences. The principle of all organized crime is to supply the addicted appetite, whether with alcohol, illegal drugs, sex, or gambling. Prohibition, of course, failed, for mere law is no match for the compelling desire to drink, which will disregard the loss of job, family, health, and life itself. But we can theorize that many people who would have become alcoholic during Prohibition did not or were delayed in the development of their disease because of the relative unavailability of drink.*

In 1935, a new movement was born in Akron, Ohio, by a desperately abstinent alcoholic named Bill Wilson and a not-yet-recovering alcoholic physician, now affectionately known as Dr. Bob. Wilson, a previously very successful stockbroker, had suffered many business losses and had been hospitalized numerous times because of his alcoholism. During one hospital stay, he had been exposed to a set of philosophical principles that he found useful in his struggle to remain abstinent. One particularly useful discovery he had made was that when the compulsion to drink was particularly strong, the simple act of talking with another

*There exists today among the ranks of addiction-treatment workers a significant contingent of "neo-prohibitionists," who point out that research demonstrates a clear and dramatic reduction in the incidence of alcoholism and alcohol-related problems wherever there is a reduction in the availability of alcoholic beverages. They point out quite rightly that if alcohol were introduced to the world today, it would never gain the approval of the Food and Drug Administration, and would be as illegal a substance as cocaine or heroin. While they acknowledge that a new prohibition would not deter people already on the developmental course of their addiction, it would dramatically reduce the numbers of new addicts continually coming "on stream" by reducing the social encouragement of and easy availability of alcoholic drink. Though most people do not develop a problem with alcohol, the sheer cost to our society in lost productivity, medical costs, and personal misery certainly makes their point worth considering.

alcoholic who also wished to remain sober often relieved the compulsion entirely. When a proposed business deal went sour, Wilson sought out Dr. Bob, not for treatment but to share their mutual burden of addiction. From their friendship grew the organization that came to be known as Alcoholics Anonymous. Wilson's wife, Lois, coming to terms with her specific problems as the wife of an alcoholic, founded Al-Anon, a Twelve-Step program for codependents, several years later.

In the years 1935–1960, AA was the only truly effective help available to alcoholics. While the religious community preached on the moral dangers of alcohol abuse and the medical community continued to offer treatment of a sort, so little was understood about the physical mechanisms of addiction that only recovering alcoholics were able to truly relate to the agonizing mental, spiritual, and emotional struggles of still-drinking alcoholics. The various Twelve-Step programs available today are discussed in more detail in chapter 14, "The Twelve Steps: The Heart of Recovery."

The post–World War II era saw the dawn of serious medical research on alcoholism as a disease entity. In 1960 Dr. E. M. Jellinek published *The Disease Concept of Alcoholism* (New Haven: Hill House), the culmination of his life's work, which has become the foundation of the modern medical understanding of alcoholism. In his book, Jellinek articulated the view of alcoholism as a disease of genetic origin and metabolic disposition, shed considerable light on the physical and psychological effects of the disease, and described the course of the illness in five different types of alcoholics, which he called the Alpha (continuous use of alcohol to relieve psychological unhappiness), the Beta (who drinks regularly and heavily to the point of medical complications but who displays no physical or psychological dependence on alcohol), the Gamma (who undergoes physical changes as a result of exposure to alcohol, withdrawal symptoms, loss of control, and catastrophic life problems), the Delta (who seldom drinks "too much" at any one time but who cannot stop drinking for even a few days without developing withdrawal symptoms), and the Epsilon (who goes on periodic binges with long periods of abstinence in between). In the ensuing decades, hundreds of researchers, theorists, and treatment workers have expanded and articulated Jellinek's original work until today we have a comprehensive, consistent, and workable body of knowledge about this tragic and terminal disease. It is ironic that alcoholism, which has been so destructive and so visible throughout the course of human history, should have been so poorly understood until the last thirty years.

Despite the tremendous advances in the knowledge of the nature of alcoholism and in the development of effective treatments for the disease, alcoholism and alcohol abuse remain this country's primary health and social problem. Consider the following facts:

- Every year, between fifty thousand and seventy thousand people die in the United States from alcohol-related diseases and accidents. This is the equivalent of wiping out the total population of a city of half a million people *every ten years!*

- Between 50 and 60 percent of all automobile fatalities involve alcohol, resulting in some twenty-five thousand deaths each year.

- Fifty-two percent of violent crime and 43 percent of all crime in the United States is perpetrated by someone who has been drinking.

- At least one third of all suicides are attempted while the victim is intoxicated.

- Sixty-eight percent of instances of spouse abuse occur when the abuser, the abused, or both are intoxicated.

- Thirty-six percent of reported cases of child abuse have involved drinking.

- Problem drinking is the primary complaint in 26.5 percent of divorces.

- Alcohol-related health problems account for 12 percent of all health-care expenditures in the United States. The tab came to $12,743,400,000 in 1975 alone.

- The total economic cost of alcoholism and alcohol abuse to the United States in 1985 was estimated to be in excess of $100 billion. That is the equivalent of $500 for every man, woman, and child in the United States.

Perhaps the most powerful testimony to the power of humankind's relationship to alcohol is the fact that despite the unbelievable cost in dollars and human suffering, we insist on preserving the right to drink. We focus our remedial efforts on rehabilitating those who develop a problem with alcohol while ensuring that the conditions of liquor availability and social encouragement to drink continue to exist. The argument is made in some quarters that if we were a sane society, we would take one look at the statistics listed above and rise up with one voice demanding the elimination of alcohol from our social and economic life.

The first step toward understanding the problem interfering with your life is to recognize that you have inherited several thousand years' worth of accumulated myth, conflicting opinion, legend, and misinformation about alcohol, and by extension, other drug addiction. Unless you can clear your mind of these myths and misunderstandings, you will find it impossible to take any constructive action.

ECONOMIC COSTS TO SOCIETY OF ALCOHOL ABUSE

	($ in millions)	1977	1983 Equivalent
Core Costs			
Direct Costs:			
Treatment		5,637	9,425
Alcoholism treatment in specialty settings	707		
Alcohol-related illness and trauma	4,930		
Support (research, training, education, construction, insurance administration)		735	1,229
Indirect Costs:			
Premature Mortality		10,715	17,916
Morbidity resulting in:		26,074	43,596
Reduced productivity, lost work time	23,593		
Lost employment	2,481		
Total Core Costs		43,161	72,166
Other Related Costs			
Direct Costs:			
Motor vehicle accidents (legal, medical, funeral, etc.)		1,782	2,979
Criminal-justice system		1,685	2,817
Social-welfare programs		142	237
Other (fire losses, fire protection, highway safety)		832	1,391
Indirect Costs:			
Incarceration of alcoholics		1,418	2,371
Lost work time of victims of automobile accidents		354	592
Total Other Related Costs		6,213	10,387
Total Economic Costs		49,374	82,553

Source: Cruze, A., Harwood, H., Kristiansen, P., Collins, J., Jones, D., *Economic Costs of Alcohol and Drug Abuse and Mental Illness—1977* (Research Triangle Institute, Research Triangle Park, N.C., 1981).

ALCOHOLISM IS NOT A PSYCHOLOGICAL PROBLEM

Probably the most pervasive myth about alcoholism today is that alcoholism is a psychological problem. It's not hard to understand how this myth got started. After all, most alcoholics who receive professional attention are seen first by counselors, psychologists, and psychiatrists, because addiction to alcohol creates disturbing behavioral and social problems. Psychologists see the world in psychological terms. When we are presented with a human problem, we naturally and automatically set about to identify the *psychological* reasons why the individual engages in the behavior that seems to be creating his problems.

Millions upon millions of dollars of private and public research funds have been spent on research to determine the psychological causes of alcoholism. Theories by the bushel-basketful have been developed to explain why some human beings seem to want to drink themselves to destruction.

Psychoanalysts, the ideological followers of Freud who believe that the child is the father of the man, advanced the idea in the 1940s and 1950s that people became alcoholics because of early childhood conflicts. Theories were advanced claiming that the alcoholic came from a family where the father was too strict, the mother was too indulgent, the father was too absent, the mother too cold, the sibling rivalry was too intense, and so on ad infinitum. One psychoanalyst even claimed that the alcoholic's fondness for the bottle represented a symbolic longing for the breast created by inadequate breast-feeding in infancy! The net result of all the psychoanalytic research was the startling finding that most alcoholics had experienced some difficulties in childhood and did not come from perfect families. It seemed to take the professional community a while to realize that everyone else experienced childhood difficulties, too, and that no one else came from a perfect family. Saying that alcoholism is caused by childhood conflict is like saying that since most criminals began their lives drinking milk, milk drinking must cause crime. If childhood conflict caused alcoholism, then everyone, or nearly everyone, would be alcoholic.

Close on the heels of the psychoanalysts came the personality theorists, who felt that if we couldn't identify the psychological causes of alcoholism, at least we could note the psychological traits and characteristics of alcoholics, and by so doing we could identify the "addictive personality." This would be important work indeed, because if we knew what personality type became alcoholic, we could identify those individuals who were at risk to develop alcoholism before they began to drink, and hopefully alter their course. The personality theorists set to work studying alcoholics and, lo and behold, they found amazing similarities in their "personalities." They discovered that alcoholics lacked a sense of responsibility, often failing to carry out their duties and obligations. They found a relationship between alcoholism and criminality, and concluded that the alcoholic personality type lacked conscience. They noted that among alcoholics there seemed to be a high incidence of fights and arguments with spouses, employers, and even total strangers, and concluded that the alcoholic personality contained high levels of hostility. They learned that alcoholics complained of more anxiety, more depression, more stress, more frustration, and more general unhappiness than nonalcoholics, and concluded that the alcoholic personality had greater degrees of "neuroticism" than normal.

The fly in the ointment was that the personality theorists were making the same mistake as the psychoanalysts, reasoning backward from the symptom to the cause. In attempting to describe the "alcoholic personality," they studied people who were already identifiably sick with alcoholism. Thinking that they were identifying the personality characteristics that would lead to alcoholism, the personality theorists succeeded only in describing the effects of alcoholism on the personality. Determining that alcoholics have an irresponsible personality is like discovering through research that paraplegics display a marked tendency toward the sedentary life.

The behavioral school of psychology, founded on the notion that all behavior, whether animal or human, is organized on the twin principles of avoiding pain and obtaining pleasure, studied alcoholism from the standpoint of the rewards, or reinforcements, of drinking for the alcoholic. They note that human beings experience pleasure from the effects of alcohol. They find that shy people find it easier to interact when they drink. They identify the relationship between alcohol and sex (one of humankind's most powerful reinforcers), noting that people report that they are less troubled by sexual inhibition and find it easier to initiate sex and find sexual partners when intoxicated. They learned that people use alcohol as a way of coping with troublesome feelings. Drinking relieves stress, diminishes anxiety, lifts depression, and dulls the pain of grief, providing the reinforcement of relief from emotional discomfort. The behavioral explanation of alcoholism is refreshingly straightforward, as psychological theories go—behaviorists claim that people become alcoholic because drinking is rewarding to them.

There are two major problems with the behavioral explanation of alcoholism, however. First, behaviorism, like psychoanalysis before it, failed to explain why everyone is not alcoholic. I kind of like the prospect of a life of pleasurable sensation, easy social interaction, lots of wild and uninhibited sex, and relative freedom from stress, anxiety, and depression, don't you? If drinking is uniformly rewarding to people, then behaviorism should predict that all human beings should display a marked tendency to drink. If, on the other hand, drinking is only reinforcing to some people (alcoholics), then behaviorism is no closer than before to an explanation of why only some people are alcoholic. Behaviorism also fails to explain why some people (alcoholics) do not stop drinking when drinking begins to bring pain rather than pleasure, and punishment rather than reward. Alcoholics, contrary to the theory of behaviorism, continue to drink right through social embarrassments, business failures, divorces, driving accidents and DWI citations, and medical complications. Among the community of recovering alcoholics today, there exists tremendous hostility toward psychologists, psychiatrists, and other mental-health professionals. And with good reason. Firm in our belief that alcoholism was a psychological problem, we killed alcoholics with our ignorance and mistreatment. We told alcoholics that their drinking was due to their "maladjustment" and their "underlying psychological conflicts" and that when these were resolved through psychotherapy, they would either return to normal drinking or would stop drinking entirely. Psychotherapists spent hundreds of hours listening to the painful and confused ramblings of the alcoholic patient, searching for the psychological key that would free him from his addictive prison. This kind of "therapy" ended only in one of two ways; either the patient ran out of money or the patient died. Unfortunately, most psychiatrists, psychologists, and counselors still practice this kind of criminal malpractice on their hapless alcoholic patients.

In the history of psychological research and theory, no consistent psychological basis for addiction has ever been found.

ALCOHOLISM IS NOT CAUSED BY POOR SOCIAL CONDITIONS

The idea that people become alcoholic because of poverty, unemployment, homelessness, or other poor social conditions is the myth favored by the sociologically minded, and it enjoys a historical respectability that goes much further back than the psychological myth. In 1986 I had dinner with an official of the Irish government who told me with an air of bland certainty that Ireland's epidemic drug and alcohol troubles were the direct result of the poverty and unemployment in that country. He was sure that if a way could be found to improve the social conditions in Ireland, there would be a corresponding drop in the incidence of alcohol and other drug addiction. Sounds logical, doesn't it? Then again, the idea that alcoholism is caused by psychological factors sounds quite logical until you give it some thought. In several weeks of conversations with Irish lay and professional people, I met no one who seemed to consider things from the other way around—that the overwhelming prevalence of drug and alcohol abuse in Ireland, and the tradition of social support for it, is a major contributor, if not *the* major contributor, to the poverty and unemployment that have plagued Ireland for so long.

There has been a long history of associating alcoholism with the "lower class." One hundred years ago Charles Dickens's novels were promoting the idea that poor social conditions caused alcohol addiction, along with crime, vice, and numerous other social problems. His contemporary, the artist William Hogarth, created images of alcoholism amidst the squalid conditions of London's inner city that still shape our thinking about alcoholism.

Every major city in this country has a skid row, and for most of us the first image that comes in association with the word alcoholic is of the skid-row bum, sitting in a puddle of his own urine or staggering down the street panhandling. Many of us first saw such people as children and were frightened by them. We realized, or were told, that this man was drunk, and since we are creatures of association, we learned to think of alcoholism as just another part of the larger picture of the poor social conditions of the inner city.

Let's conduct a short exercise in imagination. Conjure up your own image of a skid-row bum. He's dirty, unshaven, perhaps toothless, and smells of vomit and urine. He sleeps in a mission or flophouse when he can get a bed, sleeps in the streets when he cannot. His age is hard to figure, but guess him at about sixty. The key question that seldom occurs to us: How did he get to skid row?

Now, turn your imagination's clock back and imagine the same man at fifty. How do you see him now? I see him as somewhat poorly groomed, but he still has most of his teeth. His clothing is inexpensive, but he bought it himself. He's single, but he has a place to live, perhaps a modest, sparsely furnished apartment or a room in a rooming house. He's working at the most recent in a chain of marginal jobs, as a dishwasher in a doughnut shop. In his coat pocket is a pint bottle of gin, which he meters out carefully. It has to last through the eight hours of his shift.

Now picture him at forty. Well, what do you know! He looks pretty normal. If you look closely, you can see that his eyes are a bit red, but he's adequately groomed and dressed. He works as the manager of the toy department in a chain department store, and his career has kind of stalled on him, for reasons he can't understand. His employees notice that his moods fluctuate, that he's generally in a bad mood in the morning, but his mood is usually better after lunch. Only he knows that he has taken to having a couple of shots for lunch from the bottle he carries in the glove compartment of his car. His wife and two children, who are about to leave him, know about his problem, but they don't understand it. All they know is that he's become moody and irrational, impossible to live with, and that he sits in his den and drinks every night.

Now envision the same man at thirty. Amazing. Who would have thought that old bum could have been such a good-looking young fellow. He's single, having been divorced from his first wife after he got drunk and hit her for the third time. He has friends and is generally well liked because he's always the life of the party. True, he does get drunk on most drinking occasions, but everyone has faults, right? He does well on his job and is a good prospect for career advancement with the department store chain he works for.

Imagine him now at twenty. He has just gotten married to his high school sweetheart, and he plans to work hard, have babies with her, own a home someday, and generally build a normal life. Not like his bum of an old man, who loved his bottle more than his family. After watching the drinking, and because of it the family violence, the financial insecurity, and finally his father's disappearance altogether, he swears he'll never, ever allow himself to turn out like his old man.

• • •

Our little exercise in imagination illustrates the fact that seedy old bums don't spontaneously and magically appear on skid row. The few alcoholics who end up there do so by following a long downhill path of deteriorating ability to function. Most led more or less normal childhoods, had jobs, were married, have children, but ultimately lost everything to their compulsion to drink. When we see these nameless men and women for the brief ten or twenty seconds before we turn our eyes away, we automatically associate them with the environment in which we see them, and this association quite naturally leads us to assume that their alcoholism is just another part, and not the cause, of the dismal social conditions in which they live.

- Fact: Fewer than 5 percent of alcoholics and other addicts ever spend a night on skid row.

- Fact: A 1978 research study showed that 52 percent of the "lower classes" were total abstainers, while only 34 percent of the middle class and 21 percent of the upper class abstained from alcohol. The percentage of drinkers, and therefore the percentage of them who become "problem drinkers," actually *rises* as income, and education rise.

It is certainly true that as income and education rise, drinking problems become less visible. Financially comfortable alcoholics don't commit economic crimes because they have no need to. Alcoholic business executives and professors have secretaries and spouses who cover for them. Middle-class alcoholics and prescription-drug addicts sip and pop pills in the privacy of their homes, their habits supported by a spouse's salary and a caring physician's prescriptions. But make no mistake: *At any given time there are twenty times as many alcoholics in the homes, business offices, and schools of America than there are on all the skid rows put together.*

Social conditions and social class may create differences in attitudes, behaviors, and patterns of alcohol and other drug abuse, but poor social conditions play absolutely no role in the cause of addiction.

ALCOHOLISM IS NOT A MORAL ISSUE

The history of moral and religious thought about alcoholism and alcoholics is ancient. The Bible first mentions alcohol in connection with Noah, who apparently felt it necessary to stock the ship's larder liberally to help him cope with the rigors of caring for all those beasts. After they made landfall, Noah got drunk to celebrate and passed out naked. His son, Ham, made the mistake of observing his father in his shameful state. With typical alcoholic defensive anger, Noah laid a curse on all of Ham's future generations.

Most of the world's major religions tolerate and even approve of the use of alcohol on occasion but regard drunkenness as immoral or sinful. Judaism permits the use of alcohol on any occasion and requires the use of wine on Passover and certain other holidays (indeed, on Purim the celebrating Jew is encouraged to drink enough so that he "couldn't tell Haman from Mordecai in the dark," that is, to become moderately drunk). Islam and certain Buddhist sects maintain an absolute prohibition on drinking.

Religious groups of American origin or of predominantly American membership tend to place great stress on total abstinence. Methodists, Baptists, Mormons, Quakers, Jehovah's Witnesses, and Seventh-Day Adventists all formally require abstinence for members in good standing. This emphasis on abstinence is the product of the marriage of religion and the temperance movement during the nineteenth century. Drinking is considered immoral and sinful by these groups, not only because it is harmful to the body but also because it is associated by them with a life-style that may include gambling, sexual permissiveness, and other forms of vice.

Among religious groups in the United States, Roman Catholicism is by far the most progressive in its attitudes toward alcoholism and the alcoholic. No prohibition against drinking is made, but the fact that alcoholism is a disease is recognized. The Catholic church extends a "special dispensation" to parishioners and priests who suffer from alcoholism, giving them permission to refrain from partaking in the sacramental wine. Total abstinence is generally recognized by the church as necessary for recovery from alcoholism.

The position that alcoholism is a sign of moral weakness or willful sin puts the alcoholic in an awful position from a moral and religious standpoint. The religious alcoholic (and there are many) must experience not only the tyranny of her compulsion to drink but also the censure of her moral and religious convictions each time she takes a drink. Her self-esteem suffers not only from her inability to control or discontinue her drinking but also from her conception of herself as a sinner and a moral reprobate. In order to participate in her religious activity, the alcoholic must conceal and deny her drinking, forcing her into a life of "secret shame." If the sick, sad alcoholic happens to be a member of a religious group that espouses the moral view of alcoholism, she can expect no help, guidance, or support from that quarter.

No alcoholic in history ever chose to become alcoholic. No human being has ever voiced the ambition to become a habitual drunk, to damage his and his family's health and happiness, to suffer progressive sickness and loss. No sane person (and despite appearances, most alcoholics are perfectly sane people in the absence of alcohol) has ever consciously chosen the life of misery, shame, and physical pain that accompanies alcoholic drinking.

Alcoholism is a disease, not a sin or a moral weakness.

ALCOHOLISM IS NOT CAUSED BY LIFE'S TRAGEDIES

The idea that people become alcoholic as a result of difficulty or tragedy in their lives is a tricky one, because like some of the other misconceptions about alcoholism, it appears to have some surface validity. We've all heard of the man who "became alcoholic because he was unemployed for a year" or the woman who "started to drink alcoholically when her husband died." The picture of the hopeless soul who turns to alcohol to relieve the pain of grief, failure, or loss is a familiar one that appeals both to our sense of logic and to our feelings of sympathy.

It is true that people often drink very heavily under extraordinary conditions of emotional or psychological distress. Soldiers under combat conditions are known to consume large amounts of alcohol (the Viet Nam War is famous for the centrality of alcohol, marijuana, and heroin to the lives of the troops). Grieving spouses often go through a period of heavy drinking after the loss of their husband or wife. The first agenda for some men who lose their jobs is to go out and get drunk. Recently divorced people sometimes begin to drink heavily to deal with feelings of loss and loneliness. The fact that is not generally noted in this line of reasoning is that *the vast majority of such people return to their normal pattern of drinking as soon as the psychological emergency has passed.*

For reasons we will explore later, roughly one out of every ten people who begin to drink will go on to develop alcoholism. Some of these people will experience life tragedies or extraordinarily difficult conditions during some period in their lives. Because they drink as a normal part of their life-style, many of them will use alcohol as a way to deal with the tragic or difficult circumstances they face. And guess what? About one in ten of these people develop alcoholism! More accurately, about one in ten of these people will experience a permanent exacerbation in the quantity and frequency of their drinking as a result of their increased use during a time of life stress, while the other nine will return to their normal patterns when the crisis or tragedy passes.

If it were true that life's tragedies and difficulties caused alcoholism, there would be many more alcoholics than there are. Nearly everyone can point to a time in his or her life that was extraordinarily difficult, stressful, or even tragic. Many people who drink will state that during that period they drank more than normal, and more frequently than normal. The distinguishing feature of alcoholism is that the alcoholic continues to drink in the heavier pattern even after the difficulty has passed.

This does not even take into account that for the incipient alcoholic—that is, the drinker who is on her way to alcoholism but whose family, friends, and associates have not yet recognized his drinking as a problem—personal tragedies are sometimes the result of drinking. The inadequate performance that resulted in the loss of a job may have been caused by heavy drinking. The divorce and the bitter arguments that led to it may have been aggravated by alcohol. Remarkably often, neither the alcoholic nor the people around her who are aware of the drinking make the connection between the drinking and the difficulty.

Life's difficulties may exacerbate alcoholism, but only in the alcoholic. They do not cause alcoholism.

• • •

It would be the height of arrogance for me to think that in one chapter I could successfully clear your head of the legacy of several thousand years of myth and conventional misinformation about alcoholism and, by extension, other drug addiction. Hopefully, though, I've helped you to discard a few of the more unhelpful notions about addictive disease that stand in the way of your doing something constructive about it.

2

THE NATURE
OF ADDICTION

There is an old story about five blind men who encountered an elephant one day. The elephant, sensing no threat, stood by patiently while they attempted to determine its nature. The first blind man stepped forward and ran his hands over the elephant's foreleg. "Aha," he said, "the elephant is a kind of tree." "I'm sorry, but you're wrong," said the second blind man, around whose waist the elephant had companionably wrapped his trunk. "The elephant is in fact a species of snake." "No, no," said the third, firmly grasping the elephant's tail. "Elephant is a variety of thick rope." The fourth, focusing the attention of his perceptive fingers upon the elephant's marvelous ear, pronounced with dignified certainty, "I agree with our first distinguished colleague that the elephant must certainly be a tree, but of a quite unusual type, for it has the most remarkable, immense leaves." The fifth blind man, upon whose unfortunate torso the elephant had inadvertently stepped while the blind man was performing a tactile examination of his undercarriage, gasped,

"Can you all be so blind? The elephant is a dangerous beast whose power and weight can crush any human who falls under its feet!"

There has been an elephant in your home, and its name is alcoholism. Someone in the family brought it home as a pet a long time ago, and you thought it was nothing more than a large dog, inconvenient, but not entirely without its amusing aspects. Though you didn't really want it around, you tolerated it. As it grew, you found you had to make certain adjustments in your life-style. You began to spend a disproportionate amount of time cleaning up "accidents." The house began to smell, well, "gamy" might be an appropriate word. It became too inconvenient to have guests, because the elephant was just too difficult to explain.

Finally you began to consult the experts about what to do about your problem. The psychiatrists said it was a psychological problem and to get therapy for it. The clergyman said it was a moral problem and to pray about it. Friends and relatives said it was just a phase and to bear with it. The social workers said it had to do with unemployment, and to focus your efforts on getting a job, or on getting your alcoholic a job. Meanwhile, there you have been, under the elephant's foot, trying to get someone to understand that it's killing you.

Alcoholism is a physical disease. Alcoholism is genetic, metabolic, progressive, and ultimately terminal. Though it is a disease that affects the entire body, and causes a variety of health and medical problems, its primary symptoms are exhibited in the nervous system. Through the nervous system, primarily the brain, which is the organ that organizes thought and behavior, it produces distinct pathological abnormalities in the thought, emotions, and behavior of the victim.

It is absolutely critical that you understand every word of the preceding paragraph if you hope to accomplish any solution to your problem. Because it is so important, we're going to take the next three chapters taking that paragraph apart piece by piece.

ALCOHOLISM IS A PHYSICAL DISEASE

There is certainly no doubt in anyone's mind that alcoholism is, in the larger sense, a disease. There has certainly been more than enough "dis-ease" in your life to convince you. But what kind of disease? We have already looked at the mistaken and even destructive notions advanced by well-meaning experts' suggestions that alcoholism is a psychological disease, or a moral disease, or a disease of society. What basis is there for the assertion that alcoholism is a physical disease?

We know that in America, roughly one out of every ten people who drinks alcohol will develop symptoms of alcoholism. We know that people who become alcoholics have experienced no greater degree of difficulty or trauma as children than those who do not develop the problem. We know that people who become alcoholic displayed no greater incidence of troublesome character or personality traits *before* they began to drink alcoholically than those who did not become alcoholic. We know that people who become alcoholic do not have lower moral values, fewer ideals, or less religious involvement than those who do not, particularly *before* they showed symptoms of alcoholism. We know that people who become alcoholics do not necessarily come from the "lower" social classes; in fact, if any class distinction applies, it is the opposite.

We also know some positive facts. We know that people from different racial, ethnic, and national origins fall victim to alcoholism at greater or lesser rates. We know that alcoholism travels in families, and that children of alcoholics become alcoholic themselves at much greater rates than children of nonalcoholic parents. We know that the bodies of people who become alcoholic adapt to the presence of alcohol in the system in a different way from those who do not become alcoholic. And we know that alcoholics from every social class, every occupational category, every racial and ethnic group, every variation in life circumstance, and every religion find amazing similarities in the unfolding, or *course,* of their disease as they share their stories. These facts point to the presence of a common thread in alcoholism that transcends class, religion, morality, and psychology and has to do with the unique process of interaction of alcohol and the human body.

WHO BECOMES ALCOHOLIC?

The factors that determine who will develop the disease of alcoholism seem to be a complex interaction of the characteristics of the *host* (the victim of the disease), the *agent* (alcohol, marijuana, cocaine, heroin, prescription drugs, and so on), and the *environment* (the cultural, social, and personal situation of the victim). If the host has the proper genetic and metabolic *susceptibility,* and if he or she uses the agent, particularly if the environment supports the use (that is, allows it to be available, condones it, or encourages it), then the host will develop addictive disease.

The vast majority of Americans drink alcoholic beverages from time to time, some more often than others. We all began to use alcohol for pretty much the same reasons (we enjoyed the effect, it was the social thing to do, it was fun, it was associated with happy times, it enhances celebration, and so forth). A minority of us (approximately 8–14 percent) who drink went on to develop alcoholism. What was different about these people?

We do not as yet know enough about the genetic and metabolic *predisposing factors* of alcoholism to accurately predict who will become alcoholic and who will not long before the first drink is taken, but promising work is now going on at several medical facilities with precisely that aim in mind. Perhaps one day soon such a predictive ability will be possible. The ability to predict, and therefore in many cases to prevent, alcoholism would eliminate untold human suffering.

We do know that there appear to be significant differences in how the bodies of alcoholics deal with the substance alcohol. Researchers have found that the livers of alcoholics do not metabolize (that is, digest and eliminate) alcohol in precisely the same way that the livers of nonalcoholics do. A precise description of the metabolic actions of alcohol is beyond the scope of this book. However, the research indicates that the differences in the way that the alcoholic liver handles alcohol may result in the buildup of certain brain enzymes that are chemically quite similar to opiates, producing in the alcoholic an entirely different and altogether more attractive quality of "high" than any experienced by nonalcoholics. This better quality "high" is probably present in the alcoholic from the beginning of his drinking and may account for the early preoccupation with drinking that is one of the early signs of alcoholism. Dr. Joseph Pursch, the medical director of the Betty Ford Center, illustrates this "high-quality high" in a particularly down-to-earth manner:

> *Just imagine that you were the only person in your family or social group who experienced sexual orgasm. You wouldn't know that what you felt was anything different from the norm, but it would certainly make your behavior very different from that of those around you. No one would understand why you made such a big deal about sex. Your interest in dating would seem obsessive and pathological. Your interest in sexual matters would*

be taken as a sign of low moral character. The energy you spend on Tuesday arranging for a date on Friday night would seem extreme and driven. You would be considered abnormal and even sick, and after a while, you might consider yourself that way.

—Joseph Pursch, M.D., in a Seattle, Washington, public lecture, 1985

We know that genetic differences exist between alcoholics and nonalcoholics, and these will be discussed at length later in this chapter. We know that children of alcoholics, particularly sons of alcoholic fathers, fall sick with alcoholism at a much greater rate than children of nonalcoholic parents.

We know, if you grant the applicability of studies on animals to our understanding of human beings, that different genetic strains show important differences in their degree of preference for alcohol. This principle of genetic differences may explain in part the fact that different racial and ethnic groups show very different rates of alcoholism. Jews, Italians, and certain other ethnic groups have very low incidence of alcoholism, in some studies reported to be as little as 2–3 percent of those who drink. Northern Europeans, from whom the majority of people in the United States are descended, show much higher rates of alcoholism, perhaps as much as 20–30 percent of drinkers, according to some studies. Other ethnic groups, for example Native Americans, report that as many as 80 percent of those who ever take a drink become alcoholic.

We know that alcoholics report much less negative effect of alcohol, particularly early in their drinking career, in terms of hangover. While the nonalcoholic person may get drunk from time to time, he or she feels violently ill the next day, and typically does not want so much as to smell alcohol for weeks after the episode. The alcoholic, by contrast, may feel a little rocky in the morning but by afternoon feels fine, and by evening is anticipating drinking.

If we look at alcoholism as a physical disease, we can see clear physical differences in the host, that is, the person who will become alcoholic, as compared with the "normal," or nonalcoholic, population. The greater the strength of the *genetic predisposition,* the higher the likelihood that the individual will develop the disease.

It also appears that there are important differences in the addictive *potential* of various *agents,* or substances. Alcohol, as a matter of fact, would appear to have a fairly low addictive potential when it is compared with some other drugs to which people become addicted. Whereas only about one out of every ten people who drink in the United States becomes alcoholic, heroin addicts perhaps as many as eight out of ten. So we could say that heroin possesses eight times the addictive potential of alcohol. Many prescription drugs also have been shown to have very high addictive potential, some of which you may have in your medicine cabinet at this moment. People who are addicted to Valium, Xanax, Percodan, Dilaudid, Darvon, codeine, and many other prescription drugs are seen in treatment centers all across the country. The addictive potential of marijuana appears to be very much on the rise due to the recent availability of more powerful strains of the plant. The exact degree of addictive potential of cocaine is not known but is presumed to be much higher than that of either alcohol or marijuana, yet probably lower than that of heroin.

The higher the addictive potential of the agent, the greater the likelihood that the individual who uses it will develop addictive disease.

The environment also plays an important role in determining who becomes alcoholic, but not in the way that is commonly understood. We have already seen that people do not become alcoholic because of poor social conditions, family problems, life tragedies, or psychological problems. The role of the environment in which the host exists is important to the degree that it either supports or discourages the use of alcohol. Even if a person possesses those genetic qualities that would qualify him as a host for alcoholism, if he lives in an environment that forbids, discourages, or punishes the use of alcohol, or denies him access to alcohol altogether, he may never be exposed to the agent, and therefore never develop the disease. On the other hand, if he lives in an environment that supports, promotes, encourages, and reinforces the use of alcohol, the probability that he will be exposed to the agent or substance is much higher, and with it the likelihood that he will become alcoholic.

The United States is a highly supportive environment for the use of alcohol, and indeed for many other addictive drugs, though our consciousness has been changing in recent years. Although radio and television advertising of hard, or distilled, liquor and showing people actually drinking beer or wine on television have been prohibited, the alcohol industry spent $492 million in 1977 on advertising. Alcohol is richly interwoven in our American myths and legends and is associated with manliness, heroism, good times, sophistication, and affluence. Adolescents mark their coming of age by the date they reach the legal drinking age. Institutions like the "three-martini lunch" and the "happy hour" (both of which, happily, have faded in popularity in recent years) create in some business people the sense that drinking is a business necessity.

Other countries vary in the degree to which they provide a supportive environment for drinking or other drug use. Saudi Arabia, for example, prohibits the use of alcohol entirely for its citizens in accordance with the national religion, Islam, which forbids the use of alcohol for the faithful. Other Islamic countries heavily discourage alcohol use and exact stiff penalties for

HOW HOST, SUBSTANCE, AND ENVIRONMENT COMBINE TO PRODUCE ADDICTION

	Host	
Low genetic susceptibility	Host	High genetic susceptibility
Low addictive potential	Substance	High addictive potential
Low support for use	Environment	High support for use

A.   A person with a low genetic predisposition to addiction who is exposed only to substances with low addictive potential in an environment that does not encourage its use almost certainly will not become addicted.

B.   A person with a low genetic susceptibility to addiction, if exposed to substances that have only moderate addictive potential, probably will not become addicted, even when cultural and environmental support for use is high.

C.   A person with a high genetic predisposition to addiction may develop addiction to substances that have only moderate addictive potential, even when the environmental support for use is low.

D.   A person with a low genetic predisposition, even if exposed to substances with high addictive potential, probably will not become addicted, especially if the environmental support for use is low.

E.   A person with a high genetic susceptibility to addiction may develop addiction to substances that have only moderate addictive potential, especially when the environment supports use.

F.   A person with only a moderate genetic predisposition to addiction will nevertheless develop addiction if he is exposed to substances that have high addictive potential in an environment that supports and encourages use.

G.   A person with a moderate or even high genetic predisposition to addiction may nevertheless avoid addiction if he is exposed only to substances with low addictive potential and remains in an environment that discourages use.

H.   A person with a high genetic predisposition to addiction is almost certain to develop addiction when exposed to substances with high addictive potential in an environment that supports use.

unauthorized or illegal alcohol and other drug use. We would predict that such countries would have lower rates of alcoholism, not because there are fewer potential hosts, but because the environment does not support the use of the agent.

Similarly, we would expect to see lower rates of alcoholism among Mormons or Baptists, who also observe the prohibition against alcohol. This is not because fewer Mormons or Baptists possess the genetic predisposition for alcoholism but because fewer members of those faiths ever begin to drink.

We would logically expect that in those areas of our country where life is lived in the fast lane, where drinking is promoted as fun, entertaining, and glamorous, where particular religious values do not govern the customs of the area at large, where liquor is readily available at all times, the reported rates of alcoholism would be the highest. Where the opposite is true, we would expect that the rates would be the lowest. True to form, the highest concentrations of alcoholism are in the District of Columbia, Nevada, New York, and California, in that order, while the states reporting the lowest rates of alcoholism are Mississippi, Kansas, Hawaii*, and North Dakota.

The greater the extent to which the environment supports the use of the agent, the greater the number of genetically predisposed hosts who will be exposed to the agent, increasing the rate at which people will develop alcoholism.

The following examples illustrate the interaction of host, agent, and environment in the development of alcoholism.

Mike is a thirty-year-old stockbroker who lives in Los Angeles (environment). He is of Irish Catholic extraction (host), the son of an alcoholic father (host). He enjoys drinking greatly (host, agent), and although many of his friends smoke marijuana, he much prefers alcohol (agent). He really likes L.A., with its glamorous image and exciting nightlife (environment). Recently he has begun to have several cocktails at lunch (host, agent, environment). Mike is at high risk to develop alcoholism.

*The position of Hawaii probably has more to do with its high percentage of citizens of Asian descent. This is actually a genetic rather than an environmental factor.

• • •

Alice is a thirty-four-year-old lawyer who lives in Kalispell, Montana (environment). Her father was killed in combat when she was an infant, but her father's brother suffers from alcoholism (host). In law school she drank frequently at parties and was beginning to be concerned that she might be drinking too much (host, agent, environment). When she came to Kalispell, she met and married her husband, who is a recovering alcoholic, so she does not drink in their home or when she is with him (environment). It is a secret of hers that one of the reasons she so much enjoys the occasional business trip to Seattle or Portland is the opportunity to enjoy the more exciting restaurants and lounges, and the opportunity to drink freely (host, agent, environment). On the whole, however, she enjoys her "life in the slow lane" in Kalispell and her marriage (environment). Although Alice appears to have some of the genetic predisposition to develop alcoholism, the lack of support for drinking in her environment reduce her to only a moderate risk of alcoholism.

• • •

Barry is a thirty-eight-year-old owner of a retail store in Minneapolis. He is the eldest son of a prominent Jewish family, and there is no history of alcoholism in the family (host). Although Barry drinks sacramental wine at Passover and other occasions when he is expected to (environment), he finds it quite distasteful (host). He got drunk once in college trying to be one of the guys, and the result was that he was sick for a week (host, agent). For the life of him, he can't understand how some people find drinking enjoyable. Like his father, Barry considers alcoholism to be a sign of personal weakness (host, environment). Barry is at very low risk of developing alcoholism.

ALCOHOLISM IS A GENETIC, METABOLIC DISEASE

The word genetic refers to the genes, the biochemically encoded instructions that tell the body how to construct itself originally and how to reconstruct itself throughout its lifetime. Each of our parents contributed half of our genes, and they determine such physical characteristics as eye color, hair color, general body build, height, sex, race, blood type, and thousands of other characteristics that comprise our total physical make-up. Genes also determine certain mental and behavioral characteristics, such as intelligence or aggressiveness. Some genetic characteristics may be emphasized, modified, or suppressed by environmental factors (for example, a genetically "tall" person may suffer a long-term illness in childhood that prevents him from attaining his growth potential), but these characteristics remain latent in the genetic code, some waiting to be triggered by factors in the environment, others never to appear but to be passed on to offspring.

The genetic factor in alcoholism has been documented for at least two hundred years, since Dr. Benjamin Rush noted that alcoholism traveled in families. More recent studies have demonstrated without question that genetics plays an important role in deciding who will become alcoholic and who will not. Research has shown that sons of alcoholic fathers run a 50 percent chance of developing alcoholism themselves, a risk *five times* greater than random. Studies of fraternal twins demonstrate that the twin of an alcoholic stands a 30 percent chance of becoming alcoholic. In identical twins, the risk rises to a frightening 60 percent.

But how can we be sure that these studies prove that heredity, and not environment, is the factor at work here? After all, could not the son of the alcoholic father simply have learned his drinking behavior from good old Dad? And wouldn't it also make sense that Dad did his drinking in a culture that supported it, the same culture that the son would have grown up in? Couldn't the fact that a high proportion of twins share alcoholism be more simply explained by the fact that siblings learn from each other?

Maybe. But the genetic researchers also asked these questions. Medical and psychological researchers have traditionally studied children who were adopted at birth to compare the effects of heredity versus the effects of learning. In an adoption study, researchers reason that if heredity is the more important factor, the child should be more like her natural parents, with respect to the characteristic under study. If, on the other hand, learning and imitation are the more important factor, than the child should be more like her adoptive parents. In the early 1970s, Dr. Donald Goodwin reported on an important series of adoptive studies to determine whether heredity or environment was the more important factor in whether the adopted children of alcoholic parents would themselves develop alcoholism (Donald W. Goodwin, M.D. *Is Alcoholism Hereditary?*, New York: Ballantine Books, 1988).

Goodwin tracked a group of children born to alcoholic parents who were adopted at birth by nonalcoholic adoptive parents. He found that *four times as many* of the biological children of alcoholics became alcoholic themselves, even though they had no exposure to alcohol in their adoptive homes. In a second study, Goodwin compared a group of children given up for adoption by alcoholic parents with their siblings who continued to be raised by the alcoholic parents. Goodwin found that the adopted children were *just as likely* to develop alcoholism as their brothers who were raised in the alcoholic home.

Surprised? These studies clearly indicate that genetic heredity, rather than environment, is by far the more powerful factor in the cause of alcoholism. They point clearly to the notion that "alcoholics are born, not made." They suggest that the infant with the heredity predisposition to alcoholism is a genetic loaded gun waiting to go off when exposed to the triggering agent, alcohol. The importance of the environment lies only in the degree to which it permits, encourages, or makes it possible for the genetically predisposed host to gain exposure to the agent alcohol.

Another powerful indication that alcoholism is a genetically transmitted disease is the fact that while there are no important differences in the rates of alcoholism related to education, social class, psychological makeup, sex, or degree of life difficulty, rates of alcoholism do differ among groups of different racial and ethnic origin. Studies indicate that people of Asian heritage show differences in their production of certain liver enzymes responsible for the metabolizing of alcohol, causing an uncomfortable and unpleasant reaction of flushing, sweating, pounding heart, and headache for many when they drink alcohol. This natural "Antabuse reaction" (Antabuse is a drug that creates these symptoms in response to alcohol) among Asians probably accounts for the very low rate of alcoholism among Japanese, Chinese, and Korean people.*

Jews and Italians also have very low rates of alcoholism, reported in most studies at 1–3 percent of those who drink. Northern European people display startlingly greater rates, reported at as much as 30 percent of those who use alcohol. Native Americans are reported to develop alcoholism at a shocking

---

*I have often wondered whether the Asian alcohol intolerance contributed to the popularity of opium use in the Orient. Opium addiction may have been the Asian alternative to alcoholism.

80–90 percent of those who drink! Not for nothing did the early Native American chiefs and medicine men label alcohol the "white man's poison."

Dr. James R. Milam proposes an interesting theory about why rates of alcoholism differ by ethnic population. He points out that those ethnic groups who report the lowest prevalence of alcoholism are also the groups with the longest historical exposure to the agent alcohol. For a variety of reasons, alcoholics may be assumed to produce offspring at a slower rate than nonalcoholics. Alcoholics do not live as long, and therefore have a shorter reproductive life. Male alcoholics are often sexually dysfunctional. Alcoholics would not be seen as desirable mates because of their instability and unreliability as providers. Alcoholics sometimes smell bad and also are prone to more arguments with their spouses, both of which discourage sexual interaction. Fetal Alcohol Syndrome causes miscarriage and stillbirth. Milam's theory is that since alcoholics are not competitive breeders, the genetic predisposition for alcoholism should gradually, by the process of natural selection, be bred out of the gene pool of a specific ethnic population.

Milam then observes that Jews, Italians and other Mediterranean groups have had consistent exposure to alcohol throughout recorded history, and that these groups, with the genetic predisposition to alcohol largely bred out of the gene pool, show the lowest rates of alcoholism. Northern Europeans, however, whose exposure to alcohol dates only from Roman times, about two thousand years ago, report a rate of alcoholism ten times greater than that reported for the Mediterranean groups. Native Americans, among whom as far as we can tell alcohol was virtually unknown before the coming of the white man some 350 years ago, fall victim to the disease at a frightening rate. Milam's theory suggests that the longer a group has been exposed to alcohol, the greater the opportunity for the process of natural selection to eliminate the genetic susceptibility to alcoholism.

Further research promises to lend support to this fascinating theory.

While research has utterly failed to show any role of psychological or sociological factors in the cause of alcoholism, there is considerable research support for the role of heredity and genetics.

3

THE
PROGRESSION
OF ADDICTION

ALCOHOLISM IS A PROGRESSIVE DISEASE

In the course of my clinical practice I have worked with up-ward of a thousand alcoholics and other drug addicts, and while I recognize that each individual is a unique and special person, I have never ceased to be amazed by the remarkable similarity in their accounts of the effects of alcohol in their lives and the stages through which alcohol came to play an increasingly dominant role. So predictable is the course of this illness that many patients feel as if I can read their minds, anticipating before they tell me the specific trail of events and circumstances that eventually led them to my office. When I sense that a specific patient is not ready to accept the diagnosis of alcoholism at this time, I sometimes offer them predictions about what it is likely that their immediate future holds; some of these patients have

returned months or years later and have told me that the thing
that ultimately convinced them that they had the disease was the
accuracy of my predictions.

Unfortunately, I can neither read minds nor foretell the
future. My apparent clairvoyant abilities come from the fact that
alcoholism is a disease, and as a disease, follows a predictable
course. If a patient has leukemia, it matters not whether he or she
is a doctor or a clerk, a man or a woman, rich or poor, educated
or ignorant. If a person catches cold, he or she will develop a
stuffed nose and a sore throat, no matter what age, sex, social
class, or occupational category. To my mind, the most convinc-
ing proof that alcoholism is a primary disease (that is, not a
symptom of another disease) is the predictability of its course.

As we have seen, alcoholics begin to drink for pretty much
the same reasons that everyone else does. Drinking is seen in our
culture as a pleasant, adult, sophisticated, social, cultured thing
to do. It relieves tensions and enhances social and sexual situations. Alcoholics are virtually indistinguishable from nonalcoholics in the *prodromal* phase (predrinking and very early drinking).
But as the alcoholic's body begins the process of forming the
adaptive and ultimately addictive relationship with the substance
alcohol, a lengthy series of events is set in motion that affects the
thinking, behavior, and life circumstances of the alcoholic. This
series of events is called the course, or progression, of the disease.

Dr. E. M. Jellinek, generally recognized as the father of
modern alcoholism treatment and research, was the first to me-
thodically chart the progression of the disease of alcoholism,
though many others before him commented on the striking
similarities in the stories of alcoholics. The familiar U-shaped
"Jellinek chart" (the first half of a modified version of it appears
on page 62), which describes so accurately the progressions of
alcoholism and other drug addictions, is very familiar to most
workers in the addiction field.

THE PROGRESSION OF ADDICTIVE DISEASE

Born with a genetic and metabolic predisposition to addiction, the alcoholic or addict awaits only the exposure to the substance to begin the course of addictive disease.

First use occurs. Powerful positive response.

Social activities and friendships become more centered on use.

Rapid increase in tolerance. Drinks or uses substance more and more.

EARLY First blackouts occur.

STAGE Repeatedly drives while under the influence.

Increasing dependence. Surreptitious use. Gulps first few drinks. Volunteers to be bartender so others won't count his drinks.

Suffers frequent guilt and remorse over use.

Loss of control. Becomes more frequently unable to stop when he intended to. Memory blackouts increase in frequency. Refusal to talk about substance abuse.

DWI citation, possible job loss, financial difficulties

MIDDLE begin.

STAGE Offers excuses and rationalizations for use.

Grandiose, impulsive, or aggressive behavior appears.

Efforts to control begin. May "go on the wagon" but always resumes use. If alcoholic, may switch to beer or wine only or make other rules to control use.

Financial, social, and legal problems increase.

Ability to function decreasing. Sexual functioning diminished. Job performance suffering. Marital discord. Interpersonal friction.

Vows to stop but fails repeatedly.

Physical dependence. Signs of withdrawal. **LATE**

Noticeable physical deterioration. Medical **STAGE** problems. Divorce. Inability to work.

Use becomes constant. Mental functioning severely impaired, may seem crazy. Retreat to "skid row" or its equivalent.

Death from accident, violence, organ failure, or overdose.

Source: Adapted from the work of E. M. Jellinek and M. M. Glatt, M.D.

The progression of addictive disease includes legal, social, familial, psychological, and psychiatric complications of alcoholism as well as medical complications. No matter the economic class, profession, gender, psychological makeup, or life circumstance of the alcoholic, the disease follows a similar course. For most alcoholics, the tracing of the course of the disease in their own lives is a matter of filling in the blanks with the specific names, places, and life circumstances. Not every alcoholic finds every event described on the chart in his or her own life, of course, but for most, the pattern is remarkably descriptive of his life story since he began drinking.

We might argue that the chart should begin with the taking of the first drink, since we have learned that from the first exposure to the agent alcohol, the genetically predisposed host alcoholic is on his inevitable course toward alcoholism. Most professionals in the addiction field would agree that in the light of current knowledge about alcoholism, several important early warning signs appear before the beginning of Jellinek's chart. We have learned, for instance, that while most people begin drinking because they feel that it's fun, chic, sophisticated, and feels good, these reactions in the alcoholic-to-be are amplified considerably. While the nonalcoholic late adolescent who starts drinking may feel that it's fun, the early alcoholic will feel that it's *wonderful.* While the nonalcoholic teenager might say that the effect of alcohol is pleasant, the early alcoholic teenager will say that it makes him feel on top of the world. The early alcoholic's enhanced response to alcohol leads to a *preoccupation* with drinking, drinking associates, and drinking occasions. He becomes fascinated with experimenting with different kinds of drinks and different combinations of alcohol. Most teenagers, alcoholic or not, find their primary opportunities to drink on weekends, and the young alcoholic's preoccupation may result in his being the organizer of parties and drinking occasions, beginning on Monday to organize Friday night's drinking party.

Preoccupation with alcohol soon leads to changes in the alcoholic's social life. Her relationships with nondrinking friends become more distant, while she spends more and more time with drinking friends. "Straights" become boring to her as she begins to associate her drinking friends with fun, excitement, and "high times." With parents, teachers, and other adults, she appears to close off, becoming like a closed book they can no longer read. It is at this point that parents often face a dilemma: While they are very concerned about their child's new and apparently unwholesome friends, they feel reluctant to interfere and create tensions and animosity. The young alcoholic may become a stranger in the house—surly, negative, defensive, and sometimes quite intimidating.

I have portrayed early alcoholism in the teenager, because it is during this time that most young people in America begin drinking, but it should be borne in mind that these symptoms of preoccupation, social changes, and increasing isolation are seen in the earliest stages of alcoholism even when drinking begins in adulthood. I have talked with alcoholic patients who had their first drink in their thirties, and they report the same sequence of events.

Jellinek takes his starting point at the time when the alcoholic has discovered that for him alcohol is a wonderfully effective antidote for all kinds of disturbing feelings, including anxiety, stress, shyness, tiredness, and depression. Alcohol is not very effective at helping most people with these feelings, but the unique brain chemistry of the alcoholic responds to the substance, creating feelings of relief, freedom from care, and euphoria. (People who have become addicted to prescription drugs will especially relate to the relief phenomenon. Indeed, it may have been difficulty in coping with troubling feelings that caused their doctor to originally prescribe the medication. So similar are the effects of "minor" tranquilizers to those of alcohol that

Valium, a highly popular drug in the 1960s and 1970s, has been called by some addicts "the vodka pill.") The wonderful thing about using alcohol to cope, for the alcoholic, is that it works every time. What a discovery! No more relying on chancy and hard-to-learn coping skills like relaxation for stress, social skills for shyness and loneliness, healthy attitudes to cope with anxiety and depression. The alcoholic finds that relief is just a swallow away. It never fails to produce exactly the right blend of relaxation, exhilaration, and euphoria that "takes the edge off" life's difficulties. Nonalcoholics have difficulty understanding why the alcoholic would want to drink exactly at the times when one would think he or she would most need all the faculties to cope with a tense or difficult situation, not understanding that the special brain chemistry of the alcoholic actually allows alcohol to improve his coping ability in the early stages of the disease.

As the alcoholic begins to use alcohol for a variety of social and emotional reasons, his body adapts to the more and more frequent presence of alcohol in the system, and he finds that he can tolerate greater amounts of alcohol without penalty of hangover or even severe intoxication. This increased *tolerance* is sometimes a source of great pride to the alcoholic, who usually does not understand its significance and takes it as a sign that he is safe from, or even immune to, alcoholism. Often in treatment we hear an alcoholic boast that he "used to be the person who would drink everyone under the table and then drive them home." Younger alcoholics will often express disdain for their further progressed alcoholic brethren who "can't hold their liquor."*

This period of enhanced coping with alcohol doesn't last long, however. Soon, the wonderful "coping medicine"

*Older alcoholics who have significant liver damage may begin to show the effects of drinking after only one or two drinks.

becomes itself a source of stress on the body and the nervous system. Alcohol in particular ranks high among drugs of abuse as a veritable bludgeon on the nervous system. As the alcoholic comes to drink greater quantities of alcohol at more frequent intervals, his body is thrown into a constant cycle of anticipation of intoxication, intoxication, and recovery from intoxication. Normal sleep patterns are disrupted, and the alcoholic lives with a resident fatigue that is so constant he comes to regard it as normal. A vague and general feeling of illness comes to be normal also, and the alcoholic comes to expect the morning headache, the sour stomach, and the general sense of being "out of it." So strong is the sense of fatigue and unwellness that some alcoholics who stopped drinking before some terrible crisis struck report that they "just got sick and tired of feeling sick and tired."

Blackouts (alcohol amnesias) come fairly early in the progression of the disease. Blacking out is not the same thing as passing out. A blackout is the loss of short-term memory rather than the loss of function. The alcoholic in a blackout may walk, talk, drive, and otherwise behave normally. His drinking associates may not even be aware that he is intoxicated. He may or may not get into trouble during a blackout. The experience of a blackout is truly terrifying to the alcoholic, who wakes up literally having no memory of the events of the past evening, or of how he got home. Alcoholics are notorious for "forgetting" where they parked the car the previous night, because they came home in a blackout.

Most early-stage alcoholics do not let on that they have had a blackout. There is shame, but more importantly there is the chilling realization that the blackout might signify that there is a drinking problem, and this stimulates the psychological response of *denial* (pretending to oneself and others that it didn't happen). Denial asserts itself in the early stages of the disease and remains the most constant psychological symptom throughout its course. The alcoholic learns to compensate for his blackouts by making cautious and indirect inquiries about his behavior the previous evening and "covering" any suggestion of abnormality in his behavior.

As the alcoholic's involvement with and dependence on alcohol leads to drinking that approaches the limits of anyone's definition of "acceptable" social drinking, he begins to go underground and become surreptitious with his drinking. This is a particular problem for women alcoholics, who still face a cultural double standard with regard to drinking. While the man who drinks too much may be regarded by his friends and associates as a good old boy, a real hell-raiser, Mr. Conviviality, the female alcoholic is viewed as a lush and a disgrace. His sexual indiscretions while under the influence are regarded as conquests, while hers are taken as evidence of easy virtue. His irrationality is seen as "blowing off steam," while hers is proof of emotional instability or mental illness.

Surreptitious drinking is aimed at presenting to others a picture of normal drinking while consuming quantities of alcohol far in excess of normal. The alcoholic may regularly volunteer to play bartender so as to have an extra shot in the kitchen while making drinks for others. She may resort to hidden bottles so her excess consumption cannot be measured by the level of the bottle in view. She may gulp two or three drinks before leaving for a party so it will not be obvious that she is drinking more than others at the party.

With surreptitiousness comes guilt, and with guilt, denial increases. The alcoholic becomes less and less able to admit to himself that there is a problem, much less to others. So paradoxical is the nature of denial that with every step of increasing seriousness of the problem, the alcoholic is less able to see it. The vicious circle tightens as alcohol is the problem covered by denial, and alcohol becomes the fuel that keeps up the denial.

The body continues its process of forming the addictive dependence on alcohol, while the alcoholic employs ever-more-flimsy excuses and rationalizations for drinking.

It is a common misconception that the definition of an alcoholic is a person who cannot stop drinking. Alcoholics often believe this, and cite the fact that they have been able to go "on the wagon" many times as evidence that they do not have alcoholism. In fact, physical dependence on alcohol, evidenced by the appearance of *withdrawal symptoms,* only develops in the late, terminal stage of the disease. During the middle phase, the alcoholic may go on the wagon numerous times. (This phenomenon is very frustrating to the codependent spouse, who so much wants to believe that the problem can be brought under control. Most codependents have ridden the emotional roller coaster of promises to quit, followed by short periods of uncomfortable abstinence, followed by disappointing relapse and renewed denial.) The alcoholic may devise schemes to control his drinking, make bets or pacts on abstinence with other alcoholics, or use abstinence as a bargaining chip with his codependent spouse ("If I don't drink for a month, *then* will you believe I don't have a problem?").

Regardless of the alcoholic's attempts to quit or cut down, the middle stage of alcoholism is marked by *loss of control.* Loss of control is not, as one might think, that the alcoholic becomes a rampaging Mr. Hyde whenever he takes a drink, though a few do. Loss of control is rather the inability to accurately and consistently predict what will happen after the first drink is taken. Most alcoholics and their codependents know about "stopping off for a drink after work." Sometimes the intention is fulfilled, and after one drink the alcoholic goes home to dinner. But sometimes, in spite of the very real intention to have one drink, it somehow becomes eight-thirty. The alcoholic, not in too much trouble yet and being a considerate fellow, calls home to apologize for being late and states his intention to finish his drink and be home in half an hour. By ten-thirty, he feels real remorse, calls home again to say that he got into a potentially important business discussion, but he *will* be right home just as soon as he finishes his drink. At midnight he knows he's in too much trouble to call home again and angrily tosses off another drink as he contemplates how that demanding bitch just doesn't realize how hard he works and how he needs to blow off a little steam once in a while. Damn it, it's humiliating for him to have to come creeping in at two-thirty with his shoes in his hand, and if she were more understanding, he wouldn't have to. When loss of control sets in, the alcoholic cannot accurately and consistently predict whether he will leave when he intended to leave, whether he will drink only as much as he intended to drink, or whether and how much he may get into trouble.

Later in the middle stage of the disease, the alcoholic's ability to perform basic day-to-day functions begins to be affected. He may become forgetful and cease to be punctual. Bill paying and other functions involving attention to details may be too much for the aggravated nervous system. Absences from work and poor job performance may be noted. Friction disrupts relationships with friends and coworkers. He may become aggressive and argumentative or depressed and withdrawn. He may begin to feel persecuted and develop seemingly irrational resentments as fewer and fewer things seem to go right.

As the difficulties with job, marriage, friendships, financial life, and perhaps the law pile up, the alcoholic may attempt the "geographical solution," moving to another city or state in the hope that a fresh start will give him a new lease on his life. The geographical solution never works, of course, since the alcoholic must take his body, and therefore his addiction, with him. But many a codependent has been wooed by a persuasive alcoholic into uprooting the home and family and traveling to another city in the hope that things will finally work out.

Often it is the occurrence of a life crisis that pushes the

alcoholic into the late stage of the disease, and it is this phenomenon that leads naive observers to embrace the myth that life
difficulties cause alcoholism. Late in the middle stage, the crises
begin to come faster than the impaired alcoholic can meet them.
The poor job performance and work absences have resulted in
termination. The unpaid bills cause repossessions and sometimes
bankruptcy. The drunken argument has ended in domestic violence charges. The spouse has left in sorrow or disgust and filed
for divorce. The dreaded DWI citation has finally arrived.

In a desperate state of hopelessness, remorse, fear, and physical need the alcoholic turns faster and harder to the only means
of coping left to him—booze. His mental and now physical
agony are only relieved when he is drinking. Unfortunately,
while alcohol used to help him to cope, he finds that now he is
utterly dysfunctional when he is drinking and utterly dysfunctional when he is not. The alcoholic tries desperately to find the
dosage that will put him into the ever-narrowing middle ground
of just enough alcohol in the bloodstream to ward off withdrawal
symptoms but not so much to keep him from performing minimal functions to live.

This need to meter the dosage gives rise to *maintenance
drinking,* the hallmark of the late, and terminal, stage of the
illness. Much earlier in the progression of the disease the alcoholic discovered that the best medicine for the relief of the
symptoms of alcohol abuse was more alcohol. He learned from
more-experienced alcoholics that a sip of "the hair of the dog
that bit him" in the morning considerably relieved his hangover.
Now he applies this principle to controlling his shaking hands,
his aching head, his depression and anxiety brought on by a
falling *blood alcohol level* (BAL). He unconsciously learns to maintain the dosage by apportioning out a belt every six hours, then
every four hours, then every two hours, ultimately even waking
up in the middle of the night to relieve his discomfort. The
executive with a bottle in his desk drawer, the cabby with a flask

in his glove compartment, and the housewife who sips wine all day are all maintenance drinkers. The fear, depression, anxiety, and physical pain of the late stage are almost indescribable to anyone who has not experienced the tyranny of an addiction. Even if he has somehow maintained his job or stayed married, the alcoholic in the late stage is frighteningly, horribly alone. Who can she tell how bad it really is? Who would understand? And even if someone could understand, wouldn't they try to help her to stop drinking, the very thing her addiction will not permit?

He may try to reduce his life to manageability by leaving his family, quitting school, or taking a job that demands less of his impaired body and mind. All over America there are cabdrivers who used to be stockbrokers, janitors who used to be doctors, and dishwashers who used to be attorneys. Eventually, however, the mental impairment imposed by late-stage addiction prevents the alcoholic from functioning at even the most basic of responsibilities. Malnutrition may set in as she becomes unable even to feed herself properly anymore, and calories from alcohol comprise almost all of her diet. Anxiety, ranging from vague, undefined feelings of fear to horrific hallucinations, becomes utterly debilitating, and the alcoholic may come to be unable to leave home except to replenish the liquor supply. Many late-stage alcoholics commit suicide at this point, simply to obtain relief from the overwhelming anxiety and depression from which there seems no other way out.

The onset of the late stage is the vantage point form which the ultimate crossroad can first be seen. One road leads to recovery, the other road to death. Late-stage alcoholics die from numerous causes, including suicide, automobile fatalities, fires caused by burning cigarettes dropped when passing out, major organ failure, and overdose. Many people do not realize that it is possible to fatally overdose on alcohol, but many alcoholics die each year from overdoses. Most deaths by overdose come from traumatic injuries sustained in a fall, vomiting while unconscious and choking on the vomitus, or from central nervous system depression, which results in a failure of the brain to transmit the signal to the body to breathe.

One of the most insidious things about the course of this disease is that it progresses so slowly. If these symptoms appeared over a period of months or even a few years, the people close to the alcoholic would have no trouble recognizing that a disease process is at work. Though a few alcoholics do pass through all the stages of the disease in just a few years, most take from fifteen to, in some cases, fifty or more years from the onset of drinking to run the complete course of the disease.

Not every alcoholic exhibits every symptom we have discussed, of course, and not every alcoholic descends all the way to the bottom of the Jellinek U-shaped chart before bridging the gap to the right arm of the chart, the recovery side (see page 281). "Bottom," the lowest point on the chart or in the life of the alcoholic, comes to different alcoholics at different points. AA members call those alcoholics who stopped drinking when the effects of alcohol in their lives were relatively less serious "high-bottom drunks." But no matter where the alcoholic hits bottom, all recovering alcoholics ultimately reached the same conclusion: Continuing to live would not be possible if they continued to drink.

We will discuss the process of recovery at a later point in this book. For now, it is enough simply to understand that alcoholism is a progressive illness, with a course that has been well charted by researchers, treatment workers, and alcoholics themselves.

4

MEDICAL AND
PSYCHOLOGICAL
ASPECTS
OF ADDICTION

ALCOHOLISM AFFECTS THE BODY

The substance alcohol is at the same time a social and ritual beverage, a food, and a highly dangerous drug. As a food, it contains the second-highest caloric density of any substance commonly consumed by humans, higher even than sugar, and second only to pure animal fat or butter. Late-stage alcoholics can, and often do, live on alcohol, supplemented occasionally by small amounts of "real" food. The calories in alcohol are "empty," however, containing absolutely no nutritional value. While the body can utilize alcohol for energy, alcohol contains no proteins, no fats, no carbohydrates,* and no vitamins or minerals.

*Beer, wine, and other fermented beverages do contain carbohydrates, but these derive from the vegetable matter used in the mash, not from the alcohol.

Taken as a drug, alcohol has far-reaching and disastrous effects on the entire body, including all the major organ systems. Excessive use of alcohol plays a role in the cause of heart disease. Research has established a clear connection between alcohol consumption and chronic high blood pressure. In *alcoholic cardiomyopathy,* the heart becomes enlarged and flabby, and the condition may lead to complete heart failure. Excessive alcohol consumption can cause *cardiac arrhythmias,* or palpitations. Alcohol appears to affect the metabolism of *lipoproteins,* including cholesterol, and may actually reduce the risk of heart attack in very low doses.

Alcohol is strongly associated with cancer, though no studies have shown conclusively that alcohol is directly carcinogenic. It is probably the case that alcohol acts as a kind of co-carcinogen that irritates the cells of body organs and weakens their immunological response. A high proportion of alcoholics are also smokers, and alcoholics who smoke are estimated to have a fifteen-times-greater-than-normal chance of developing cancers of the mouth and throat. Of the victims of *esophageal cancer,* 60 to 80 percent report a history of alcohol abuse. Alcohol is the primary cause of *liver cancer,* and a high proportion of liver cancer victims have also been found to suffer from *cirrhosis,* a disease almost exclusively due to alcohol. Cirrhosis is an irreversible, frequently fatal condition caused by the severe scarring of the liver from cellular breakdown. These long, thin scars on the liver resemble cirrus clouds, hence the name.

The liver is the organ directly responsible for the metabolism of alcohol and, as we might predict, is the most commonly damaged organ in alcoholism. The most common liver ailment associated with alcoholism is *fatty liver,* a condition characterized by the buildup of nodes of fat tissue in the liver; though serious, it is usually reversible with permanent abstinence. Fatty liver may be a preliminary condition to the development of cirrhosis.

The list of medical conditions associated with the chronic

and heavy use of alcohol is almost endless, ranging from *esophageal varices* (varicose veins in the throat, which can burst and result in bleeding to death) to *rhinophyma* (whiskey nose). Alcoholism affects the reproductive system, causing *dysmenorrhea* (cessation of menstruation) in women, and *gynecomastia* (development of breasts), *testicular atrophy,* and *impotence* in men. Alcoholism affects every organ system of the body.

No organ system so obviously displays the effects of alcohol as the nervous system, however, because the nervous system produces the observable behavior of the alcoholic. Most people have felt the effects of *hangover,* which appears eight to twelve hours after the excessive consumption of alcohol. Hangover is actually a fairly complex condition in which the body is called upon to deal simultaneously with the toxic impact of alcohol on the endocrine system, the gastrointestinal system, and the blood. However, there is no doubt that the primary symptoms of hangover—shakiness, headache, sensitivity to noise and light, anxiety, guilt, and depression—are symptoms of the nervous system. Ironically, early and middle-stage alcoholics appear to suffer less from hangover than do their nonalcoholic counterparts. Often alcoholics will cite the fact that they do not have hangovers as proof that they do not have a problem with alcohol.

When physical dependence on alcohol develops in the later stages of the disease, however, alcoholics suffer hangover to a degree unimaginable for the nonalcoholic in the form of *withdrawal symptoms,* a kind of general protest of the nervous system caused by the absence of the substance alcohol to which it has become *habituated.* Withdrawal is characterized by shakiness, tremors of the hands, headache, nausea and vomiting, cramps, and generalized anxiety. In severe withdrawal, *delirium tremens* (DTs) can occur, with convulsions and hallucinations. DTs are sometimes fatal.

Alcohol can actually cause serious-enough changes in the nervous system to bring about *psychosis* (insanity). In *Korsakoff's psychosis,* a generally irreversible organic psychosis (insanity caused by damage to the brain), the patient is confused, disoriented, and uncomprehending. A precursor condition to Korsakoff's is *Wernicke's encephalopathy,* a condition of general confusion and loss of short-term memory. These conditions have often been lumped together under the general diagnosis of *"wet brain."*

Alcoholic neuropathy is nerve damage due to the irritating effect of alcohol, and results in pain, numbness, and cramping, usually of the legs.

Through the brain, alcoholism affects the thoughts, emotions, and behavior of the victim.

Though the nervous system effects of delirium tremens and psychosis are pretty frightening, of much greater concern to most alcoholics and their codependents are the effects of alcoholism on the *personality* of the alcoholic. We learned earlier that no one has ever demonstrated the existence of a prealcoholic personality, that is, a particular psychological makeup that would dispose a person to become alcoholic. However, as the body of the alcoholic undergoes the adaptive changes to alcohol that result in psychological dependence and physical addiction, the personality of the alcoholic undergoes corresponding changes. While the personalities of prealcoholics differ infinitely, the personality attributes of alcoholics advanced in their drinking careers resemble each other strikingly.

It is important to understand that when a psychologist uses the term personality he does not mean by it exactly the same thing as the commonly understood layperson's meaning of the term. Because of the way our language is constructed, most people come to believe that personality is somehow a thing, a kind of mental or spiritual black box located somewhere in the human brain that determines how an individual will behave. If we meet Mary on five separate occasions, and on each of those occasions she laughs and tells jokes, we say that Mary has a "humorous side to her personality," as if by saying so we were explaining why Mary tells jokes instead of simply describing the fact that she tells jokes. By doing so, we create the illusion that the personality is a thing inside of Mary that dictates that on any given occasion she will laugh and joke.

When psychologists use the term personality, we are simply talking about the general principles upon which a person's overall behavior is organized, including his *mental behavior* (thinking), his *emotional behavior* (feeling), and his *physical behavior*. A few of these principles are inherited, but the majority are learned in the course of living. These principles that govern and organize an individual's behavior come into being because they are useful to the individual in dealing with specific kinds of situations that arise in life. For instance, Mary may have learned early in her life that humor was a good tool to break the ice at social gatherings, or that it drew favorable attention to her and made her popular.

Personality can change as the conditions in an individual's life change, though these principles of behavior sometimes tend to persist long after they are useful to that individual. Much of the work that is done in counseling and psychotherapy can be viewed as an attempt to help a person reorganize the principles that govern his behavior so that they fit the circumstances of his or her current life rather than the previous circumstances of life. For example, Mary might horribly embarrass herself by telling a really inappropriate joke at a funeral reception, and come to feel because of it that maybe humor is not always so appropriate. This new principle will cause her to become more discriminating about when and where she tells jokes.

The increasing presence of alcohol in a person's life, and the events that occur because of it, radically change the circumstances of that person's life, whether that person is himself alcoholic or whether he lives with or loves an alcoholic. As the body's relationship with alcohol becomes stronger, the alcoholic's behavior unconsciously changes to accommodate that relationship.

As the alcoholic becomes less reliable and more out of control, the personality of the codependent unconsciously changes to become superreliable and very controlling. These psychological changes occur very gradually, but after a twenty-year drinking career, both the alcoholic and the codependent appear to be literally different people, their personalities more resembling other alcoholics and codependents than the people they were before the drinking started.

For computer buffs, a good analogy to personality is the Disk Operating System (DOS) of the computer. The computer is a truly wonderful machine when it comes from the factory, and it has certain built-in potentials and characteristics (like the relatively few inherited personality characteristics built into the human infant). But when you bring your wonderful new computer home from the store, the first thing you discover about it is that it won't *do* anything. In order to get your computer to do the things you want it to, you must first give it a personality, a series of operating instructions to tell it what to do when you strike a particular key on the keyboard. The computer gets its personality in prepackaged form from the DOS, a special program that contains a very complex and sophisticated set of instructions that organize and govern the computer's behavior in any given computing situation.

Now imagine that someone is tampering with your computer without your knowledge or consent. This mysterious and mischievous programmer (addiction) at first makes such subtle alterations to your computer's DOS (personality) that you hardly notice it at first. Gradually, you become more and more upset as your computer does strange things and doesn't react the way it's supposed to in certain situations. You consult a computer psychiatrist who theorizes that you bumped the computer when you brought it home from the store, and that's what makes it behave abnormally now. Unsatisfied, you consult a computer priest, who tells you your brand of computer is noteworthy for its underpowered morals module, and advises you to pray that your computer will soon be restored to full functioning. Meanwhile, your computer is going increasingly haywire as that devilish programmer continues his clandestine operations. Finally things get so bad that you're considering junking the whole machine, but the thing that stops you is that you've got hundreds of hours of your time invested in entering volumes of personal information into it that now you can't even get at. The idea of going through all that arduous work with another computer discourages you, and besides, how do you know that the same thing won't happen with a new computer, since you don't know what the problem is? Your behavior has changed noticeably in response to the personality changes in your computer. You've become irritable and short-tempered, and you've adapted to your computer's quirks by adopting all kinds of abnormal computing techniques.

Think how wonderful it would be if someone came along and said, "Look here, the problem is that your program's been tampered with. We can fix the program, but the first task is to stop the molesting programmer from having any contact with your computer. If he can't be stopped, you have no hope of leading a normal computing life." At least you would know what the problem was, and you could set about doing something about it.

A second analogy may be more helpful to nontechnical types. As a devoted horror-movie buff, I recently saw a wonderful remake of the classic *The Fly*. The movie's hero is a scientist who is conducting experiments in teleportation. In the process of sending himself from one terminal to another, a tiny housefly lands on his arm, and the teleportation device, thinking that the fly is part of the scientist, mixes the fly's genetic material with the scientist's. The scientist is reassembled at the new location, and at first the viewer sees no change in him. As the movie progresses, however, we observe subtle changes in his "personality." He becomes much more athletic and displays a marked preference for raw, aged meat. He becomes slovenly in his personal habits and takes to climbing on the walls. The fly's genetic material (addiction) has invaded the scientist's (his personality) and is gradually taking him over, literally transforming him into a fly. Toward the end of the movie (the later stages of addictive disease), the changes come fast and furious. The scientist descends into a hellish existence as a fly, disgusted with his appearance and behavior and horrified at what he has become. The disease has shut him off from the love of his girlfriend and from the comfort of any human contact. Ultimately, he kills himself.

It is as if with the first drink the alcoholic's otherwise normal personality is invaded with the foreign genetic code of addiction, which sets about to reshape his personality to conform to its own structure. By the end of the process, little is left of the personality of the unique and special individual, and in its place is the characteristic personality of the addict.

The personality changes that occur during the course of addictive disease directly parallel the course of the disease. With each step in the development of the physical course of the disease, a corresponding change occurs in the personality of the alcoholic. When drinking begins, the alcoholic's body discovers the powerful response of the high, with feelings of expansiveness, euphoria, and elation. Because of the physical response, the personality changes so that he becomes *preoccupied with alcohol,* and highly motivated toward drinking situations. Because alcohol enhances his ability to relate, converse, express his feelings, and have fun, he increasingly chooses friends who drink and unconsciously starts to avoid friends and situations where drinking is not encouraged.

When the alcoholic's body, via the nervous system, discovers that negative feelings—stress, anxiety, depression, and loneliness—are relieved by alcohol, it becomes a part of his personality to drink when he has such feelings. Conversely, it is important to note that he develops fewer skills to cope with such feelings when he does not drink.

As the body begins to depend on alcohol to maintain its state of well-being, and the alcoholic's drinking begins to exceed normally accepted drinking standards, she begins to drink surreptitiously. Her personality changes to become sneaky in a way that she never was before. With the sneakiness come *feelings of guilt* and a *loss of self-esteem.* These personality changes that occur in the early stage already represent important changes to the personality (the organizing principles of behavior) of the alcoholic.

As the realization that his drinking is not normal begins to dawn, the alcoholic becomes increasingly sensitive to criticism or even mention of his drinking habits. If the subject should arise, he tries to change the subject, or to excuse his drinking with elaborate excuses, or to angrily reject the concerned person who offers the feedback. As the body's relationship with alcohol has become more noticeable, *evasiveness* and *defensiveness* are added to the alcoholic's personality.

When the alcoholic begins to experience the physical phenomenon of blackouts, she becomes *confabulatory,* that is, she learns to make up stories to cover the missing details from her memory. As the occurrence of loss of control increases in frequency, she becomes skillful in *rationalizing* each episode, so that it seems to make sense if taken as an isolated event. As she becomes physically and neurologically unable to perform routine tasks such as bill paying or keeping appointments, *unreliability* is added to the list of her new personality traits.

As he is less and less able to do his job and misses opportunities and promotions, the alcoholic comes to feel that he is being discriminated against and begins to accumulate what will become a long list of *resentments* and grudges. He will assert with *grandiosity* that he is capable of great achievements and that someday he will accomplish them, by God, if someone will just give him the opportunity.

The more neurologically impaired the alcoholic becomes, the less safe it is for him to take part in the kinds of activities from which most people derive interest and pleasure. Skiing or sailing becomes too hazardous. Horseback or even bicycle riding is out of the question. Even moderate exercise becomes distasteful in the light of his physical discomfort. Sex becomes both less interesting and less possible as alcohol inhibits his hormonal and neurological responses to sexual stimulation. As the alcoholic acquires his addicted personality, he becomes *avoidant* of what were formerly pleasurable activities.

As the body's demand for alcohol rises and drinking becomes more frequent and increases in quantity, the alcoholic's former sense of well-being is replaced by physical feelings of *unwellness* and *fatigue,* and his psychological state becomes dominated by *anxiety* and *depression.*

When the body's need for alcohol finally takes the alcoholic into the late stage of the disease, her nervous system is so completely ravaged by alcohol that she may become *irrational* and perhaps *combative.* Her view of the world will have become so distorted that she seems to have *impaired thinking.* (I once had an alcoholic patient who was near death and knew it but wouldn't enter the hospital because she felt she needed to stay at home to feed her cats!)

I have deliberately italicized the descriptive adjectives so that you can see how the disease changes the alcoholic's personality over a period of years or even decades. The advanced alcoholic can be described as preoccupied with alcohol and highly attracted to drinking friends and situations. He drinks to cope with negative feelings and has fewer than normal skills to cope with these feelings other than drinking. He is surreptitious, sneaky, has feelings of guilt, and low self-esteem. He is evasive and defensive. He is confabulatory and rationalizing. He is unreliable, resentful, grandiose. He generally avoids activities that give other people pleasure. He feels unwell, fatigued, anxious, and depressed. He is irrational, demonstrates impaired thinking, and may appear to be mentally ill.

It's not hard to see how psychiatrists and psychologists imagined that there must be one common personality type that would predispose a person toward alcoholism. After all, they only got to study those patients who had already been diagnosed with alcoholism, and they all appeared to be so similar! Little did they suspect that they were dealing with a physical disease so powerful in its impact that it actually changed and re-formed personality according to its own characteristics. It was not true that the patients all had alcoholism because their personalities were so similar. The truth was that the patients' personalities were so similar because they all had alcoholism!

It's also not hard to see why the friends of the codependent who first met the alcoholic at some point in his or her drinking career can't see why the codependent stays with the alcoholic. "Honey," they urge, "you should leave the bum!" They never knew the kind, caring, sensitive, and beautiful person you fell in love with. Their only acquaintance has been with the addiction-transformed personality your alcoholic exhibits now.

Now you know the truth about alcoholism and other addictions. As you struggle to deal with your situation, you will undoubtedly find that the myths and misconceptions you have held for so long will often interfere with your ability to think clearly about your alcoholic's situation and yours. As you work with professionals, even in the addiction field, often they will say things that appear to support the misconceptions rather than the realities. It may even help you to memorize our working definition of alcoholism and to check your thinking against it as you proceed:

Alcoholism is a physical disease. Alcoholism is a genetic, metabolic, progressive, and ultimately terminal disease. Though it is a disease that affects the entire body and causes a variety of health and medical problems, its primary symptoms are exhibited in the nervous system. Through the nervous system, primarily the brain, the organ that organizes thought and behavior, it produces distinct pathological changes in the thought, emotions, and behavior of the victim.

5

ADDICTION
TO DRUGS
OTHER THAN
ALCOHOL

Throughout the previous chapters, we referred to all addiction as alcoholism, because alcoholism is probably the best researched and best understood of the major drug addictions. Most workers in the addiction field believe that addiction is addiction. While various drugs differ in their addictive potential, and the circumstances may vary depending on the legality, availability, and method of use of the particular drug in question, the processes of genetic susceptibility, physical adaptation, dependence with its attendant personality changes, and physical addiction remain essentially the same. I would urge the reader who is addicted to a drug other than alcohol or who is involved with someone who is addicted to a drug other than alcohol to read Dr. Stanley E. Gitlow's definition of the word *alcoholism* on page 22. However, it's quite natural that you would want to know more about the particular drug you or your addict may be using. In this chapter, we're going to discuss some specific information about the three major drugs of addiction other than alcohol—cocaine, marijuana, and prescription drugs.

COCAINE

Like marijuana and alcohol, cocaine is a naturally occurring drug. The alkaloid compound is found on the leaves of a few varieties of the *coca* plant, a moderate-sized bush found in the Andean regions of South America. Coca cultivation has been attempted in other parts of the world but without much success, and today the countries of Colombia, Bolivia, and Peru produce the vast majority of the world's cocaine crop.

Archaeological evidence indicates that South American Indians in ancient times used cocaine regularly, as a food source as well as a ceremonial and medical drug. Coca leaves supply protein and carbohydrates and are rich in vitamins A, B, and E. The Incas of Peru probably chewed the leaves mixed with a small amount of ash, swallowing the juices much as a tobacco chewer uses a chew.

The use of cocaine was probably pretty well controlled by tribal custom and the chiefs and medicine men who governed the tribes, but all that changed when the Spanish conquistadors arrived. Just as modern scientists have discovered that laboratory rats will go to a great deal of time and trouble to earn a cocaine reward, the Spanish conquerors found that coca leaves would motivate the Indians to perform the backbreaking labor of mining silver, gold, and other metals, while diminishing their appetites and enabling them to work many more hours at a time without fatigue.

Europeans did not become generally familiar with cocaine until the middle of the nineteenth century, but when they did, it was "Katy, bar the door." Researchers in Germany identified the alkaloid compound in coca leaves that caused the curious numbing of the tongue when tasted. A few years later an Italian pharmacist and entrepreneur named Mariani concocted a magical tonic that he called Vin Mariani, which was little more than red table wine laced with cocaine. Mariani, a brilliant promoter, provided free samples of his product to famous people in exchange for their testimonials and support. He was successful in obtaining effusive praise for his elixir from personages no less famous than the sculptor Auguste Rodin, author Jules Verne, composer Charles Gounod, inventor Thomas Edison, President William McKinley, and even Pope Leo XIII! Vin Mariani was praised for lifting the spirits, restoring energy, stimulating the creative drive, and even for extending life.

Sigmund Freud, the father of modern psychiatry, became fascinated with cocaine in the 1880s and published his now-famous paper, entitled "On Coca," in 1884. While his public papers described various medical applications of the drug, including its use as a local anesthetic (which became its primary medical application for many years), his private letters to his fiancée, Martha Bernays, praised its psychoactive properties of promoting a feeling of mental clarity, increased energy, and enhanced writing ability. With a dubious medical judgment that may have been influenced by his positive attitude toward the drug, Freud used cocaine to treat a physician friend's addiction to morphine. The treatment was a disaster and resulted in his friend's owning not one but two addictions.*

In 1886, an enterprising American pharmacist introduced a

---

*Medicine repeated the error of attempting to "cure" one addiction by substituting another addictive drug several times in the subsequent hundred years. Morphine was used to "treat" alcohol addiction. Both cocaine and heroin were used to treat morphine addiction. In the 1950s and '60s, barbiturates and later Valium were used to treat alcohol addiction. Today, the United States government spends tens of millions each year to "treat" heroin addiction with methadone, which is just as addictive.

"soft" drink named Coca-Cola, a carbonated beverage flavored with cola and laced with cocaine. Coke, as it came to be popularly called, was single-handedly responsible for transforming the American pharmacy from the European-style chemist's shop of the 1800s to the soda fountain–emporium we know today, because as one researcher notes, it was "the first popularly advertised product that directed the general public to the drugstore." Cocaine was eliminated from the preparation of Coca-Cola in 1903, but even today, Coca-Cola's advertising contains indirect references to cocaine's mood-elevating properties: "Things go better with Coke," and "Coke adds life."

Most individual addicts to any drug experience tremendous initial benefits from it, only to have the piper arrive demanding payment later. Entire societies seem to mirror this process. In the early 1900s a reactive outcry arose from a number of sources warning of the dangers of cocaine. Numerous medical papers appeared pointing out the harmful medical and psychological conditions arising from cocaine use. Freud withdrew his earlier advocacy of the drug and called it "a far more dangerous enemy to health than morphine." Various medical societies adopted official positions recognizing dependence upon and addiction to cocaine. The Pure Food and Drug Act of 1906 limited the use of cocaine in tonics and patent medicines. Finally, in 1914, the Harrison Narcotics Act made the possession and use of cocaine illegal except for medical treatment.

America's second cocaine epidemic began in the mid-1970s. Cocaine has never really been absent from the American scene since its introduction, but in the decades from the 1920s through the 1960s, its popularity, like that of marijuana, was limited primarily to the night world of entertainers and musicians, gamblers, and petty criminals. No one is sure about the exact route by which cocaine rose to its current level of popularity, but it seems reasonable to link this rise to a fundamental change in the American attitude toward drugs in general that occurred in the mid-1960s. Americans have always used alcohol and other drugs, but the 1960s, with its atmosphere of rebellion and revolution, emphasized the use of drugs for the express purpose of experiencing their mind-altering effects. Timothy Leary, a once highly regarded psychologist, publicly advocated the virtues of "mind expansion" through psychedelic drug use. His "Tune in, turn on, drop out" became the battle cry of a generation. Popular rock music, and eventually even country music, made frequent reference to alcohol and drug use, often in a highly positive way. Getting high became an important social, recreational, and for some, spiritual activity.

As the flower children of the 1960s grew up to become the yuppies of the 1980s, they brought their orientation to drugs with them. Cocaine's rediscovery was inevitable in the search for the better high. The "rush," the feeling of euphoria, heightened perception, ego expansion, and increased self-confidence, mental alertness, and sexual excitement achieved with cocaine give it an aura of glitter and glamour that make it highly attractive to many people, and particularly to the driven, upwardly mobile, image-conscious young people of the 1980s. In 1982, the National Institute on Drug Abuse (NIDA) found that almost 10 percent of Americans had tried cocaine at least once, and that 5 percent of Americans had used it during the preceding year. The same study estimated the number of regular users of cocaine (at least once a month) at 4.2 million. In another NIDA study, 16 percent of high school seniors admitted to having used cocaine at least once, nearly double the percentage reported in a 1975 study. With the tremendous increase in cocaine users, emergency room admissions related to cocaine use have soared, increasing an incredible twenty-nine times from 1975 to 1985.

It doesn't take an economist to figure out that anytime you have 20 million people occasionally using a product, and 5–10 million of them regularly using it, you're dealing with a major business. The National Narcotics Intelligence Consumers Committee conservatively estimated that in 1981, forty-five metric tons of cocaine were smuggled into the United States. These estimates are made on the basis of arrests and confiscations. Because of the nature of drug smuggling, no one really knows how much cocaine actually enters the country, but we can assume that the actual figure is much higher than the official estimates.

Americans spend an estimated $40 billion on cocaine every year—and this is just the direct cost of the product itself. Add to that figure the cost of operating the various law-enforcement agencies, of providing medical care to cocaine casualties, and of lost, delayed, or faulty production of goods and services in the workplace, and you begin to get some idea of the enormous impact of the cocaine economy on American life. If the total of all the above comes only to $100 billion, which is probably conservative, it means that the cost of cocaine to every man, woman, and child in these United States is five hundred dollars.

Coca leaves are almost entirely produced in the Andean countries of South America. Only the leaves of the plant are harvested, and only in quantities small enough to ensure the survival of the plant. The leaves are baled and transported to processing centers, where they are rendered into a paste containing the cocaine alkaloid. It takes about one hundred pounds of leaves to manufacture one pound of cocaine paste. The paste is then transported to laboratories, where it is purified by a relatively simple chemical process to the finished product, *cocaine hydrochloride.* The finished salts vary in their concentrations of cocaine, but it is in the best interests of the smugglers to find the purest cocaine available, allowing them to transport the most cocaine per unit of weight. The cocaine is then smuggled by boat, land, or air into the United States. The smuggler is richly rewarded for his efforts, realizing a profit of 400–700 percent.

Once the cocaine has entered the country (the United States accounts for the vast majority of world consumption of cocaine), it enters a trickle-down system of distribution. The importer, often an organized crime syndicate, "steps on" (adulterates) the product using a variety of substances, which may include milk sugar, powdered baby laxative, lidocaine, procaine, benzocaine, aspirin, or amphetamines. The specific composition of the "cutting" agent will affect the action of the drug, so that different batches of cocaine will affect the user differently. The cutting process turns the original one hundred kilos into a substantially greater amount of the compound, perhaps as much as 150 kilos. The importer then sells smaller quantities of the "stepped-on" product to regional distributors, who step on the product again. The original importer may have paid the smuggler $3,000 per kilo for the one hundred kilos, making his total investment $300,000. He sells the 150 kilos of stepped-on product to regional distributors for, say, $8,000 per kilo, realizing a profit of $900,000 (300 percent) on his original investment of $300,000. Each regional distributor, who may have bought perhaps ten kilos, cuts the compound again, increasing his supply to fifteen kilos, and selling each kilo for about $15,000, realizing a profit of $145,000 (180 percent) on his investment of $80,000. The bigger street dealers buy individual kilos for $15,000, and sell to smaller street dealers in ounce quantities for perhaps $800 per ounce, realizing a profit of approximately $30,000, or 200 percent. The smaller street dealers step on the product again, increasing the ounce to 1.5 ounces, and sell the product by the gram for $100–$150 per gram, earning a tidy profit of $2,000, or 250 percent. It doesn't take much imagination to see why a commodity that turns such profits in cold, hard, nontaxable cash should quickly become big business.

Just as with alcohol, addiction to cocaine seems to depend on the interaction of host, agent, and environment. Good studies do not yet exist to identify host variables that may render a person susceptible to cocaine addiction. The evidence suggests, however, that cocaine has a much higher addictive potential than alcohol or marijuana. Of particular concern is that during the period of 1975–1985, the environment in the United States became immensely more supportive of cocaine use.

The first exposure of the cocaine addict-to-be is almost always experimental. A friend or business associate touts the drug as the greatest thing since sliced bread and urges or even pressures the user to try the drug. Usually the first administration of cocaine is nasal, the finely chopped white powder inhaled into the nose and sinus cavities through a tube, where it is absorbed by the nasal mucosa. Many people have an indifferent or even unpleasant response to the drug (as with alcohol, there are individual differences in the user's response to the drug), and these people may never progress beyond experimental use. The cocaine addict-to-be experiences the very pleasurable effects of the drug from two to five minutes after "snorting" it. He feels a sense of heightened perception, increased mental alertness, enhanced self-confidence, and general euphoria.

Because of the positive feelings he associates with cocaine, the user quickly adopts a pattern of *social use* of the drug. As is the case with alcohol addiction, he finds that he gravitates more and more to a circle of friends who also use cocaine. Use at parties and social gatherings becomes standard.

The user may then discover that cocaine helps her out in certain specific circumstances or situations. A "toot" before a party may increase her social confidence; a gram used over a weekend may help her to lose those five pounds she needs to look good in her bathing suit for the upcoming pool party. Coke helps him stay up all night completing the term paper that's due tomorrow.

As addiction sets in, the emerging addict displays a pattern of *intensified use,* increasing both the amount and frequency of use. During this stage the user may experiment with other forms of administration, "freebasing" (dissolving the cutting agents with a chemical solution and smoking the purified residue) or "mainlining" (injecting the drug directly into the bloodstream). The user will at this stage begin to go on "coke runs," using the drug continuously for hours or even days until the supply is exhausted.

Intensified use is, of course, quite expensive. Often the intensified user begins to deal in the drug to support his or her use. The businessman in intensified use may embezzle from his company. The woman in intensified use may turn to prostitution or position herself as the girlfriend of a dealer. The blue-collar worker may moonlight as a burglar or resell goods stolen from his company. Intensified users often spend more than a thousand dollars a week on cocaine.

Finally, cocaine use becomes *compulsive.* One of the most pernicious aspects of cocaine addiction is that, unlike addiction to alcohol or marijuana, its use is not self-limiting, that is, the user does not pass out or stop after a certain level of intoxication is reached. Like animals in research studies, who will ignore food, water, and sex to use cocaine until they die, the compulsive user abandons his work, fails to pay his bills, neglects his appearance, stops eating and sleeping. Constant cocaine use becomes necessary to stave off the severe depression characteristic of cocaine withdrawal. The addict loses all ability to function. He deteriorates physically and mentally until finally he is arrested or goes bankrupt or dies.

Cocaine addiction follows a course similar to other drug addictions. It begins with exposure of a predisposed host to the agent. It progresses to a preoccupation with the drug and a gradual social isolation and segregation of friends. Use increases in frequency and quantity until the user must continue ingesting cocaine constantly in order to remain free of the symptoms of withdrawal. As with alcohol, if the use is not arrested, death is the inevitable outcome.

THE

800-COCAINE

TEST

Source: Mark S. Gold, M.D., *800-Cocaine* (New York: Bantam Books, 1984). Reprinted by permission.

The symptoms of cocaine addiction are as plain to see as the signals warning that addiction is perilously close. The questions that follow spell them out in detail. Anyone who answers "yes" to as few as ten of them is teetering on the thin edge of addiction. An affirmative answer to more than ten is a clear signal that coke has taken over, that the user is addicted and is in urgent need of treatment if he is to have a chance to return to decent health and normal living. As a guide for anyone taking the test, we have provided brief explanations and comments to make clear why an affirmative answer means trouble.

Yes   *No*

_____ _____   1. Do you have to use larger doses of cocaine to get the high you once experienced with smaller doses?
(This means you have developed a tolerance to the drug, that is, that you need more of it by a more direct route to achieve the same effect.)

_____ _____   2. Do you use cocaine almost continuously until your supply is exhausted?
(This is called bingeing, and it signals loss of control over drug use.)

_____ _____   3. Is the cost of cocaine the major factor limiting your use, and do you wish you could afford more?

(Your internal controls are virtually gone. The drug is in charge, and you will find yourself doing anything to get it.)

_____   _____   4. Do you use cocaine two or more times a week? (If you do, you are in the highest risk group for addiction.)

_____   _____   5. Do you have three or more of the following physical symptoms? Sleep problems, nosebleeds, headaches, sinus problems, voice problems, difficulty swallowing, sexual-performance problems, nausea or vomiting, trouble breathing or shortness of breath, constant sniffling or rubbing your nose, irregular heartbeats, epileptic seizures, or convulsions?
(Three or more of these indicate severe loss of bodily function related to coke abuse—addiction.)

_____   _____   6. Do you have three or more of the following psychological symptoms? Jitters, anxiety, depression, panic, irritability, suspiciousness, paranoia, problems concentrating, hallucinations (seeing things that are not there), hearing voices when there are none, loss of interest in friends, hobbies, sports or other noncocaine activities, memory problems, thoughts about suicide, attempted suicide, compulsive, repetitious acts like combing the hair, straightening of clothes or ties, tapping the feet for no reason?
(Cocaine abuse is causing psychological problems that are not within the individual's capacity to control.)

Yes   *No*

____ ____   7. Have any or all of the problems specified in the previous two questions caused you to stop using cocaine for a period ranging from two weeks to six months or longer?
(If not, the acquired disabilities are not strong enough to overcome the addiction.)

____ ____   8. Do you find that you must take other drugs or alcohol to calm down following cocaine use?
(You are trying to medicate yourself so as to maintain your cocaine habit without suffering the terrible side effects of addiction. You are, of course, flirting with becoming addicted to a second drug.)

____ ____   9. Are you afraid that if you stop using cocaine, your work will suffer?
(You are psychologically dependent on the drug.)

____ ____   10. Are you afraid that if you stop using cocaine you will be too depressed or unmotivated or without sufficient energy to function at your present level?
(You are addicted and afraid of the withdrawal symptoms.)

____ ____   11. Do you find that you cannot turn down cocaine when it is offered?
(Use is out of your control.)

____ ____   12. Do you think about limiting your use of cocaine?
(You are on the verge of addiction and are trying to ration use of the drug.)

Yes   *No*

_____ _____ 13. Do you dream about cocaine?
(This is related to compulsive use and the total domination of the drug.)

_____ _____ 14. Do you think about cocaine at work?
(This is also a part of the obsession with the drug.)

_____ _____ 15. Do you think about cocaine when you are talking or interacting with a loved one?
(Obsession with the drug dominates all aspects of living.)

_____ _____ 16. Are you unable to stop using the drug for one month?
(This is certainly a sign of addiction.)

_____ _____ 17. Have you lost or discarded your precocaine friends?
(You are stacking the deck in favor of cocaine by reducing negative feedback.)

_____ _____ 18. Have you noticed that you have lost your precocaine values, that is, that you don't care about your job or career, your home and family, or that you will lie and steal to get coke?
(Addiction causes slow but steady changes in personality and the approach to life to reduce intrapsychic conflict.)

_____ _____ 19. Do you feel the urge to use cocaine when you see your pipe or mirror or other paraphernalia? Or taste it when you are not using it? Or feel the urge to use it when you see it or talk about it?
(This is called conditioning and occurs after long-term, heavy use.)

Yes *No*

20. Do you usually use cocaine alone?
(When addiction sets in, this is the pattern. Social usage ceases.)

21. Do you borrow heavily to support your cocaine habit?
(You can be pretty sure you're addicted if you are willing to live so far above your means to get the drug.)

22. Do you prefer cocaine to family activities, food, or sex?
(This is a sure sign of addiction. Cocaine need overrides fundamental human needs for food, sex, social interaction.)

23. Do you deal or distribute cocaine to others?
(This kind of change in behavior signals addiction because it is an accommodation to the need for the drug.)

24. Are you afraid of being found out to be a cocaine user?
(Addicts usually live a double life, preferring not to choose one or another alternative.)

25. When you stop using the drug, do you get depressed or crash?
(This is a sign of withdrawal—a symptom of addiction.)

26. Do you miss work or reschedule appointments or fail to meet important obligations because of your cocaine use?
(The drug has taken over your life.)

27. Is your cocaine use a threat to your career or personal goals? Has your cocaine use caused

Yes   *No*

you to lose interest in your career? Has cocaine caused you job problems? Has the drug caused you to lose your job? Has your cocaine use caused you to lose interest in or to have violent quarrels with people you love? Has your cocaine use caused you to lose your spouse or loved one?

(You would hardly sacrifice so much if you were not addicted.)

28. Do people keep telling you that you are different or have changed in a significant way?

(Addicted people are indeed different from the way they were precocaine. Such comments are a clue to addiction.)

29. Have you used more than 50 percent of your savings for cocaine? Has your cocaine use bankrupted you and caused you to incur large debts? Have you committed a crime to support yourself and your cocaine habit? Have you stolen from work and/or family and friends?

(If you are not addicted, would cocaine be worth these dreadful problems?)

30. Do you believe that your cocaine use has some medicinal value in treating a problem you have with energy, motivation, confidence, depression, or sex?

(Users who believe this are the most likely to develop addiction.)

31. Do you think you have had withdrawal symptoms when you stopped using cocaine?

(Only addicted persons experience withdrawal.)

Yes   *No*

32. If you had $100 to spend would you spend it on cocaine rather than on something for your house or apartment, or a gift for someone you love, on theater, records, movies, going out with friends or family?
(Addicts become so fixated on their drug they can think of nothing else, no one else, and no other form of entertainment.)

33. Do you think that you are addicted?
(If you think so, you probably are.)

34. Do you use cocaine compulsively despite your recognition that the drug is a very real threat to your physical and psychological well-being, relationships, family, and job?
(This is addiction.)

35. Did you ever enter psychiatric treatment or therapy for a cocaine-related problem and not tell the doctor or therapist about your cocaine use or how current or recent it is?
(When an addicted person is pressured into getting help, he may not only try to cover up the extent of his drug abuse, but may also use his treatment as a cover for his continued use of the drug.)

36. Did you have a cocaine problem that was cured either through your own efforts alone or with the help of friends or with professional treatment?
(The critical word is "cured." No addict is really cured—rather, he has a remission of a chronic disease that can recur should he become a user of cocaine again.)

Yes   *No*

—— ——   37. Have you ever used cocaine and had hallucinations, a convulsion or seizure, angina (severe pain around the heart), loss of consciousness, the impulse to kill yourself or others? And when any of these side effects passed, did you figure that you would use less next time or use a purer quality of the drug?

(These side effects are related to addictive use, but the addict prefers to ascribe them to overdose or to the adulterants used to make the drug go further. He then can continue to use the drug under the illusion that it will be okay the next time.)

—— ——   38. Do you leave paraphernalia or a supply of cocaine at work?

(This may be a call for help by a person who feels that his life is out of his control. It is like a suicide note left so that people will find it and prevent the act.)

—— ——   39. Do you sometimes wish that you would be discovered as a user by someone who would see to it that you got into treatment and recovered?

(If so, you know you need help and want it.)

—— ——   40. Do you use cocaine three times a week or even more often, and still try to maintain an interest in diet, health, exercise, and fitness?

(The interest may be there, but the fact is that such heavy use of the drug makes it virtually impossible to act on the interest. There is too great a conflict in values.)

Yes   *No*

41. Have you switched from intranasal use to freebasing or intravenous use?
(This usually means that tolerance to the drug has developed, and it is very likely that you will binge and become addicted in short order.)

42. Have you been using cocaine more than once a week for three or more years?
(With this much use, any stress or change in your life can turn you into a daily user with a high probability of addiction resulting.)

43. Do you find yourself choosing friends or lovers because of their access to cocaine or their cocaine use?
(This kind of behavior usually indicates a life out of control.)

44. Do you wake up in the morning and wonder how you could have let cocaine gain control over your life?
(You are addicted if you have these thoughts.)

45. Do you find it almost impossible to fall asleep without a drink or sleeping pill or tranquilizer?
(You now have a second addiction.)

46. Since you started using cocaine, have you ever wondered whether you would be able to live without it?
(We find that people who raise this question are generally hooked on the drug.)

47. Have you wondered whether you would be better off dead than continuing to use cocaine?

Yes   *No*

(This question usually suggests an addiction so profound that the addict feels himself terminally ill.)

——— ———   48. Have you ever wished that you would die of an overdose in your sleep?
(Same as above.)

——— ———   49. Do you use cocaine in your car, at work in the bathroom, on airplanes, or in other public places?
(You are so desperate you want to be caught—and helped.)

——— ———   50. Do you use cocaine and then drive a car within six hours after use?
(Cocaine has impaired your judgment and you are out of control. Don't wait to get help until after you have impaired or killed a pedestrian.)

MARIJUANA

Marijuana (Spanish for "Mary Jane") is a substance comprised of the finely chopped or shredded leaves of the *cannabis sativa* plant. In and on the leaves is a sticky resin that bears the psychoactive (mind-altering) chemical compound *tetrahydrocannabinol,* or THC. Marijuana is most commonly ingested by smoking a rolled cigarette (a "joint"), a pipe, or a hookahlike affair called a bong, which contains and concentrates the marijuana smoke (this method probably originated in Southeast Asia). Adolescents in particular are often quite inventive and ingenious in constructing homemade bongs from wood, metal, or glass tubing, and even disposable bongs made from empty toilet-tissue tubes. Marijuana is sometimes eaten, in the form of Alice B. Toklas brownies, although this method of ingestion has become less popular in recent years, as marijuana's THC concentration has increased.

The marijuana plant grows prolifically in most tropical regions of the world. It is botanically related to hemp, and stem fibers from the plant have been used in the manufacture of rope. Like alcohol, its mind-altering properties have been known since time immemorial, and it probably played a significant role in the pharmacopeia of tribal medicine men as far back as prehistoric times. Physicians used marijuana as medicine from the Middle Ages until the development of modern drugs that were more specific, more concentrated, and easier to administer.

Drugs have frequently played a role in the process of economic exploitation of subjugated peoples, and marijuana is one of them. Just as the Spanish conquistadors encouraged the chewing of coca leaves by their South American Indian slave workers, the British colonists in North America grew marijuana for use by their slave laborers to keep them pacified and docile. Dr. Mark S. Gold, founder of the National Cocaine Helpline (1-800-

COCAINE), points out that evidence suggests that George Washington grew marijuana on his estate at Mount Vernon and maintained his own personal "stash."

Marijuana remained a legal drug in the United States, but its use never gained widespread popularity until the 1960s. During the first few decades of the twentieth century, its use was generally associated with jazz musicians. In the 1930s and '40s, Harlem was the center of marijuana use in this country.

Ironically, the greatest force for the popularization of marijuana was Harry J. Anslinger, the first director of the Federal Narcotics Bureau, created in 1933 by President Franklin D. Roosevelt. Anslinger launched a hysterical witch hunt against marijuana, claiming that it was part of the "international communist conspiracy," intended to destroy America's moral fiber. Official releases from the Federal Narcotics Bureau stated that marijuana use caused permanent insanity, violent crime, and total disintegration of the social fabric. It was in this climate and with the support of the Federal Narcotics Bureau that the cult classic film *Reefer Madness* was produced.

Anslinger's misinformation campaign, with its gross distortions and obvious scare tactics, backfired in the 1960s in the atmosphere of mistrust of all authority and the questioning of all laws. Rock musicians, whose music symbolized and unified the youth movement of the '60s, openly advocated the use of marijuana in their music. Marijuana became the drug of the antiestablishment, and it clearly contrasted the defiant, antiauthoritarian young from their conformist, Establishment, alcohol-drinking parents. The fact that Anslinger's claims about marijuana were clearly not true became just another example of the Establishment's hypocrisy and lies. "Reefer Madness" became the term used to describe any claim or warning that the use of marijuana could be dangerous or harmful. Anslinger himself was caricatured in underground cartoons as a policeman named "Bull" Slinger.

The marijuana that was generally available during the '60s would barely qualify as what is called "dirt weed" by today's marijuana users. With a THC concentration of around .05 percent, it produced a relatively mild high characterized by a slowing of response, a subjective enjoyment and awareness of music and color, and a "mellow" feeling. Hashish, produced by extracting the THC-bearing resins and compressing them into cubes or slabs, created a correspondingly stronger high.

In the 1970s, soldiers returning from Southeast Asia brought with them seeds from much stronger strains of Asian marijuana.* Thai sticks and Maui Wowie began to replace on the marijuana marketplace the much weaker but previously valued strains of Acapulco Gold and Panama Red. By 1975, the average concentration of marijuana sample obtained by researchers had reached 1 percent, twice as strong as ten years before. Amateur botanists continued to refine their product by selective breeding of the plants, and corresponding studies by the National Institute on Drug Abuse showed steady rises in average THC concentrations every year, until in 1985, average concentrations were measured at 5.5 percent, eleven times more potent than the marijuana of 1965. These are average concentrations and do not include the concentrations of special strains like sinsemilla, a premium product at a premium price, containing THC concen-

---

*The use of marijuana was extremely widespread among American troops during the Viet Nam War, presumably because it provided them with substantial relief from the trauma, terror, and horror of the war. As with alcohol in previous wars, many soldiers who used marijuana heavily discontinued or decreased their use when they returned home. Some, however, in whom the addiction process had been set in motion, continued their use after their return from combat, experiencing a progression in their addiction very similar to the progression of alcoholism. Posttraumatic stress syndrome, the "Viet Nam vet's syndrome," is a very real psychological condition; however, I have seen a number of people whom psychologists and psychiatrists have diagnosed as suffering from posttraumatic stress syndrome, ignoring or regarding as a psychological symptom very obvious indications of alcoholism or marijuana addiction. When will we learn to stop explaining away addiction as a psychological problem?

trations of up to 14 percent, a stunning twenty-eight times as powerful a drug as the comparatively innocent marijuana smoked by the '60s flower children.

As concentrations rose, so did prices. Marijuana of the '60s was sold by the ounce, in plastic bags called lids. A lid of average marijuana sold for $10–15, while the specialty strains like Acapulco Gold could command as much as $25–$40. Today marijuana is sold by the gram (there are approximately twenty-eight grams to the ounce), and a gram costs as much or more as an ounce did in 1965.

It doesn't take an economics genius to see that at these prices marijuana soon became an important cash crop for the agriculturist who wasn't particular about the law. Dr. Mark Gold cites statistical estimates that suggest that marijuana is the third-highest crop produced in the United States, higher than soybeans, grapes, lettuce, or tomatoes, bringing in some $10 billion annually. The economic advantages of growing marijuana are enormous for the farmer prepared to risk criminal penalties. Marijuana is grown as a cash crop in backyards, in houses that are not occupied but are rented under assumed identities, and in remote areas of public lands. The legitimate farmer raises, say, lettuce, for which he might get fifty cents a pound, on land he had to buy, after harvesting it with equipment and workers he had to pay for. The illegal horticulturist who raises marijuana may get as much as five thousand dollars a pound (if he handles all aspects from growing to selling himself). He can obtain his seed without risking smuggling by simply purchasing a small quantity of marijuana from someone else, and get high to boot. He has no need to invest in land, and he can perform all labor himself with no special equipment. And if he is reasonably discreet and careful, his risks are limited to the possible loss of his crop by confiscation. It is no mystery why the growing of marijuana has become a huge underground agribusiness.

Who smokes this $10 billion worth of marijuana? The citizens of these United States. Marijuana is not an export crop, though it continues to be imported heavily, mainly from South America. There are few places in the world where people can afford to pay the kind of prices that marijuana commands in this country. Studies suggest that as many as sixty million Americans have tried marijuana, and at least fifteen million are regular users.

An upsetting proportion of marijuana users are kids. One third of all marijuana addicts admitted to treatment centers across the nation said that they began to use pot before the age of fourteen. A recent study conducted by the National Institute on Drug Abuse showed that marijuana use among kids aged twelve to eighteen is twice that among adults. One in ten high school seniors smokes pot every day and averages more than three joints per day. Half the high school seniors studied reported that they had used grass at least once in the preceding year. Numerous studies show that it is not at all unusual for children to begin pot smoking in the third or fourth grade.

Parents may have a difficult time even suspecting, let alone detecting, that their child is involved with marijuana. The psychological and behavioral symptoms of marijuana addiction are almost perfectly camouflaged by the "normal" abnormal behavior of adolescence. Rebelliousness, defensiveness, negativity, the tendency to be isolated, and the cultivation of nonconforming styles of dress and hairdo are all taken as normal, or at least not indicative of drug involvement in adolescence. To complicate the picture even further, many of the parents of today's adolescents were the adolescents and young people of the '60s, who still maintain the attitude that marijuana is an essentially benign drug, and who may themselves be addicted to it. I have heard numerous parents state that they would "rather have my kid smoking dope than drinking any day."

There are some definite signals that can help the parent distinguish between normal adolescence and drug involvement.

PARENTS' CHECKLIST FOR ADOLESCENT DRUG ABUSE

1. Has your child's overall grade average fallen markedly during the past year?

2. Has your child been arrested during the past year?

3. Has your child been suspended or otherwise disciplined by the school during the past year?

4. Has your child been cited for DWI or another driving offense during the past year?

5. Are you aware if your child has ever used alcohol, cocaine, or marijuana?

6. Does your child consistently seem depressed, sullen, and withdrawn?

7. Does your child consistently seem defiant, uncooperative, and irritable?

8. Does either parent regularly use alcohol or other drugs in the home?

9. Have you observed drug paraphernalia among your child's possessions?

10. Have you observed eye drops or mouthwash among your child's possessions?

11. Have there been repeated disappearances of cash?

12. Does your child express sympathetic attitudes toward drug use?

13. Has your child been repeatedly truant from school or in violation of his nighttime curfew?

14. Does your child have a persistent cough, reddened eyes, or stuffy nose, especially when there is no history of allergy?

A yes answer to three or more of these questions indicates that you should suspect that your child is involved with alcohol and/or other drugs.

A sudden (over the period of a year) drop in overall grade average indicates a decrease in attention span and general mental functioning. Disappearing cash may signal drug purchases. While emotional instability is characteristic of adolescence, a chronic condition of depressed, sullen, withdrawn irritability is a signature of drug dependency in the adolescent. Drug paraphernalia is of course indicative of use. (You should take the time to familiarize yourself with the amazing variety of devices to contain and to use drugs. Most local police departments have collections of paraphernalia and are glad to show them to parents.) If your adolescent even owns eye drops, it is virtually guaranteed that he or she uses them to cure the reddened eyes that result from smoking marijuana. While it is natural and normal for the adolescent to want to emphasize his or her individuality and to stake out her own territory (a DO NOT ENTER sign on the door of the adolescent is normal), the presence of a sullen, angry stranger in the house is not. A persistent cough may indicate either cigarette or marijuana smoking, but generally marijuana smoke is the much more irritating to the lungs. Nonconformity in dress and grooming is normal, but trappings suggesting violence, sadomasochism, or satanism may be associated with drug abuse.

Today's marijuana, as we have pointed out, is a very potent intoxicant that induces a profound slowing of motor responses, drowsiness, an inner "glow," sensitivity to music and color, and in some cases distortions of light and sound so powerful as to be similar to hallucinogenic effects. Under some conditions, it may also induce deep anxiety and paranoia.

Tolerance (needing more and more of the drug to produce the same high) develops fairly rapidly with marijuana, primarily because, unlike either alcohol or cocaine, THC stores in the body's fat cells for a considerable length of time, and the body adapts to its presence. The principle here is that to achieve the high requires that the user raise his body's THC content over normal. Naturally, if the normal THC concentration in the body is zero, it requires relatively little of the substance to get high. But if the user has stored a considerable amount of THC in his or her body by regular pot smoking, then a substantially greater amount of the drug is required to raise the THC concentration above the acquired "normal" level.

As tolerance develops, withdrawal symptoms are seen. The withdrawal symptoms of marijuana are relatively mild when compared to those of alcohol, manifested primarily by irritability, low tolerance for frustration, inability to concentrate, diarrhea or constipation, and very strong cravings for the drug. Because marijuana stores in the body's fat tissues, the period of *detoxification* (the process by which the body cleanses itself of the poisonous chemical) is very lengthy when compared with other drugs of abuse. Clinicians note that marijuana addicts often do not seem to be "clear," that is, mentally alert and fully intact, for as long as three months after terminating their use. This is in marked contrast to alcohol or cocaine addicts, who seem to be in pretty good shape mentally one to two weeks after use is discontinued.

There are serious medical and psychological consequences to marijuana addiction. The respiratory system (nose, mouth, throat, and lungs) are irritated by the smoke, which is much richer in tars than even the smoke of cigarettes, causing colds, sinus infections, bronchitis, asthma, and cancer. Because marijuana is "fat seeking" (that is, the THC stores in fat cells), it invades the fat-rich reproductive glands, the ovaries and the testicles, reducing the amount of reproductive hormones they produce. The result is that ovulation is disrupted in women and sperm count is lowered in men, interfering with fertility.

The nervous system, primarily the brain, is also an extremely fat-rich organ system and attracts the THC molecules from marijuana. Because we use our brains to organize and govern our behavior, it is through the brain that the physical processes of marijuana use and addiction become translated to psychological symptoms seen in the thinking and behavior of the addict. The long-term marijuana user becomes irritable, has difficulty concentrating, shows evidence of reduced short-term memory, appears mentally confused, and often behaves in an irrational manner. He eventually develops the well-known *amotivational syndrome,* appearing to lose interest in former activities and projects, becoming careless about his personal hygiene and appearance, and functioning poorly at work or at school. Probably this failure of motivation is related to the addict's diminished ability to perform even the simple and basic tasks required of him. When people can't do a thing successfully, they become frustrated and soon lose interest in doing it at all.

Those codependents to marijuana addicts who have watched the person they care about use more and more of the substance more and more frequently have no doubt about the truly addictive nature of it. Like alcohol addicts of an earlier time, they listened to "experts" deny that addiction to marijuana exists while sinking deeper and deeper into the physical need for the drug with all its psychological complications. Though marijuana is not known to kill directly by overdose, the life of the marijuana addict is ruined just as surely and thoroughly as the lives of addicts to alcohol, cocaine, and other drugs.

PRESCRIPTION DRUGS

Almost 20 percent of the drugs prescribed by physicians in the United States are *psychoactive,* or mind altering. It is unclear exactly how many of these drugs work, but they appear to alter the chemistry of the brain in a way that changes the way it interprets the signals that are brought to it by the nervous system.

Painkillers, for instance, do not of course "kill," or eliminate, pain—they change the way the brain interprets pain signals.

There is something very American about taking a drug to "cure" a feeling. We are a nation of people who expect instant gratifications. When we want something, we want it yesterday. We lack the patience to examine the meaning of feelings, and to respond to their meaning with constructive changes in our lives. Instead, we regard negative feelings as a nuisance, a kind of psychological static to be eliminated as quickly as possible. If we have a headache, we don't take a walk or a nap; we take an aspirin. If we are constipated, we don't exercise and change our diet; we take a laxative. If we are depressed, we don't search for the causes of our depression and modify our lives accordingly; we go to a psychiatrist and get a prescription for antidepressant medications. Of course, some people are genuinely in pain, are clinically depressed, or suffer other conditions that legitimately require the use of psychoactive medication, but the majority of users of these drugs are people who have made the mistake of regarding their feelings as problems to be solved instead of useful information about their lives.

Using a drug to deal with a feeling creates a very dangerous exposure to the possibility of addiction. The general rule of human behavior is "Any behavior that is reinforced tends to be repeated." To be relieved of an unpleasant feeling is a very powerful reinforcement. So the tendency is created to repeat the behavior of taking the drug whenever the feeling is experienced. As you know by now, repeated exposure to any agent that has addictive potential will result in addiction if the host has the proper genetic and metabolic disposition.

There are several major groups of psychoactive prescription medications. *Antidepressants,* as the name implies, are most commonly used in the treatment of certain forms of depression that

NAMES OF COMMONLY PRESCRIBED PSYCHOACTIVE MEDICATIONS

Antidepressants
Adapin
Amitriptyline
Asendin
Elavil
Ludiomil
Nardil
Norpramin
Sinequan
Tofranil
Vivactil

Antipsychotics
Compazine
Haldol
Mellaril
Narvane
Prolixin
Stelazine
Thorazine

Tranquilizers
Ativan
Equanil
Halcion
Librium
Miltown
Serax
Tranxene
Valium
Vistaril
Xanax

Sedative Hypnotics
Amytal
Butisol
Dalmane
Nembutal
phenobarbital
Placidyl
Seconal
Tuinal

Stimulants
Biphetamine
Dexedrine
Fastin
Pondimin
Preludin
Ritalin
Tenuate

Narcotics
codeine
Darvocet
Darvon
Demerol
Dilaudid
heroin
methadone
morphine
Percocet
Percodan
Talwin

result from biological disturbances of brain chemistry (they are not useful or advised to treat depression that results from a loss, grief, loneliness, or other such life circumstance).

Antipsychotics are used to treat schizophrenia and certain other forms of mental illness.

"Minor" tranquilizers, which are not minor at all, and which account for a very great percentage of prescription-drug addiction, are prescribed rather casually by many physicians to patients who suffer from anxiety, tension, and stress. There are legitimate medical uses for the minor tranquilizers, but they are very rare. You should question your doctor's prescription of tranquilizers very carefully indeed.

Sedative hypnotics are dangerous, highly addictive drugs that account for the second-greatest percentage of prescription-drug addiction in the United States. Used widely in the 1940s and '50s as sleeping medications, this group includes the widely abused and recently banned methaqualone.

Also banned in some states and prescribed only with great caution by doctors in other states are *stimulants,* primarily compounds in the amphetamine group. The amphetamines were heavily abused during the 1960s by students cramming for examinations, women who wanted to lose weight, pilots, truck drivers, and others in occupations that demand alertness and wakefulness under long and boring circumstances. Amphetamines have a very high addictive potential and should never be used except for very specific medical conditions, and then under the close supervision of a doctor (if my doctor prescribed amphetamines for me, I would obtain a second opinion).

Narcotics are used by physicians to control acute pain resulting from medical procedures or traumatic injury. These drugs are immensely valuable in controlling shock, inducing anesthesia, relieving immediate posttraumatic or postoperative pain, and alleviating the suffering of terminal cancer patients. They are for the most part either derived from or chemically patterned on opium, and they carry a tremendous addictive potential. Even very short-term use can result in physical dependence and addiction. Narcotics are also dangerous in that the body of the user rapidly builds tolerance to them, requiring greater quantities to produce an intoxicating effect. Narcotics pose the greatest danger of death by overdose.

Many patients fall victim to *iatrogenic addiction,* that is, addiction to a medication prescribed by a physician for a medical reason, but a great many more develop *cross addictions* when they use alcohol, cocaine, marijuana, or prescription drugs in combination with each other to heighten or amplify the effect of their drug of choice. Cross addiction is not thoroughly understood yet, but it appears that as a general rule whenever a drug is used to gain its psychoactive effect within the context of addiction to another drug, cross addiction to the secondary drug will result. Thus, a cocaine addict who drinks will develop alcoholism secondary to his cocaine addiction. An alcoholic who uses Valium or Librium will develop a secondary addiction to these drugs. The founders of Alcoholics Anonymous obviously had an intuitive understanding of cross addiction when they adopted the standard of "complete abstinence from all mind- or mood-altering drugs."

Determining who becomes addicted to prescription drugs is virtually the same as for alcohol, cocaine, marijuana, or other drugs. The interaction of the host (does the user's body have a genetically predisposed responsiveness to the drug?), the agent (does the drug have addictive potential?), and the environment (is the drug readily available, and is the culture permissive or supportive of its use?).

The course of addiction to prescription drugs is also quite similar to the other addictions. The fact that prescription medica-

---

FACTORS THAT DETERMINE THE INCIDENCE OF ADDICTION

Host

Low Risk	*High Risk*
no parental history	addicted parents
low-risk ethnic group	high-risk ethnic group
no sibling addiction	sibling addiction
late onset of use	early use

Agent **Environment**

Moderate Potential	*High Potential*	*Low Support*	*High Support*
alcohol	narcotics	drug illegal	drug legal
marijuana	tranquilizers	social disapproval	social approval
caffeine	nicotine	no availability	easy availability
antidepressants	sedative hypnotics	discouragement	promotion
antipsychotics	cocaine	high cost	low cost

---

tions are carefully controlled and access to them is limited to either physicians' prescriptions or the street market is an inconvenience to the prescription addict and requires her to go to some lengths to get them. Most prescription-drug addicts must cultivate several different physicians and learn exactly what symptoms to complain of in order to obtain their drug of choice. A few wealthy or important drug addicts have actually employed their own physicians to prescribe any drug that suits their current fancy, and several notable celebrities have died of drug overdoses as a result. Of course, physicians and pharmacists stand at very high risk themselves because of their easy access to these drugs.

Whether you or the one you love is addicted to alcohol, cocaine, marijuana, or prescription drugs, it is important that you understand that you are dealing with one disease. Whether you choose to call it alcoholism or addiction is of no real significance.

In all cases, the process of contracting addictive disease is similar. It depends on the interaction of a predisposed host, an addicting agent, and some degree of support from the environment.

In all cases, the course of the disease is similar. It begins with the initial exposure to the agent followed by a powerful, pleasurable response of the host. It progresses to more frequent social use, with preoccupation of the user with the drug, and the narrowing of the user's social circle to the exclusion of nonusers. Relief usage to combat negative feelings follows, and usage becomes covert and sneaky. Life difficulties in job, marriage, interpersonal relationships, medical problems, and troubles with the law may ensue. Decreasing ability to function is noted with the more frequent use of greater quantities. Psychological changes are noted as the user becomes depressed, anxious, unable to meet responsibilities, defiant, defensive, and denying. Physical dependence and the presence of withdrawal symptoms mark the onset of the late stages of addictive disease. With some drugs, most notably cocaine, the course is quite rapid, the entire progression compressed into a few months or years, while with others, such as alcohol or marijuana, the progression may be quite gradual, taking years or even decades to reach the late stage.

In all cases, the outcome is the same. Unless the addiction is arrested by complete and permanent abstinence, the addict dies an untimely and miserable death.

In the next chapter, we'll try to envision a composite addict, again using alcoholism as the model for addictive disease. It is quite unlikely that you or your addict will demonstrate all the symptoms that John does, but if addiction is the problem in your life, you will almost certainly feel a sense of kinship with John or with his wife, Mary.

6

JOHN'S STORY

A numbing sense of unreality came over John as the flashing lights of the police cruiser parked behind him illuminated the night. "Oh, shit," he groaned to himself, "this just can't be happening."

It had been, after all, a night just like a hundred others. He and a few of the other attorneys from work had stopped off for a couple at Callahan's. How many times had they discussed the strictness of the new drunk-driving laws and how much new business they had brought into the firm? He'd never thought much about the fact that gradually a new seriousness had entered everyone's voice when they uttered the ritual good-bye: "Drive carefully." And now here it was.

Not that he was actually drunk, of course. John was a great drinker, always able to handle his booze, seldom getting sloppy or out of line (*tolerance*). And he knew his limit. He would never have more than five or six drinks if he had to drive, except of course on those very rare occasions when the conversation be-

came so engrossing he just couldn't leave right away. Sure, tonight he was a bit high, just like many other nights. He knew
he'd have to be careful driving home. But drunk? Come on. He
was as steady as a rock (*denial*).

And this kid, who was obviously a rookie trying to make his
mark in the force, obviously wasn't going to be reasonable at all.
"God," John thought, "I hope I get this kid on the stand someday. I'll crucify his ass!" Couldn't he understand that they were
both in the fraternity of the law, brother officers of the court?
He'd tried to be congenial. "Ya got me, lawman," he'd said,
grinning as he'd stepped from the car raising his hands in a
parody of a wild West badman. The kid hadn't even cracked a
smile. Instead of a couple minutes of reasonable conversation
and maybe at worst an escort home, he, John Williams, a respected attorney and citizen, was forced to walk a line, touch his
nose with his eyes closed, and breathe into that goddamned
Breathalyzer, which probably wasn't even calibrated right anyway, all with cars driving right by to witness his humiliation.
"First I'll defend myself on this ridiculous DWI," he thought,
"and then I'll sue the ass off this kid, the police force, and the
city. I'm not only getting real mad, but I'm going to get real
even."

"I'm sorry, Mr. Williams," the young officer said, returning
to the car, "but the Breathalyzer shows that your blood alcohol
level is above the legal limit for safe driving. I'm going to have
to cite you for driving while under the influence of alcohol, and
to ask you to come with me to headquarters. You may either
leave your car parked here, or I can radio for assistance and
another officer, with your permission, can drive your car to headquarters."

"Oh, come on, guy! Be reasonable, willya?" John pleaded.
"I'm not drunk, you know I'm not drunk! Okay, I had a couple
after work, don't you? Is that some reason to single me out and
wreck my life? Come on, do you know what you're doing to me

here? Look, I'm an attorney, you're a cop, we're in the same
business, right? Wouldn't you want me to give you a break if the
situation were the other way around? Look, I'll tell you what I'll
do; I'll park the car right here and call a cab. That way you've
done your job and I can get on with my life, okay?"

Sitting in a holding cell at police headquarters, surrounded
by other inebriates, some as well dressed as he, John's fury
continued to mount as the possible consequences of this unbelievable miscarriage of the system occurred to him one by one.
His experience defending drunk drivers told him that if he
pleaded guilty, there'd be a substantial fine, loss of his license for
a year, a day in jail, and a huge increase in his insurance rates.
Maybe the judge would make him go to those AA meetings and
get religion. "No way," he thought. "I'll find a way to attack this
charge on procedural grounds or something."

"Mary's just gonna love this," he thought bitterly. For
going on two years now she'd been bitching about his drinking,
as though it were some kind of problem. The only real problem
about it had been the night he'd lost that personal-injury case that
would have fixed them for life, and he'd gotten well and truly
blitzed. She'd started to scream at him, something about booze
ruining their lives, and at midnight, for God's sake, after all the
liquor stores were closed, she started to pour his bottle of Scotch
down the sink. Okay, he'd smacked her, and he felt real bad
about it, too. Still did. It had been the one and only time he'd
ever hit a woman. Next day, he'd been filled with remorse, and
he'd quit drinking for a month. Of course, when he thought
about it later, he realized that the problem wasn't the booze but
Mary's shrill and hysterical reaction. He certainly hadn't been
proud of the way he'd handled the situation, but then what was
a guy supposed to do with a screaming woman (*denial, rationalization*)? Of course he wasn't an alcoholic like his father (*genetic
predisposition*); after all, he'd been able to stop for a month, hadn't
he? Nevertheless, for the first six months after he started drink-

ing again, he followed some strict rules just to be sure that there was really no problem (*attempts to control*).

The old man, he thought with a wry shake of his head. Most times John just didn't think much about his father, dead ten years now, but whenever the thought of that awful night he hit Mary came to him, memories of the old man and his drunken rages filled his head. Now there was an alcoholic! In John's memory, the old man was a demon who'd made his life and the lives of his mother and two older sisters miserable. He'd been a teamster for many years but had lost his job when John was eight because the company inspector had found a bottle in the glove compartment of his truck. After that, the only thing he'd done steadily was drink. John remembered well the nightmare evenings, when everybody would hold their breath waiting for the inevitable explosion. Mom tiptoeing around, trying to stay out of his way, John and the girls in their rooms, wishing they could go down to watch TV but fearing the results if they did. The only nights they could breathe were when he got together enough of a stake to go down to the corner bar, and then there was always the anxiety of wondering what would happen when he got home. Having friends was difficult, since John really couldn't have them over to visit. Worse still were the beatings, which always seemed to single out John, since he was the boy. You just couldn't tell when they were coming, or for what reason. John still got regular ear infections from the broken eardrum he had sustained from a blow to the ear.

But the worst times were when the old man would beat on Mom. He'd wondered a thousand times why she'd just cower and take it, why she didn't leave him or at least have him thrown in jail a few times to teach him a lesson. All she would say about it was "I have you kids to think about," but Jesus, what did she think the effect on the kids was to live in terror of their father and watch their mother get beaten up every Saturday night? It hurt really bad for John to see the fear come into his daughter,

Jennifer's eyes every time he took a drink for several months after that bad time with Mary. It was a relief when the old man finally died ten years ago, when John was twenty-five, of cirrhosis of the liver. At his funeral, John had promised himself for the thousandth time that he would never, ever, become like the old bastard.

Of course, the old man had been thirty-six, one year older than John was now himself, when John had been born. Sometimes John wondered if he'd always been a drunk, and if he had, why Mom ever married him in the first place (*disease progression*).

It was because of the old man that John didn't drink or do drugs in high school, even when there was a lot of pressure to do so (*phenomenon of abstinence in the children of alcoholics*). John was in the high school class of '71. The era of the Beatles, the Viet Nam War, the Stones. Long hair, tie-dyed jeans, and flower children. Lots of his friends were drinking, but not John. Oh, sure, he smoked some pot, liked it even, but it never got out of hand.

John's first drink came unusually late in his life, during his senior year in college. He'd been going with Mary for two months now, and had put enough aside from his student's budget to take her out to a really special dinner. Sharing a bottle of wine just seemed like the right thing to do under the circumstances (*alcoholics begin to drink for the same reasons that nonalcoholics do*). And it was amazing how good it made him feel, even though he'd been a little scared of the first sip, what with the old man and all. Normally, he was too serious and uptight, but the wine loosened him up and made him relaxed and charming. Mary evidently thought so too, because they ended up in his room making love. John had only been with one girl before, and that had not been a satisfying experience, because he'd been nervous and it was over too quickly, but with Mary he was great. The wine had made him feel relaxed, confident, and sensual. She'd even said, in the luxuriant aftermath of their lovemaking, "We'll have to get you drunk more often!" (*initial positive experiences with alcohol*).

Gradually, John developed a more "normal" relationship with alcohol. He looked forward to seeing Mary, because drinking some wine had become a normal part of their path toward the bedroom. One of the guys in his frat house had a wet bar in his room, and John looked forward to the little happy hour that the "in guys" in the frat enjoyed several times a week. It felt good to be one of the guys, too, and not a geek like he was in high school because he'd been so hung up on the old man's problems. He had Mary to thank for showing him that a couple of little drinks didn't turn you from Dr. Jekyll to Mr. Hyde (*preoccupation with alcohol and changes in social life*).

John never got really drunk until nearly seven months after his first drink, when he was accepted to law school. The guys, his fraternal brothers in arms, got together and threw him a party that went on into the wee hours of the morning. Somewhere between his third and sixth drink, he proposed a drinking contest, with prizes for the most drinks taken, the strongest drinks, the most creative combinations of booze, and the most proficient chugging of beer. Next morning, sick with headache and nausea (*hangover*), he found he couldn't remember much that happened after about midnight, but the guys assured him that he'd been the life of the party until almost 4 A.M. (*blackout*), when he finally passed out. When Mary heard about it, her big concern was whether there had been girls at the party.

In law school, drinking became a normal part of John's life. The law students, like a fraternity of their own within the university, had a favorite lounge across the street from the law school, cleverly called The Bar. The students called their daily after-school meetings at The Bar the Law Review. In many ways, these sessions at The Bar were as important to John's education as an attorney as were his classes. John and his fellows debated legal cases and discussed principles of law over pitchers of beer, or if there were faculty members present, as there often were, over pitchers of martinis. John would always think of The Bar fondly, but there were times when he had fleeting concerns about how much he was drinking, particularly on those few occasions when he missed his morning classes because of the drinking the night before. He regarded it as a welcome restraint when he and Mary were married after her graduation from college at the end of his first year, since married life would have to cut down the frequency of his visits to The Bar.

And it did cut them down, though since Mary worked until six o'clock and didn't get home until six-thirty or so, there were plenty of opportunities for John to participate in the Law Review sessions, though he did not nearly so often close the place down. Mary seemed to understand that the law students, particularly the L-2s, were under terrific pressure, and that they needed to blow off some steam. John particularly felt the pressure of his studies, as it seemed the further he got in school the harder it was to compete (*beginning to lose effectiveness*). The pressure really got to him, and more and more by the end of the day he really felt the need for a drink or two to unwind (*relief drinking*). However, there were no major problems that arose from his drinking, other than a few nasty arguments with Mary because he hadn't gotten home when he said he would. Well, actually, once he didn't get home at all because he passed out at a friend's house. That one took a bit of explaining before Mary was satisfied that he hadn't been with a woman (*losses of control*).

After graduation, John got a job with a good firm and found out that the pressures of professional life made law school look like a Sunday outing. Soon after going to work, he and Mary bought a house nicer than anything either of their parents had ever lived in. John smiled as he remembered how the fears about how he would make those huge house payments for thirty years used to wake him up sweating in the middle of the night, and how he would sometimes go into the living room to sit in the dark and have a drink or two just to calm down (*relief drinking, psychological and neurological aggravation, sleep disturbance, beginnings of physical dependency*). Now that he thought of it, it would have looked pretty strange if Mary had found out he was drinking in the middle of the night (*surreptitious drinking*), and he was glad she never caught him.

John's thirtieth birthday ushered in the beginning of the toughest year of his adult life. Mary got pregnant with Jennifer, which they intended, but what they had not intended was for him to be turned down for partnership in the firm. The senior partner, a pompous old fool who lived off the labors of his junior-partner slaves, had informed him in oh-so-smooth tones that his "production was just not up to par" and that he "had dropped the ball on a couple of important cases" (*increasingly ineffective performance*). The hell with him! John still got angry every time he thought of the old son of a bitch who had taken three years of his professional time and then refused to cut him in on the real action! So what if he was not a "detail person"? Isn't that what God made secretaries for? And besides, he always suspected that secretary, what's her name, of sabotaging his work (*alibis, distorted thinking, harbored resentments*).

Well, he'd shown them! Even if he did have a pregnant wife and those huge house payments, he was still a man, by God, and he'd submitted his letter of resignation that very afternoon, and within a week had a better spot at a better firm, sponsored for hiring by two of his old Law Review drinking buddies. And he'd done well, too, though he was still not a detail person, because he had an aggressive courtroom style into which he poured all the angry energy he had for his father against his legal adversary.

"Oh, my God!" John thought, remembering that he was up for partnership in six months. "If this drunk-driving charge gets out, I'm finished as a partnership candidate. Most of the guys are pretty good drinkers, but I don't think they'll go for this." Frantic, and still drunk despite the coffee that the officers had given him, John began to think of alternatives to the humiliation and defeat that seemed sure to come. One option would be to go into solo private practice, where he'd be his own boss with no one to pass judgment on him or his performance, or how he handled his cases or spent his time (*isolation*). Another choice might be to divorce Mary, leave Jennifer in her custody, and move to another city, another state even, where things would be better for him (*the geographical solution*). As an unbidden tear rolled down his cheek, John thought that suicide might be still another option, and maybe not such a bad one at that. It seemed as if his life might be over anyway, so why fight on (*alcoholic despair*)?

John stands, fearful and alone, at a crossroads in his life. At thirty-five, his disease has progressed fairly rapidly, indicating his strong genetic predisposition to alcoholism. His exposure to the agent alcohol was almost inevitable, despite his early intentions to abstain, since his cultural surroundings were so supportive of the use of alcohol and other drugs. An undeniably good man who loves his wife and child and is committed to his chosen profession, he has nevertheless been reduced by his illness to the status of a wife beater, an inattentive and frightening father (like his own father, whom he swore never to be like), a sloppy and incompetent professional, and now an offender against the law he swore to uphold.

The saddest fact is that at the very moment John faces the most crucial decision in his life, he is not really aware of that decision or its implications. At this moment when his life may depend upon making the right decision, which depends on him seeing himself as he really is and seeing things as they really are, he is most blinded by his denial, his distorted thinking, his rationalizations and alibis, his confusion, and his physical and emotional pain.

At this point in his life, John is still what AA members call a "high-bottom drunk," that is, an alcoholic who may have "hit bottom" at a point that is still not so very low, comparatively.

There has been no divorce, no bankruptcy, no loss of his professional license to practice, no default on his house payment, no physical illness, or warnings from his doctor . . . yet. He is still filled with denial and rationalizations, anger and resentments. Not yet has he been brought to his knees by his illness, to the point where the only two alternatives left to him are recovery or death.

The problem is that every time an alcoholic stands at this crossroads, neither he nor those around him know how many more opportunities God or fate or whatever Higher Power oversees the events of our lives will give him to make the crucial choice. On the one hand lies the road of continued drinking. John may get out of this one relatively unscathed, though public authorities are doing a better job each year in intervening in the illness of alcoholics through the instrument of the DWI citation. He may continue to drink through his divorce from Mary, after continued conflict, repeated instances of physical violence, and the psychological scarring of his daughter, Jennifer. He may continue through bankruptcy, the loss of his professional license. He may, like his father before him, continue to drink until he dies a lonely and miserable death of accident fatality or terminal disease.

On the other branch of the crossroads lies the path of recovery. If John could somehow see clearly that the *single factor* affecting his marriage, his career, his emotional condition, his physical state, is alcohol; if he could be made to understand that he suffers from a disease that has, by tiny bits and pieces, taken over his personality and behavior; if he could make the connection between himself and his father, whose disease had roughly progressed to the same degree at roughly the same age that John is now, and realize that what his father and he have in common is a genetic illness; if he could even begin to imagine the possibilities that recovery would hold for his life, for his marriage, for his career . . . if, if, if. But the central fact of John's disease is that through its actions on his nervous system, the very functioning of his brain is affected, so that the brain events on which the "ifs" listed above depend, that is, "seeing clearly" . . . "understanding" . . . "making the connection" . . . "imagining the possibilities," are not likely to occur.

Unless something extraordinary occurs, John is most likely to leave jail that night bitter, resentful, and full of angry denial. He will probably fight the citation, and he may even win. His conflict with Mary is likely to escalate now that there is an identifiable event that clearly says he has a problem with alcohol. His fears, feelings of guilt, anger, and defensiveness will be increased, provoking a step-up in his drinking for relief, and thereby accelerating the already rapid course of his disease.

PART

III

UNDERSTANDING

CODEPENDENCY

As recently as 1980, when I was the partner of an alcoholic in treatment, the role and personal plight of the spouse of the codependent partner was as yet little understood. After a relatively brief checkout by her counselor to be sure that I was not also alcoholic, the general assumption was that I was a pretty normal person who, though somewhat the worse for the wear of living with a late-stage drinking alcoholic, was essentially stable and well adjusted. The focus of treatment for me was to be sure that I was properly advised about my addict's disease, that I understood that my addict needed AA and could never safely drink again, and to encourage me not to drink alcohol, at least in her presence.

Little or no acknowledgment was made of my suffering and sickness. To be fair, I was encouraged to attend Al-Anon, the Twelve-Step group for codependents, but no one confronted the fact that I was clinically depressed, anxiety ridden, and still carrying the burden of my lover's recovery as my own.

If you love a drinking alcoholic or a using addict, you are sick, too. I don't mean that you are sick to love that person, or that you started out sick and therefore chose an alcoholic or addict to love (though for some people that may be the case). I mean that, like any person who has lived for any period of time in a distorted, topsy-turvy, chaotic, and punishing environment, your entire system of perceptions of the world around you and your reactions to it have become distorted and inappropriate. You have gotten used to and live with conditions that are neither normal nor healthy, and your body, mind, and spirit show it.

New developments in the field of addiction treatment during the 1980s have led to the recognition of codependency as a clinical syndrome of its own, requiring appropriate diagnosis and treatment. Indeed, we have seen over and over again that unless the spouse receives some form of treatment for codependency, the alcoholic's or addict's recovery will be significantly impeded or fail entirely.

In the following chapter we'll explore the syndrome called codependency and try to trace the route by which you came to your current state of physical exhaustion, emotional desperation, and spiritual emptiness. You'll see that the condition you're in is not a mystery and that in fact it is the normal and reasonable result of living with and loving an alcoholic or addict. You'll learn that the very circumstances with which you've been coping (or not coping, as the case may be) have caused you to learn some self-defeating, if not downright weird, reactions and behaviors. And you'll see how what was once your fundamentally loving and decent response to the problems of the person you love has changed so that you feel as if a monster controls your behavior and your life.

It may be that you, like many people, came to the role of the codependent with on-the-job training that came from being the child of one or both alcoholic or addicted parents. If you grew up with an alcoholic in the family, the nightmarish life of caring for, fearing, covering for, and coping with your addict may seem natural to you. The repressed rage, the chronic depression, the illness, and the absence of joy in your life may be such familiar inner feelings that they may seem normal to you. Chapter 9, "Am I Codependent?" will pay special attention to the effects of growing up in an alcoholic family. You'll learn that you're not alone, and that whether you are twenty, forty, or eighty there is hope for you to learn a way of being that allows joy and inner peace.

The friends and lovers of alcoholics and addicts are a courageous and stalwart, but for the most part, misguided group of people. I hope that in these chapters you will learn that your personal suffering is not the key to your addict's salvation but is really just another part of the problem. You can truly help by working toward your own well-being as well as toward your addict's.

THE
CODEPENDENCY
SYNDROME

The fact that you're reading this book indicates that you're in, or about to be in, or have recently been in a *codependent crisis*, which means that something has recently happened to heat up your situation to the point where you feel that something must be done. The "something" may have happened to your chemical dependent, such as a DWI citation, a job termination, a bankruptcy, a heart attack, or stroke. Or the something may have happened to you—you tried to kill yourself, your addict struck you in an argument, you struck your addict in an argument, your doctor diagnosed an ulcer, or your alcoholic vomited on your dinner guest's shoes. In part II we tried to gain some understanding of the disease that is affecting your partner's life and therefore yours. In part III, we'll take a closer look at you, the codependent, and try to understand the ways that your emotions, your thinking, and your behavior have become warped and distorted as a result of living with this killing disease.

As you read in part II, addiction is a disease, so we are able to predict its course, often with amazing accuracy. Codependency isn't exactly a disease in the strictest sense, because there are no physical causative factors that we know of, but it's close enough to one to be often called a disease by workers in the field. Codependency is actually a *syndrome,* that is, a collection of psychological, physical, and behavioral symptoms that present themselves in an equally predictable order in certain kinds of persons under certain kinds of circumstances.

You may feel the same eerie sense that I am describing you as you felt when you read the section about alcoholism and addiction. Don't worry; there are no spies under your bed. It's the predictability of the symptoms and progression of codependency that allow us to make such detailed descriptions of the codependent and his or her life. As we examine the progression of codependency, I hope you will begin to understand what on earth has been happening to you and perhaps to get some clues about what you must do for your own recovery.

It may be that you can remember back to the time when you were a happy, relaxed, and relatively normal human being. Chances are that if you didn't grow up in an alcoholic, addicted, or otherwise dysfunctional family, you once had a properly functioning internal guidance system that motivated you in the direction of meeting your own needs, taking care of yourself, running your own agenda, and generally engaging in what Thomas Jefferson called the pursuit of happiness.

On the other hand, if you were a child of a chemically affected or otherwise dysfunctional family, you may have no recollection of ever living in the normal manner described above. You would have come to your relationship with your addict by being already well prepared for a life of depression, nasty surprises, conflict, and despair.

Either way, living in a codependent relationship has turned you into a psychological mess. You're a bundle of raw nerves, and in the rare times when you're not, you're too exhausted to do anything but sleep or watch TV. You can't get the problems caused by your spouse's addiction out of your mind; you chew over them like a dog with a bone, as if you believed that if you only think about them and worry about them long enough, you'll be able to solve them. Your sleep is disturbed; either you're finding it nearly impossible to get out of bed in the morning or you're up at 3:00 A.M., unable to sleep any more. Your eating patterns have gone crazy; either you've lost a frightening amount of weight, or you can't keep your food down, or you've gained an enormous amount of weight. Your temper is entirely out of control, and you can't predict when it will erupt, usually inappropriately. You may be developing alcoholism or other drug addiction yourself. It's been so long since you really paid attention to yourself that you may feel that you don't know who you are anymore.

It often comes as a shock for codependents to think that they may have problems of their own; most codependents labor under the delusion that if their alcoholic would only stop drinking, or if their addict would only stop using drugs, everything would be all right. So little do codependents typically focus on themselves and their own problems that while they are in the very midst of profound psychological, physical, and behavioral problems of their own, the idea that there may be something wrong with them usually strikes them as a very foreign idea. It is almost amazing to watch how difficult it is for them to understand that they, and not just their addicts, have a serious problem. Later, we'll see how the course of codependency directly parallels the course of addiction, but for now it's useful to note that the codependent's failure to recognize his or her own problems is the exact counterpart of *denial* in the alcoholic or addict. Just as the addict denies that he or she has a problem, and stoutly maintains that the problem has to do with the nagging wife, the demanding boss, or the impossible world, so also the codependent denies that he or she has any problem. The codependent is so convinced that his or her alcoholic is the problem that he will go on for hours describing the bad behavior and ugly situations of the alcoholic without ever referring to his or her own misery.

Codependency has only just been recognized as a syndrome of its own, usually connected with but not identical to alcoholism or other dysfunction or addiction. As recently as ten years ago, the only real attention paid to the spouse or partner of the alcoholic or addict by the professional community was in the way of giving advice on how the spouse might help the addict with his recovery. The reasons why codependency could remain hidden for so long are not really so complex, if you think about it. Codependents are in their own form of denial and don't usually state their problems as if they were their own. Professional addiction counselors, until quite recently, were almost always themselves recovering alcoholics or addicts, who were much more aware of and familiar with the problems of the addict than of those of the addict's spouse. Even today, I find that many highly respected old-timers in the field continue to minimize the problems associated with codependency, in part because while they lived and suffered the problems of alcoholism and addiction, in their drug-affected state of insensitivity they were simply not aware of the suffering of those around them. The general recognition of the codependency syndrome has only been developed as more and more nonalcoholic children of alcoholics and spouses of alcoholics have taken up professional roles in the field.

This chapter is not intended as the last word on codependency. Many fine scholars and workers in the field have recently written on the subject, and I would encourage you to explore their works in greater depth (see Appendix C: Recommended Reading, page 308). Claudia Black and Sharon Wegscheider-Cruse have written about codependence from a family perspective. Melody Beattie has explored the problem from an intensely personal viewpoint. Dr. Timmen L. Cermak has addressed the medical and psychiatric aspects of codependence. Anne Wilson Schaef has provided extensive discussion of the syndrome from a professional and social perspective. Each of these authors has developed his or her own definition of codependence, as have most workers in the field. Some define codependence as an addiction to another person, as has Robin Norwood in her book *Women Who Love Too Much* (Los Angeles: Jeremy P. Tarcher, 1985). Others view codependence as a developmental problem, resulting from learned behaviors in a dysfunctional family of origin. Still others regard codependence as a special case of posttraumatic-stress syndrome, the emotional devastation resulting from growing up in a chemically affected family. Each of these definitions makes good sense, and since they don't contradict each other, it seems clear that each perspective has value.

The definition of codependence that seems most useful for our purposes follows.

> Codependency is a collection of psychological symptoms including depression, anxiety, decreased self-esteem, phobia, and obsessiveness, guilt and shame, physical symptoms such as gastric disorders, skin disorders, cardiovascular disorders, back problems, and behavioral symptoms such as "people pleasing," controlling, isolation, hyperresponsibility, work dysfunction, and compulsiveness. These symptoms present themselves in predictable order in persons who are prone to love, care for, and take responsibility for others under circumstances of chronic dysfunction in the other due to alcoholism, addiction, mental illness, personality disorder, or chronic medical illness.

THE CLIMATE OF THE CODEPENDENT RELATIONSHIP

Codependence almost always occurs in a relationship in which one party has become impaired in his or her ability to function. Some of the common causes of this dysfunction are long-term physical illness, mental illness, personality disorder (a kind of psychological problem in which the individual is not mentally ill but nevertheless consistently behaves in ways that are not normal and cause problems), and, of course, alcohol or other drug addiction. Other compulsive disorders, such as gambling, eating disorders, or sexual addiction also usually foster codependency in the other partner in the relationship.

The codependent is usually a pretty responsible, competent person who feels a powerful inner imperative to see that things are right, that obligations are met, that appearances are maintained. As the impaired partner loses the ability to function, or at least the ability to function reliably, the codependent partner gradually begins to take up the slack, assuming more and more responsibility for the effective functioning of the relationship, and in doing so, assuming more and more responsibility for the life of the dependent. He may pay off her gambling debts, extracting meaningless promises from her that it will never happen again. He may call in sick for her at work while she sleeps off a hangover.

The more the codependent takes over the personal responsibilities of the dependent and the joint responsibilities of the relationship, the more the dependent is able to practice his or her addiction, compulsion, or other disorder in relative freedom from suffering the consequences of his failure to meet his responsibilities. If she pays the gambling debts, he will only feel freer to lose large amounts of money without worrying about how to pay the losses. He has her to worry about that.

This pattern of assuming responsibilities that are not one's own was one of the first characteristics of codependents that was noted by the addiction treatment field, and was called *enabling*, because it enabled the alcoholic, addict, or otherwise disordered individual to continue his or her disordered behavior without experiencing its negative consequences. The idea of enabling was a hard one for codependents to take, because the implication was that the codependent somehow had an unconscious motive to preserve the status quo by helping the addicted partner stay addicted.

The first time I was presented with the idea of enabling, I became so angry that it felt as if I was close to physically assaulting the person who "accused" me of doing it. I had reached the point where I knew something was terribly wrong in my lover's and my life and that it was somehow connected with her use of alcohol. A friend had referred me to an alcoholism counselor:

AW: *(after a lengthy recounting of our difficulties with her drinking):* . . . *So it feels as if our lives are falling apart, and I just don't know what to do.*

Counselor: Have you given any thought to how you're helping her continue to drink?

AW: *Me? Are you kidding? I do everything I can think of to stop her from drinking! Haven't you been listening?*

Counselor: Well, sure I've been listening, but maybe I'm confused. How does she get the money to buy booze?

AW: *Well . . . ah, she works.*

Counselor: She does? I'm amazed. If her drinking is as serious as you describe, what kind of employer would tolerate the poor job performance that would undoubtedly be the result?

AW: *Oh, well, uh, I'm her employer. It's true that she's performing badly, but . . .*

Counselor: I see. So you write the paychecks with which she buys her booze, and you tolerate the poor performance that would cause her to be fired from any other job? Is that right?

AW: *(Getting angrier) I . . . I suppose if you want to put it that way.*

Counselor: Okay. Another thing I'm confused about is this: If she's spending all her money on booze, how can she afford a place to live?

AW: *C'mon. I told you we live together.*

Counselor: Oh, yes, that's right. So is it correct that you make the house payment out of your salary?

AW: *(Seeing where this is leading) . . . Yeah.*

Counselor: So it wouldn't be stretching the truth, really, to say that you provide her a place in which to do her drinking?

AW: *Well . . . I suppose, but what do you expect me to do? Fire her? Kick her out? What would happen to her then? I love her, damn it!*

Counselor: Sure, I understand. Let's look at another question. How does she take care of herself? Eating and so forth?

AW: *Well, when she's really drinking hard, I try to stay pretty close to home to be sure she's okay. I usually try to get her to eat some soup or something, and I coax her into taking vitamins whenever I can.*

Counselor: Let's see if I've got it right. You provide her with a job, which she couldn't hold down elsewhere in her alcoholic condition. You pay her money, which she uses to buy her booze. You provide her with the place to do her drinking in relative affluence and comfort. And you do your best to make sure she doesn't get sick because of the way she's treating her body. But you don't think you're helping her to continue to drink?

Enabling is the behavioral symptom of some underlying ideas that, to put it bluntly, are wrong. When we enable our addict, we think (in the moment) that we are helping. We think that if we can only intervene to avert this crisis, if we can just cover this embarrassment, if we can just prevent him or her from doing something stupid, things will get better. We believe that if we can only give our addict a break, that he will get his feet under him and shape up. We feel that it would be terrible to just stand by and let the consequences of her behavior hurt or even destroy her. Enabling is like standing in front of a dam, sticking our fingers into the little holes until we have no more fingers and toes left, as if we thought that if we could only hold on long enough, the dam would repair itself. And still the dam continues to spring leaks. We forget, deny, or don't understand the fact that addiction is progressive, that it gets worse, not better. As a general rule, the longer we can keep our alcoholic or addict from crashing, the worse the crash will be.

The more enabling that takes place, the more out of control and the less responsible the addict becomes. Gradually, the code-pendent takes on more and more of the job of controlling the addict's behavior—or tries to. The fact is, of course, that the responsibility for controlling one's own behavior is the proper job and responsibility of each individual human being, and except in the case of very young children, no one can do it for us. But somehow, in the heat of the day-to-day crises that mark the lives in a chemically dependent family, that fundamental fact of life gets ignored or forgotten.

Some codependents who were the children of addicted parents never learned that each person is responsible for himself, because their parents, who literally held their lives in their hands, were made so fundamentally irresponsible by their addiction or dysfunction. For them, the hopeless situation of having to control the behavior of an out-of-control alcoholic is well-known territory, and they settle into it with a kind of comfortable despair.

Codependents who grew up in homes where there was severe psychological disorder or mental illness behave in similar ways.

Codependents who grew up in homes where there was chronic and severe illness learned an overly responsible and caretaking style of behavior. The family's response to the sick member was to assume a greater proportion of that member's normal family responsibilities, to pitch in and care for that member, and to accept a loved one's inability to function as a fact of everyday life. They fit right in with a relationship partner who has been rendered dysfunctional by the disease of addiction.

Other codependents seem not to have had childhood or other experience with alcoholism. Probably there is such a thing as adult-onset codependency. The most likely scenario for its development would be in a relationship with an addict or alcoholic who showed no symptoms of the disease when the relationship was forming, where the codependent partner adapted so slowly to the emerging and progressive symptoms that the changes in his or her attitudes and behavior were hardly noticeable. These folks may respond in a codependent manner to the growing dysfunction out of a framework of salt-of-the-earth beliefs. Typically they came from families in which propriety, religious beliefs, and philosophical values were placed above emotional realities. This type of codependent says things like "We don't air our dirty laundry in public," and "People like us work hard, pay our bills on time, and don't embarrass ourselves." As often as not these codependents married or became involved with their addict long before there were any obvious signs that addiction would later become a problem. They seem to have regarded each new step in the progression of their partner's addiction as a temporary aberration that would correct itself in time if only they would hold the fort while their partner was on a vacation from personal responsibility. Of course, addiction being progressive, things don't get better; they get worse and worse until finally the codependent is forced by some crisis to abandon the front of propriety and cry out for help.

Either way, the codependent partner's attempts to control the addicted partner's behavior become more intense as that behavior goes more out of control. Gentle suggestions about watching how much he drinks turn to angry harangues after each embarrassing drunk. What may have been once an equal financial partnership now sees the codependent partner playing the role of Chancellor of the Exchequer, paying all the bills and doling out small-enough advances of cash to try to prevent the addict from buying more cocaine. The codependent becomes a detective, checking the whereabouts of the addict, trying to be sure she is where she's supposed to be at all times.

When the addict can't or won't cooperate by shaping up, the codependent starts to get angry. Not that the anger is very obvious or direct, of course. Oh, no, we're much too involved in being nice, loving people. We express our anger only very indirectly toward our addicts, with sarcastically negative comments, sighs and rolls of the eyes, by sexual and interpersonal withdrawal. Or we turn our anger inward upon ourselves, becoming depressed martyrs, anxious phobics, stressed-out nags, or frantic and oppressive restorers of order. Or we get sick. Or we vent our anger inappropriately, kicking the dog, abusing our children, or screaming at other drivers on the freeway.

The more wild and out of control things become, the more energetic and manipulative we become in our efforts to get things under control. We monitor the amount of our addict's drinking or using. We locate all the hiding places and pour the booze down the drain or flush the drugs down the toilet. We develop a song-and-dance act to delay the taking of the first drink. The greater our efforts to control our addict's use, the wilier he becomes at outwitting us, and the harsher and more violent the arguments become when we win.

PSYCHOLOGICAL PROBLEMS OF CODEPENDENTS

You really can't blame the codependent for trying. A chemically dependent relationship is a pretty unsafe place to live. One never knows when one will be embarrassed in front of family and friends. Every phone call when our addict isn't home could be a death knell. Every drinking bout could be the end of our marriage, or result in our being physically hurt. All people, whether codependent or not, when faced with a threatening or unsafe situation, will try to do what they can to remove or reduce the threat. Attempting to control the situation is a natural, but unfortunately unhelpful, response. The only result it produces in this situation is frustration, more anger, and, ultimately, severe depression.

Research has established that when subject animals are trapped in an unpleasant, punishing, or threatening situation, their first response is to try to do something about it (the main difference between rats and codependents being that rats, apparently the smarter of the two groups, focus their efforts on escaping). Once a rat finds a way to escape his unpleasant situation, he quickly becomes quite good at it. However, if the rat is prevented from escaping, and is therefore rendered helpless, sooner or later he just gives up. He curls up into a little ball and suffers silently in a pit of rat depression, refusing food or water. If it goes on long enough, he just dies. Researchers have termed this form of giving up "learned helplessness," because the rat, having learned that he cannot escape, lapses into a profound, helpless depression.

Phyllis described the helpless depression of the codependent: "After ten years of watching him get worse and worse no matter what I did, one day I just gave up. It seemed as if I stopped feeling, stopped thinking, and stopped doing anything in my life except what was absolutely necessary to get from today to tomorrow. I don't know why. I knew tomorrow would always be just the same as today. One more fight, maybe, one more unpaid bill. Who cared anymore?

"And the scary thing was that it felt good, for a change, not to care about anything. At least it didn't hurt. I stopped going out. I'd send the kids to the store. Then I stopped getting dressed. Who was there to care what I looked like?

"I finally knew I had to get help the morning I just stepped over his body, passed out on the kitchen floor, as if he wasn't there, and served the kids breakfast with him just lying there."

Why didn't Phyllis leave? Why did she behave like the rat who can't escape, when for ten years the front door was right there? Why did she behave as if she were totally helpless, when she could have just "left the bum," as many of her harder-headed and more pragmatic friends had advised? In Phyllis's case, the answer was that she had learned a long time ago that it was hopeless to try to escape. The eldest daughter of an alcoholic mother, she first watched her poor father practice his tolerant, long-suffering codependency for years, and more and more assumed the burden as she grew up. Children know they can't escape from their parents, because when they're little, they literally couldn't survive without them. By the time they would be able to survive without their parents, the role of codependent, depressed caretaker has become so "normal" to them that the thought of leaving their situation never occurs to them as a realistic option. Phyllis's apparent helplessness was learned, and she will have to unlearn it before she can recover from her depression and her codependency.

. . .

Mindy learned how to be guilty along with her depression and codependency: "I was only three when my brother was born with a severe handicap. I learned from the earliest of times to care for him when Mom was 'sick.' My parents always praised me for my help, saying that they didn't know what they'd do without me.

"As I grew up and my mother's drinking got worse and worse, it began to seem as if it was my destiny to spend the rest of my life caring for Tommy. I knew Mom and Dad couldn't do it forever. Mom's drinking had reached the point where she really couldn't be relied on to take care of him, and Dad's response to the whole situation was to lose himself in his work, so that he wasn't home nearly enough to see to Tommy. That left me.

"Boys became a problem. I knew that their interest in me threatened someday to 'take me away from all this,' and I knew that I couldn't leave. What would become of my family? My solution was to gain weight. I weighed 350 pounds before I was twenty. The weight guaranteed that no one would take me away from my obligation in life, which was to take care of my mother and my brother."

When Mindy came to treatment at age twenty-seven, she weighed 370 pounds, had no friends, was a virgin, and lived in her parents' home. Though she had a good job and a large amount of savings (there was nothing for her to spend money on except food), the idea that she could have a life of her own was as foreign to her as the idea of flapping her arms and flying to the moon. She had learned very early on that there was no escape or, more accurately, that to try to escape would create in her an intolerable amount of guilt. Today Mindy is working at unlearning her helplessness. She has lost a substantial amount of weight, participates actively in Overeaters Anonymous and Adult Children of Alcoholics, has a place of her own, and is in a relationship with a caring man. She is working at recovering from her guilt, depression, and codependency.

. . .

Codependents, as a result of living in close proximity with an alcoholic or chemically dependent parent or spouse, develop serious psychological problems. Whether the codependency syndrome began in childhood by living as the child of an alcoholic or addicted parent or whether the problem emerged in adulthood, developing in rhythm with the spouse's emerging alcoholism, the psychological symptoms are similar. All codependents suffer from chronic anxiety, which is the result of living on "red alert." All codependents seem controlling and manipulative as they try so desperately to create a zone of safety for themselves and their families. All codependents suffer from chronic depression, the inevitable emotional reaction to the fact that no matter how hard they try, they cannot control or overcome their partner's drinking. All codependents experience serious erosion of self-esteem, except possibly those who had little to begin with, as their lives become progressively unmanageable; they experience shame and guilt over the financial difficulties, family discord, and social embarrassments caused by the family addiction. Many codependents become symptomatic with disorders of impulse control. Eating disorders, phobias, and compulsive neuroses are common by-products of the ongoing anxiety built into the codependent relationship.

MEDICAL AND HEALTH RISKS IN CODEPENDENCY

In addition to these complex and very serious psychological symptoms, codependents often suffer from a variety of physical illnesses, just like their chemically dependent partners. While liver damage is seldom observed in nonalcoholic codependents, and the source of the physical problems is stress and depression rather than abuse of alcohol, the physical health consequences of codependence are scarcely less serious. Chronic back problems due to muscular tensions, low-grade infections due to psychological stress on the immune system, migraines, treatment-resistant hypertension, and gastrointenstinal problems, such as ulcers, diarrhea, and colitis, are commonly seen among codependents. Cardiovascular difficulties, such as angina and stroke, may be aggravated by the stress of codependency. Alcoholism or drug dependencies, which might have lain indefinitely as latent tendencies in the codependent, are often triggered into active process by drinking or by using drugs with the addicted partner, or by drinking or using drugs for relief. Suicide is by no means unknown among codependents as the ultimate way out.

Medical problems are often complicated and allowed to become more serious because of the reluctance of the codependent to discuss with his or her doctor the real truth about how awful things are at home. The tendency to cover up, to deny, to protect the addicted spouse is like a reflex in the codependent, and as much as he or she would like to reach out for help and support, the inner imperative to keep the family secrets is often stronger still. In recent years, many more physicians have become sensitive to the possibility that alcoholism or drug abuse may underlie many of the chronic complaints of frequently seen patients, but few have yet learned to search out codependency as a chronic, underlying source of stress upon the patient.

BEHAVIORAL PROBLEMS OF CODEPENDENTS

With all due respect to the seriousness of the psychological and medical problems associated with codependency, it is the behavioral style of the codependent that creates the most devastating and life-quashing effects. The life-style that evolves from fighting the hopeless battle to control or overcome your partner's addiction is a joyless, unspontaneous, rigid, and depressing one that precludes pleasure, negates accomplishment, and denies any possibility of establishing spiritual meaning or personal growth. Codependency is boring.

Codependents are, first and foremost, caretakers. We seem to derive our sense of self-esteem from meeting, or trying to meet, the needs of others. We create relationships with other people based on their needs and not our own. We behave as if we believe that if we make ourselves valuable to other people by meeting their needs, they will love us. Many codependents become professional caretakers, entering fields such as nursing, medicine, psychology, counseling, and social work. Usually, we are very, very good at it. No wonder!

Wally is an addictions counselor, and a recovering alcoholic. When he came to therapy some five years after getting sober, his complaint was that he felt like a "hollow man," a man who was to all outward appearances successful in his sobriety, respected in his profession, but who experienced no inner happiness or peace. He owned a nice home, drove a terrific car, and made plenty of money, but at the same time he had no wife or girlfriend, few friends, and was 150 pounds overweight.

I asked Wally to keep an accurate log of his daily activities for one week. The log showed that he spent nearly sixty hours in his office working with clients in counseling, devoted fifteen hours per week to volunteer work at the local Crisis Line telephone center, spent an average of two hours a night on the phone with his clients, was the sponsor (a kind of part big brother, part counselor) to fourteen AA members, and "for fun" volunteered on a Coast Guard Auxiliary search-and-rescue team.

Wally spent every waking moment responding to the needs of others. Caretaking was a reflex for him, and he seemed not to be able to imagine doing things just because they were fun, or because they made him feel good. When asked, he could not state, beyond the obvious needs for food, water, and shelter, what *he* needed in his life to be happy. For Wally, private time equaled wasted time. His inner emptiness and unhappiness came from the fact that while he was there for everyone, no one, least of all Wally, was there for him.

I chose Wally as an example of codependent caretaking because he is male and because his caretaking had the social masquerade of "meaningful" and "important" activity. There is an inherent sexism in our tendency to characterize the alcoholic as male and the codependent as female. The fact is that there are as many female alcoholics as male and as many male codependents as female. Wally's case is also interesting because it demonstrates clearly that codependence is an independent problem; you don't have to be in a relationship with an alcoholic or addict to actively practice codependency. Wally inherited his alcoholism from his father. Once his alcoholism was arrested in his recovery, he began emulating his mother's behaviors of taking care of her husband, her children, and everyone else but herself. As we'll see later, if we grew up in an alcoholic or otherwise dysfunctional family, we may learn to be codependent at a very young age, and as an adult our whole behavioral style will be codependent.

· · ·

Marcia's case, however, fits a more stereotypical picture of the female codependent. Marcia was thirty-four years old and had been married for ten years to her husband, Bill. The couple had two children, ages four and seven. Marcia is employed as an administrative assistant to the head of a large local corporation. Marcia came to treatment because she was concerned and wanted information about what appeared to be a drinking problem that Bill was developing.

Although Marcia clearly wished to keep our discussions centered on Bill and his problems, she herself appeared quite depressed to me. Generally she showed little emotion and spoke in a quiet voice. Often, however, she appeared on the verge of tears, even when the subject did not seem particularly sad. A physical history revealed that she had gained thirty-eight pounds over the past three years, was having some trouble sleeping, and was developing psoriasis. When I suggested she might be suffering from depression, however, she denied it, saying it was "only a bit of stress, probably no more than normal for a busy person."

As I did with Wally, I asked Marcia to keep a log of her daily activities. She resisted this task for several sessions, stating with some irritation that she didn't see how this was going to help Bill's problem. When she finally completed her weekly log, it showed that she rose at 4:30 A.M. (she explained that her boss arrived at work at 7:00, and that he expected coffee ready when he arrived). She described her job as "meeting My Lord and Master's every need, complete from answering his correspondence and picking up his clean shirts to booking international travel arrangements and even writing a speech or two." She observed that her boss did not make her job any easier, because although he had often put in a full day's work before noon, he had an annoying habit of disappearing in the afternoon, particularly if there was drinking at lunch. She observed that covering for him was becoming a job in itself.

Marcia left work at 5:30 and normally drove straight to the day-care center to pick up Danny, age seven, and Kim, age four. She confessed that it had been a source of ongoing irritation for her that Bill, who was an outside salesperson with a schedule almost entirely under his control, almost never picked up the children. Her irritation, she was quick to state, was not because this made her day harder but because she felt guilty about the children spending as much time as they did in day care. She would have preferred to take a job with shorter hours, she said, but the family needed to rely on her fairly substantial income since Bill's could go up and down so dramatically.

Marcia spent from 6:15 until 8:30 preparing dinner for the family and spending "quality time" with the children. Her concern about Bill's drinking had to do with the fact that he was now not home for dinner on two or three nights during the week, usually phoning from one cocktail lounge or another to explain that he was "doing business." Bill's contention was that, at thirty-eight, this was the make-or-break point in his career, and that she was just going to have to deal with the fact that for the next several years he was going to be married to his job. Marcia was careful to explain that it was not that Bill was not home to help her with the children that bothered her so much as that she was concerned about his drinking (his speech often seemed to be slurred when he called to say he'd be late) and about his driving home after drinking.

As soon as the children were in bed, Marcia's habit was to call her mother, who lived alone since her father's death (of liver disease). Marcia called every night because "Mom lives alone and just needs someone to chat with, and because I feel better knowing she's okay." By the time the phone call was complete and the dinner things cleaned up, it was normally 10:00. "By that time, I really need to get to bed," Marcia sighed, "but if Bill's not home, I can't get to sleep for worrying about him, and lately, if he is home by that time, we seem to get into stupid arguments that last sometimes for hours. I've learned *never* to comment about his drinking. That's sure to start an argument."

Marcia reserved most Saturdays for a thorough housecleaning. She was glad when hunting season arrived, because it got Bill out from underfoot while she cleaned. She felt guilty, she said, because she didn't get the children out to the zoo or to the movies on a Saturday as often as she'd like, but she explained with a sigh that she also felt guilty if the house hadn't been cleaned. "How can you win?" she asked with what seemed to me a painful chuckle.

On Sundays, Marcia taught Sunday school. "It gets kind of

hectic around the house on Sunday mornings," she said, laughing. "The kids are at that age where they're so easily distracted, and it's hard to get them fed and dressed and not wake up Bill." (She explained that Bill had stopped going to church several years ago, saying that he was sure that "God would approve of any man who works at the pace I do taking one morning a week to sleep in, and besides, isn't Sunday called the 'day of rest'?") After church, she spent the afternoon watching football with Bill. "I really hate football," she explained to me with the air of one disclosing a great secret, "but I believe that marriage takes quality time spent together, and Sunday afternoon is the only time, really, that we can be together." Marcia shyly disclosed that this time together was of such high quality that often they made love during half time!

Marcia continued to be quite difficult to work with because she felt impatient with all of my curiosity and concern about her state of mind and well-being. The problem, she insisted, was Bill, and she wanted advice and information about what to do about him.

Marcia was consuming herself and her life in her compulsive need to meet the needs of others. Every waking moment was devoted to the needs of her husband, her boss, her children, her church. There was no time to take a walk, read a book, enroll in a class, watch television, or to do anything else that was solely and exclusively *for herself.* So powerful was her inner demand that she attend to the needs of others that she could not even tolerate the idea that counseling might be for her, and not to solve her husband's problem.

Marcia is typical of tens of thousands of codependent women who live with and love alcoholic or otherwise chemically dependent men. To the world around them they are saints and heroines who bear up mightily under the demands of life with a worthless drunk of a husband. To their husbands they are either uncomplaining fixtures to be both ignored and depended upon, or irritating martyrs whose silent or not-so-silent suffering fills them with rage. To the chemical-dependency counselor they are codependents in deep and powerful denial. To themselves they are no one, counting for nothing except to the degree that they fulfill their obligations and meet the needs of those around them.

*   *   *

Codependents are blamers. Paradoxically, they seem at one moment to blame themselves for everything that is wrong in their world and at the next moment to be blaming everyone *but* themselves. Because codependents typically have very low levels of self-esteem, they tend to be very hard on themselves, believing that if only they were smarter, or nicer, or more Christian (or Jewish or whatever), or stronger, or had a better faith, they would find the solutions to all of the problems that the people in their lives are suffering. On the other hand, because they are so little focused on themselves and their own experience, and because their own denial is so strong, they obsess self-righteously on the idea that if only the others in their lives would "straighten up and fly right," the problems over which the codependent labors day and night would not exist.

Codependents are compulsive people pleasers. Because they tend to believe that they are not worthy of love or happiness or getting what they want and need, their consistent tendency is to attempt to get love by meeting the needs of others, to gain happiness in the happiness of others, and get what they need and want by creating obligation in others. One bit of Al-Anon (the organization for spouses and partners of alcoholics) wit says that "Codependents don't make friends—they take hostages!"

Codependents are notoriously poor communicators. It's not that they're not verbal—most are. It's that directly communicating wants, needs, and feelings is experienced by the codependent as a terribly dangerous thing to do. Many codependents who were raised in alcoholic families learned that they could not directly acknowledge a situation for what it was. "Daddy's not drunk, honey, he's sick." Many believe that if they don't give the people in their lives what they want that they will be deserted, either emotionally or physically, so they fear expressing contrary wishes or opinions. Many learned that if they expressed anger or displeasure, the retaliatory response would be overwhelming, so they don't say when they're hurt or angry. (If you think it's silly to be afraid to get somebody mad at you, *you* try being five years old and getting a thirty-year-old inebriated father angry!) Many learned that if they said what they wanted, they would be denied or, sometimes worse for a child, that they would be promised it only to be disappointed, so they are reluctant and even unable to state wishes or preferences. From codependents you get a lot of responses like "Whatever . . ." or "I don't care; whatever you'd like," or "It makes no difference to me." (I don't want to tell you that I feel like eating Chinese food tonight because maybe you really want Italian, and then you'd be disappointed, and then you wouldn't love me, and maybe you'd desert me. . . .)

When codependents do communicate, they're very indirect about it. They sigh, roll their eyes, lapse into cold silences, withhold sexually, burn food, leave notes lying around, slam doors, and generally do anything that might communicate their message without actually saying it. Some codependents adopt a "communication style" not unlike that of a prosecuting attorney on cross-examination. "What time did *you* get home last night?" "And what did I just *tell* you about that?" "*Why* must you get drunk and spoil every nice time I plan?" The questions manage to convey the anger and the implied judgments without ever exposing the codependent to the direct expression of what he or she actually feels. Of course, the chemically dependent partner feels put down and angry at these barbed reminders of what a piece of dirt he is and, inflamed by anger and shame, goes off and drinks some more. (Codependents don't make alcoholics drink or addicts use drugs, but they certainly provide them with plenty of great excuses!)

Codependents, like their alcoholic and addicted loved ones, are deniers. Sometimes they learned to deny as children, to protect themselves from the knowledge of the awful realities around them. Often they learned from their codependent parent that reality is what you say it is ("Daddy is taking his medicine, honey, because it helps him calm down from working too hard"), so they feel that if they say things are just fine, it will make it true that things are just fine. Often codependents use denial to protect themselves from feeling a deep sense of shame about themselves and everything connected to them. (If I admit my wife's a drunk, what does that prove about me?)

Codependents fail to see the distinctions, or boundaries, between themselves and the people they are close to. They dream of a love relationship in which two become one, and there is a complete fusion of identities. They think that love means that they will be perfectly understood, perfectly accepted, and cared for. They think that in that perfect world, everything will be perfect, including themselves and their partners. They believe that all they need to do is work hard enough to shape themselves and their partners into that model of perfection, and in the end, all will be wonderful. They become confused and frustrated when others do not share their notions about what is good and right, and believe that it must be because they have failed to make themselves properly understood. Usually, they believe they know better than others do about what is good for them. They help when their help is not asked for, they advise when their advice is not appreciated, and when others fail to heed their advice or accept their help, they try to manipulate situations and people so that things come out right anyway. They can't understand when people become angry with them. They were only trying to help, right?

Codependents all seem to have a deeply held conviction, a

core belief, that they can control themselves, the people around them, and indeed the course of history itself. Not that they would ever say so in so many words, of course. It sounds too silly, even to the codependent ear, to actually express such an idea. But the behavior of the codependent reflects the idea that if I just try hard enough, and if I work long enough at it, I can make things go the way I think they should be. Alex, another codependent man whose marriage was destroyed by addiction and who has been very helpful to me in my recovery (his name isn't really Alex, but he'll know who he is), talked about controlling in a very moving and personal way:

"Things in my home, as a child, were wildly out of control from my earliest memories. My aunt tells me that my parents would take my baby carriage into the bar at night, and they'd put beer in my bottle to put me to sleep when I'd cry too much. I don't remember that, of course, but I remember hiding under the bed while the screaming and fighting went on outside my bedroom door.

"I didn't know things were out of control, of course; I just thought that was the way life was, and it was horrible to me. I can remember wondering at age five or six if I could hold my breath long enough to die. It's ironic that my earliest solution to how to gain control over the terror and pain I was feeling was to figure out how to die.

"I don't know how old I was when I began to realize that not *all* of life was horrible, that it was just *my* life that was horrible. I saw that it was not being alive that caused the misery, it was just being alive in my circumstances. I don't know that I could have said that, but I know that I got the idea that if things were different, I wouldn't be so unhappy. Anyway, I began to make up a life for myself in my head. I imagined that I lived in a town called Niceville, and that I was the child in a family named Good. Yep, little Alex Good, that was me. My fantasy mother's name was Betty Good, and my fantasy father's name was John

B. Good (I don't know if Chuck Berry was singing his song yet at that time). We even had a dog, which I called Pretty (Good). (I actually had a real dog once, but my father kicked it one night when he and my mother were fighting, and it died. Mom wouldn't let me take it to the vet, I think because she knew we'd have to explain what happened.)

"Anyway, living in Niceville with the Goods was sure a lot happier than living at home with my folks, and I spent as much time there as I could. I spent hours making up stories about Alex Good, the things he did, the nice times he had with his Mom and Dad and his dog. There was no drinking and no fighting in Niceville, and the families all sat down and had dinner together, and said grace, and stuff like that. Nobody ever got hit in Niceville. My 'Good' dad took me fishing, and my 'Good' mom would come in and tell me a story and tuck me in at night. I guess I must have already been in school before I gave up the world of Niceville, because I remember one time I got in trouble because I printed 'Alex Good' on my paper by mistake.

"I was eight or nine when we got our first TV. Boy, was that an eye-opener! For the first time I saw (I thought) the way other, 'normal' people lived. I studied programs like *Father Knows Best* and *The Donna Reed Show* as if they were some kind of a road map to the land of normality. I saw a world in which no one ever got angrier than a frown, where dads all came home from work at five, where there were no fights, *and nobody drank.* Kids got to be kids, and do kid stuff. Beaver Cleaver never had to cook his own dinner, and David Nelson never had to stop his parents from fighting before they killed each other. When I realized (or thought I did) the way everyone else lived, I was filled with a terrible sense of shame about my home, my parents, the filth, the fighting, the drinking, the poverty that came from my father's never being able to hold a job. Since I was filled with shame about everything *about* me, it wasn't a long jump to become deeply and profoundly ashamed of *myself.*

"I adopted a slightly more mature version of the Niceville strategy, this time not to control my inner misery but to control the shame I felt about myself and my life. I constructed a carefully designed fiction about how I lived along the lines of the TV shows I'd seen and represented it to my friends and teachers. I became, just by working at it, to all appearances a normal, well-adjusted kid from a normal, well-adjusted home. Of course, it was dicey having to avoid ever having friends over or even having anyone know where I lived, but I solved that by just not letting anyone get close enough to find out the truth. I even learned a pretty fair imitation of an adult woman's handwriting so that the answers I provided to occasional school correspondence looked as if they came from a responsible parent! The point is that I was achieving happiness (well, at least a little less misery) by controlling the appearance of reality. It was hard and it was lonely, but it worked, sort of.

"High school was the best time in my life. It was easier to keep up my biographical fiction, because home was farther away from school, and I was able to spend most of my time at school and in extracurricular activities and at my job in the evenings. For the first time I had real friends, and I could manage to have them without ever bringing them home. As long as I lived my facade, I could feel good about myself, but I would have died of embarrassment if anyone had really known me. I had never learned to talk about my feelings, so I assumed that they were just another part of the ugly and shameful world of my private life. It continued to be well worth it to me to play a role I believed was normal and acceptable to other people. The reward was that I could have friends and live a normal life, at least away from home.

"Things had settled down a bit at home, too. My father died when I was a sophomore, and I was glad. I know it sounds awful to say it, but I hated him. He was a brutal, angry, shameful excuse for a man. I suppose I could have forgiven him more easily if he were someone else's father, but he was my father, and as I look at it now, I had to bear all the shame he should have felt for himself. I still couldn't bring anyone home; the place was still a pigsty despite my best efforts to keep it clean, and Mom kept herself in a state of contented buzz pretty much around the clock. She did it quietly, though, I'll give her that. But I wasn't really sorry when she ran off with another barfly during my senior year. I haven't seen her since.

"It was a bit of a trick to manage as a high school senior living alone in a slum apartment while trying to be David Nelson to the whole world around me, but, hell, I could do it. I could do anything! I was, after all, little Alex Good, Master and Lord Creator of Niceville! I continued to cash my mother's welfare checks, paid the rent on the apartment, and survived somehow. When I finally left for college, I was filled with triumph. I had survived hell at home and managed to become accepted and live a halfway normal life out of the home, and I had actually pulled it off, with very few slip-ups, for seventeen years! Wow! Was I ever in control!

"I honestly believed that once I'd gotten out of Akron and was in college and on my own, I'd won the game. I thought I had truly succeeded at making my fantasy world my reality. Things were okay now, I thought. You couldn't tell me from the other college students, and as long as I didn't think about my family or my past, I felt just like my fellow students seemed to feel. I was popular and well accepted, and I did well in my studies, but I became subject to depressions, which became more and more frequent and more and more serious. Some days I couldn't even get out of bed. Other nights I couldn't sleep all night. Why, I wondered in my frustration, was I feeling so bad when things were going better for me than they ever had? Of course it never occurred to me to get counseling. I'd spent a lifetime covering up the inner truth about me, and I wasn't going to start uncovering it now!

"The episodes of depression got worse and worse until I met Amy. She was pretty, she was sexy, she was more fun than the circus, and she just didn't give a guy time to be depressed. Even in college, she loved the fast lane. She used to get high on marijuana and go riding her motorcycle on back roads at a hundred miles an hour. I rode with her on the back of her cycle a couple of times, but I had to get drunk to do it. No sexual novice, she was just as adventurous in bed. God, I loved her!

"The closer Amy and I became, the more I found out that the party-girl surface concealed someone who had suffered as much in her way as I had. Amy's father was an alcoholic, though her mother was not. Her father had sexually abused her from grade school until she finally put a stop to it in high school. She'd hated herself and felt ashamed of herself and had put on an act all her life just as I had. I learned that she was sick and miserable inside, and since I had won my battle (I thought), I could help her win hers. I saw it all—she'd win her inner battle with my help, settle down with me, and we'd all live happily ever after (that was how Alex Good ended all his stories). We were married right after graduation.

"As I reflect on it, I see that my depression seemed to get better when I met Amy because I began to focus more and more of my attention on her problems and away from my own. Her life and her happiness became my project. I'd spent my life learning to manufacture reality, and, by God, I'd just manufacture a new and happier reality for her.

"I set about the task with enthusiasm. My every thought and action was designed to assure Amy. 'Don't worry about a thing, baby,' I used to say. 'It doesn't matter what happened before. You've got ol' Alex at the helm now, and everything's gonna be all right.' My first book sold that year [Alex writes fiction, and as you might guess, he's *very* good at it], and I bought us a house. That was where she and I were going to live happily ever after.

Then we set about to get pregnant. That was the 'and baby makes three' part of my self-constructed blue heaven. Unconsciously I was trying to reconstruct the *Leave It to Beaver* household, with Amy in the role of Mom and my son, Alan, starring as 'the Beav.'

"Problem was, Amy wasn't having any of it. Her depression was getting worse, not better. She was smoking a lot of grass by this time, and I started to worry about leaving Alan alone with her. Fortunately, I wrote at home, so I was there for the most part to see that things didn't get out of hand. Of course I didn't get much actual writing done during that time, and what I did wasn't very good, but I didn't know that. I was having too much fun living in Niceville. The fact that Amy started each day by getting high, stayed high all day, and claimed she couldn't go to sleep without getting high again was just . . . well, something I overlooked, I guess. The fact that she now got drunk every time she drank just didn't have a lot of significance to me, or if it did, it was a reason to be angry at that son-of-a-bitch father whose abuse of her was making my job of making her happy so difficult.

"No matter how hard I worked at it, Amy just didn't seem to be getting any happier. She started going out at night with her 'girlfriends,' and coming home drunk in the wee hours. I was living more and more of a housebound existence, between writing, taking care of Alan, and working on Amy. By this time, I'd at least figured out that if she would only lighten up on the grass and the booze, it might be easier for her to accept the happiness I was creating for her.

"Getting her to smoke less dope and drink less became my occupation and preoccupation. I made bargains with her (if you can go a week without smoking, I'll buy you a fur coat; if you can go on the wagon for a month, we'll take a trip to Mexico). I lectured her (How on earth can you expect to feel good when you've been out three nights this week drinking?). I'd arrange family trips, and while loading the car, I'd surreptitiously unpack her stash of grass, which I soon stopped doing, because the net result was always a terrible argument when we got to the hotel. Nothing worked. Alexander the Great, who had single-handedly created reality out of fiction in his own life, was a total flop at the business of making the woman he loved happy.

"In the process, my own sense of self-esteem was going to hell. The only way I'd ever managed to feel good in my life was by controlling my own reality, and now I couldn't, because Amy wouldn't let me. Every day she found a new way to screw up my grand plan for personal happiness. I couldn't make her happy, I didn't even try to make myself happy, and Alan was beginning to act as I had as a child, increasingly distant and withdrawn. I didn't see that my life was getting emptier and emptier. I didn't see the friends we had. I didn't work out or go to the movies or do anything else that normal people do. I was depressed all the time now, but I didn't recognize it as depression, because it wasn't the sharp, searing emotional pain I used to have. It was only a dull gray, numb emptiness that grew larger every day.

"Somehow, it didn't come as a total surprise when Amy didn't come home one night. When she showed up at noon the next day, she had some crazy story about how she had car trouble and couldn't call home, but I knew the truth. We had a gigantic argument, and she went out again that night. I never saw her again. About a month later I got served with divorce papers originating in Arizona, giving me all the property and sole un-contested custody of Alan. Poor kid hasn't seen his mother in three years now. That'll be his battle to fight, I guess.

"I guess the moral of the story is that he who believes he controls history or other people is a fool. I don't know, it seems as if I needed my ability to fictionalize reality in order to survive as a kid, but the payback was that it nearly destroyed me as an adult. In my Al-Anon program now, I'm trying to learn that the only person I can really take care of is myself, and within limits,

Alan. And surprise, surprise, it turns out that I don't even know
how to take care of myself very well, although I feel I'm learning.
Seems as if all those years I spent paying attention to Amy and
her problems would have been better spent paying attention to
me. Learning to mind my own business is the hardest thing I
think I've ever had to do. I still find I want to get in there and
create another reality for Alan and for my friends who are having
trouble. But slowly I think I'm making some progress at figuring
out that I'm not God. I didn't make other people unhappy, and
I can't make them happy. I'm trying to learn to take my own life
'one day at a time' and to 'live [my own life] and let [other
people, even people I love] live [theirs].' "

I have included Alex's story in its entirety, with his gracious
permission, because he really says it all. He shows us the roots
of his codependency in an out-of-control alcoholic environment.
He explains the foundation of his denial as an infantile way of
protecting himself against the constant trauma of his experience.
He shows us all how we developed the mental trick of changing
reality in our heads to give us the sense that we can control
something. He makes it clear how, if our real world is crazy and
abnormal, we have no idea what normal is and try to learn as best
we can from public images (in his case, TV) about what normal
private life is really like. He shows us our own fundamental sense
of shame about ourselves, and our compulsion to go underground with our real needs and feelings while presenting to the
world what we think it wants or will accept. He confronts us with
our sad deceptions to make other people think we're okay, while
we are convinced at the deepest levels of our being that we're
not okay, not by a long shot. He hints at the power of our
posttraumatic depression, which assails us once we've gotten out
of the battlefield of crises and emergencies. He explains how we
attract troubled people, and how easy a solution to our own
troubles it is to focus on fixing their lives. He admits with rare
courage the fact that fixing Amy's life was only a part of his

master strategy for fixing his own life and making Niceville a real place on Earth. He owns up to his sneaky and manipulative attempts to control her for her own good, and ultimately for his. Most important of all, he surrenders to his complete defeat in the effort to control reality, and helps us to see the absolute bankruptcy of such an approach to life.

Thanks, Alex.

8

PROGRESSION

IN

CODEPENDENCE

We saw in chapter 3 how alcoholism and other forms of drug addiction are *progressive* diseases, that is, their symptoms unfold and worsen in an orderly and predictable manner. We saw that it was possible to make very accurate guesses about what kinds of things would be happening in the lives of addicts depending on whether they were in the early, middle, or late stages of their illness. What about codependency?

Because codependence is a *syndrome* and not a disease, that is, because codependence is not caused by any physical disease process that we know of, there are more individual differences in the specific symptoms that will appear in any one codependent and in the order in which they will appear. But the essence of the syndrome is that it is reactive—codependent behaviors are learned and habituated by reacting to the sick and out-of-control behaviors of the alcoholic or addict. We know that addiction is progressive, so as long as the codependent remains in a situation where he or she is reacting to the progression of addiction, we can be sure that the syndrome of codependency will also be progressive and predictable.

Once the codependent has gotten out of his or her situation with the alcoholic or addict but has not yet begun to recover, that is, to actively deal with the problem behaviors associated with the codependency, the codependent behaviors may take on a more random pattern. Many nonrecovering codependents are out there alone and frustrated, either because they can't find anyone interested in their way of being in a relationship, or because they are afraid to allow a relationship to develop, intuitively knowing that any relationship is fertile soil for their sick and self-destructive codependency to take root. These are the people that everyone knows, who are just the nicest folks, salt of the earth don'cha know, who just can't seem to find anyone to love, or to love them, despite the best efforts of their friends and relatives to set them up. They remember everyone's birthday, show up on your doorstep when you're sick, and are always there to comfort you when something bad happens. They're wonderful hosts, perfect entertainers, and energetic charity workers. They make terrific "helping professionals," because their drive to make others feel better is so strong. If you have a friend like this, don't worry about him or her being lonely. Sooner or later the right alcoholic, addict, or otherwise-dysfunctional relationship partner will be attracted to the beacon that flashes "help offered here." Worry instead about what's in store for your friend once that relationship comes about!

For right now, our concern is you. You need to understand that whether you came to your relationship with your alcoholic or addict with your codependency already in place (if you're the child of an alcoholic or otherwise dysfunctional parent, this is probably the case), or whether you have developed your codependent symptoms as a product of spending the past five or ten

or twenty years with your alcoholic, the symptoms of your codependence have developed in direct response to the symptoms of
addiction that have appeared in your alcoholic.

You have gotten sick right along with and more or less on
the same schedule as your addict. Every time his or her behavior
patterns have changed as a result of the disease, your manner of
thinking, perceiving, feeling, and behaving have changed in response. Oh, it's subtle and hard to detect at first. Was it the
beginning of denial on your part or just simple naïveté that first
led you to accept the idea that drinking should liven up every
social occasion? But once you get down the road apiece, there's
no other way to explain the facts than to observe that you've
gotten sick and distorted, too. Who else do you know whose
main occupation in life is to get someone else to stop drinking?

What we want to do in this chapter is to get you to look at
your own symptoms of codependence, so that you can more
easily admit the truth about yourself and so that you can pinpoint
where you are in your syndrome and identify where you need
help. On the following page is the first half of a modified version
of Jellinek's famous chart of the progression of alcoholic stages
and symptoms superimposed on to a similar graph of the symptoms of codependency. As we explore the progression, you'll see
that the development of your addict's disease has pretty much
determined the progress of your syndrome.

When we met our addict, he or she was probably already
drinking. Some addict–codependent relationships began in teen-
age years, before use was a factor, or at least before it had
become anything that we reasonably could be expected to recognize as a problem, but most began after the initial use had begun.
Either way, most spouses of alcoholics or addicts report that the
addict made a powerful initial impression. To our eyes, which had
no scale to measure what might be normal or not, the alcoholic seemed exciting and romantic. Her impulsive behavior made
her seem at the same time daring yet touchingly vulnerable.

THE DOWNWARD PROGRESSION OF ADDICTION AND CODEPENDENCY

The addict is reacting to the changes produced by his use of his substance.
The codependent reacts to changes in her addict.

First use of substance occurs.
Attraction to potential alcoholic/addict. Seems an exciting, romantic, "glittering" person.

Social life begins to change to include substance use.
"Goes along" with social changes. Works to fit in with new friends and aquaintances.

Growing preoccupation with substance.
Accepts substance as part of normal life. May obtain substance for addict.

Increase in tolerance to substance.
Accepts, ignores, even defends, increased use. Puts down her own fears.

Onset of memory blackouts.
Frustration with addict's lapses. Sometimes wonders if it is she who is crazy.

Increased guilt about drinking. Surreptitious drinking.
Is appeased by addict's guilt about drinking. Accepts his promises, feels morally superior at his admissions of remorse.

Refusal to talk about substance use.
Accepts prohibition against acknowledging or talking about drinking. Is intimidated by addict's defensive anger. Begins to "act out" hostility.

Loss of control. Inability to stop when others do, or when intended.
Loss of control. Thoughts, attitudes, decisions, become governed by partner's excesses. Life becomes coping with a series of emergencies.

Rationalizations and excuses.
Rationalizations and excuses for codependent behavior. "Someone's got to take care of things." Buildup of anger and loss of respect toward alcoholic. Punitive, sometimes brutal acting out.

Grandiose, aggressive behavior.
Disgusted by the gradiosity, terrified by the aggressiveness, codependent becomes increasingly withdrawn, silently enraged.

Attempts to control use fail.
Codependent attempts to control addicts use by finding hidden supplies, manipulating activity, withholding sex, extracting meaningless promises, lecturing, haranguing.

Use becomes constant; family and friends avoided. Work, money troubles, build up.
Codependent accepts social isolation. Socializing is not worth the embarrassment. Assumes more responsibility for breadwinning and financial management.

Irrational thinking, buildup of resentments.
Engages in endless, irrational arguments and discussions. Takes partner's resentments personally.

Complete inability to function socially, sexually, occupationally.
Accepts social withdrawal. Secretly grateful for partner's sexual disinterest. Completely takes over breadwinner role.

Physical symptoms of dependence: shakes, unconsciousness, liver disease, withdrawal symptoms. Psychological symptoms resembling mental illness.
Develops stress-related physical problems. Seems crazy to friends. Traumatic medical emergencies occur.

"Hits bottom." Reaches the point where using substance and living becomes an either-or choice Next step is either death or recovery.
Codependent hits bottom. May leave alcoholic, commit suicide, or begin to recover.

Here was someone who could open up our dull and limited lives and spark our experience with excitement. Here was someone who could use our already well-developed capacity for disciplining and organizing our lives. Here was someone who could accept our latent desire to nurture and take care of. Many codependents later describe their addicted partners as "takers" or "users," but in fact it was that very quality, which we perceived at an unconscious level, that drew us to them in the first place. They were taking what we were giving!

As the addict began to become fascinated with his substance, and its use began to change his circle of social activity, you went along with the changes that were happening in his life. The new friends and acquaintances, drinking buddies some call them, seemed to you to be terribly interesting people, and if they drank too much, well, isn't that what chic and exciting people do? These people appealed to your low sense of self-esteem. They seemed smart, sophisticated, and interesting. How lucky that dull, uninteresting old you had an opportunity to enter their company. You worked at fitting in to your addict's new circle. Perhaps you drank or used drugs with them. Certainly you tried your best to fit in with them, to be accepted, and to make your addict proud of you among his new friends.

As your addict developed a life-style that included substance use, you came to accept her use as a part of everyday life. You had seen movies and television shows in which the heros drank before dinner, had drinks to relax, drank as a prelude to sexual encounters. Even if you had very negative experiences with alcohol use in your own family, you reasoned that your experience and your feelings were probably distorted, and that probably your addict's behavior was more normal. Certainly she was not out of control, mean, and obnoxious like your parents were when they drank. In fact, she was often nicer, more attentive, funnier, and more charming when she drank. Certainly she never got out of control. You were probably happy to stop by the liquor store while you were shopping, and it may have pleased you to keep the liquor cabinet stocked, so that your partner would always have what she wanted, without even having to ask.

As time passed, your alcoholic was drinking more and more often. His tolerance to the drug was increasing (it took more of it to affect him), but if you noticed, it certainly didn't bother you. He was a wonderful man, wasn't he? So if he liked to drink, even every day, even three or four or five drinks, well, so what? Okay, it was unusual. But *he* was unusual. Isn't that what attracted you to him and isn't that why you were so lucky to have him? Unusual people have unusual tastes, unusual life-styles, and the thing about them is they do exactly what they want. They're totally themselves. If he chose to drink a lot, well, that was part of the package. Who were you to question it? Besides, as he pointed out, you were probably neurotic about drinking because of the way your parents drank. His drinking was certainly nothing like that. You were probably just being silly to even waste a moment's concern over it.

It took several years before you began to notice very slight lapses and abnormalities in his behavior. At first it seemed funny when he couldn't remember where he parked the car, and you both had to go out looking for it the next day. But as time passed it became frustrating. You would have intense conversations with him about something that concerned you in your relationship, but the next day nothing would change. You would make agreements to do something or other about a project or a social commitment, but when the time came, he'd forgotten the thing you specifically agreed on. With your orderly and conscientious mind, it appalled you when he forgot to pay the utility bills that month, and getting the past-due notices were like a traumatic shock to your system. In your saner moments, however, you were sure that you were making mountains out of molehills.

Most of the time you were probably mistaken anyway. Who knows, after all, if you really made that agreement or reached that conclusion during that discussion. You had been drinking, too, you know, and you both knew that you didn't hold your liquor nearly as well as he. Maybe it was you who were supposed to remember to pay that bill. He seemed so sure that you said you'd take care of it.

After "The Party" (isn't it funny how that awful evening always has capital letters in your mind?), you became sure that there was a problem. She'd been so nervous about hosting a Christmas party in your new home, and by this time you were so accustomed to her drinking that it didn't seem unusual when she poured a stiff one while she was making the hors d'oeuvres at three o'clock. But you were definitely alarmed when you realized that she was three-quarters lit before the first guest arrived at seven. By this time you knew that she was unpredictable and impulsive when she drank, and there was a lot riding on this party. Your division manager, a Mormon, was invited, and although you knew he was pretty tolerant of other people drinking, you'd been around him enough to know his private views about people who got drunk. You'd carefully explained to her that a promotion could depend on the success or failure of this party, yet here she was, drunk before it even began! How could she! She'd reassured you not to worry, that she'd take it easy, but you knew from experience that once she got started, there was no telling how things would end up. You'll never forget the chilling, mind-numbing shock you felt when you came out of the bathroom to see her blithely performing, to the shocked silence of the guests, her famous striptease. Thank God you got to her before too much came off, and hustled her off to bed. Mercifully, most of the guests had left shortly, with embarrassed excuses for leaving early.

You were mad enough to get a divorce over that one, and

she knew it. After you gave her the "silent treatment" for a day or so (no, that's not fair; you weren't using silence to punish her—you were really *mad*), you made up. But only after she came to you, tearful, and promised it would never happen again. Damn well better not, you thought. You told her then that you just couldn't understand why she didn't control herself better. People who weren't responsible about their drinking behavior disgusted you, you told her. They reminded you of your drunken mother who was a constant embarrassment to your father. She was most of the reason your father had never really made a success of himself, and by God, you told her, that wasn't going to happen to you! In the end, though, you were satisfied with her promise that she'd take care of the problem, and you were delighted when she announced that she was going on the wagon for a while. Indeed, when she did begin to drink again about a month later, it seemed as though she'd learned her lesson, because you could see her being careful about it.

· · ·

Things really changed over the next two years. There were more episodes of behavior out of control. There was the time you caught him having an affair, but you hadn't gone to see the divorce lawyer because he swore it was just because he'd been drinking and met her in a bar. He didn't even know her name, he claimed, and besides, he'd told you with a sheepish grin (it was that damn grin that always got you; how can you stay mad at a little boy?), they hadn't really "done it" because he'd been drinking and couldn't get it up. But after that it was as if you weren't allowed to mention the drinking. When you tried, it seemed to start the worst arguments the two of you had ever had. He'd called you a nag, a bitch, a neurotic killjoy, a controller, a manipulator, and a lot of other things you'd just as soon not repeat. Pretty soon you got the idea; this was a subject that was no longer open for discussion. That was okay with you, too. You'd gotten pretty tired of talking about it and getting nowhere but in trouble. Who needs to be abused, anyway? Since then, you've found that there are other ways to make your feelings known. You don't sleep with him anymore unless he hasn't been drinking, which is pretty damn seldom. If he's not home in time for dinner, he can just make his own, and you won't sit with him while he eats as you used to. In fact, you felt, you just didn't care to have anything to do with him when he'd been drinking, and you didn't.

Somehow, you adapted to a life-style of missed appointments, neglected responsibilities, and disrupted plans. Seems as if you learned to go from one emergency to another. It became normal for you to call home several times a day to remind her about that bill that needed to be paid, the parent–teacher conference or whatever other event that one of you had to attend, though the secret reason for your calling was to check whether she was high. It was a heavy load to try to run two lives, but you just didn't seem to be able to stop. You didn't even want to think about what would happen if you did. If that wasn't bad enough, there were the emergencies that punctuated your already too-busy life. *You* had to find her a lawyer when she got arrested for possession of marijuana, *you* had to find a body shop to fix the car after she banged it up, *you* had to take time off to take your son to the doctor for the asthma attacks he'd started having, you, you, you.

· · ·

The stress of living like this was getting to you. Even you, the superwoman, felt constantly overtired, overstressed, and out of control. You were running a hundred miles an hour to stay in place. What was the alternative? Let him run the family into bankruptcy? Kill himself on the road (maybe that wouldn't be so bad, as long as the kids weren't in the car with him!)? The jerk!

Oh, you still loved him, you supposed, but you couldn't remember the last time you felt respect or admiration for him. Sometimes you actually hated him when he got into that disgusting cocaine-generated "lord of all he surveys" mood. God! Here you were with the credit cards maxed out, behind on every bill, him unemployed and *selling* the stuff, for goodness sake, and he would sit in the middle of the whole mess talking about starting his own company. It made you sick, but heaven help you if you said so. You learned that the best strategy was to just ignore him. He wasn't even worth your attention anymore anyway.

Finally, things reached a point where something had to be done. You were tired of her promises that she'd straighten up, and you just couldn't be anything but negative and unsupportive about her attempts to get her drinking under control. You were optimistic at first when she decided to drink only wine and beer, until you found out she could get just as messed up on those. When she promised to limit it to two drinks per sitting, you got hopeful for a bit, until she figured out how it was possible to have four or five "sittings" a day! You'd gotten good at finding where she kept her bottles (well, you were good at it, but she had become so obvious that her attempts to fool you were pitiful) and pouring them out, but there always seemed to be more that you hadn't found. You tried watering her vodka but only once. You had her watch that program on alcoholism, and you got her those books to read, but she never remarked about it either way. You tried reasoning with her, but she'd just sit there in stony silence while you explained and explained, pleaded and pleaded, threatened and threatened. Sometimes she'd promise to take your advice to heart, but it was really just to shut you up.

• • •

After the bankruptcy, the responsibility of supporting the family had fallen to you. He just didn't seem to care about anything anymore. He hadn't worked in four months, and judging from his current behavior, it didn't look as if he'd ever work again. You knew that he was smoking marijuana first thing in the morning now, and you assumed he was smoking all day. It made you feel awful on those days when you knew he was picking up the baby from day care, but you had to work, didn't you?

Your friends had all but given up inviting you to dinner or to their parties, because you'd turned them down so many times. Who needed the embarrassment? There was a time when you forced yourself to go alone because he just didn't care (oh, he always had excuses: "I never liked him anyway" or "She's just a materialistic bitch who only invites us over so she can show off their new furniture"), but in time it just hadn't seemed worth the effort to think up excuses for him, and it wasn't any fun to be the only single person at a party. When he was willing to go, it was no fun because you spent all your time worrying that he'd drink too much or go outside and smoke grass and then do or say something embarrassing. You don't even see your own friends anymore, because all you do is complain about him and his drinking and drugging. You bore yourself, not to mention your friends. It was simpler to just give up on a social life.

· · ·

Lately, it's gotten to feeling really crazy even to be with her. Her drinking goes on around the clock now, and she talks and acts like an insane person. You wonder if indeed she has lost her mind. She has terrible nightmares. She shakes, her skin has either a terrible pallor or it looks like raw hamburger. She wakes you up in the middle of the night and gets you involved in long, serious discussions that, in the end, just don't make any sense. You try to reason with her, but it's as if her reasoning ability is gone. Every time you use a sentence of more than ten words, she seems to lose the point. You feel tricked into these discussions and arguments, and end up losing your temper with her, which makes you feel bad and guilty. Last week you hit her, and you're not sure if you'll ever be able to forgive yourself for that.

Your health is breaking down, too. You hate to go to the doctor, because you hate to take the time off, you hate to spend that much money, but most of all, you know that the doctor suspects that something is very, very wrong in your life. You don't want to talk to him about it because he won't understand, and he'll probably tell you to do something you either can't or really don't want to do. So you suffer along with your ulcer, or you bear up under the pain of your back, or you just don't stray very far from the toilet so you can deal with you spastic colon.

Although you really don't spend much time thinking about yourself, you're dimly aware that your friends and coworkers don't seem to know what to make of you anymore. You're always in a hurry, you never smile, your work is failing (and God help everybody if you lose your job!), you can't concentrate, you had to miss four days last month alone to deal with emergencies at home. Her drunken phone calls are now coming in through the front switchboard. People know you're having terrible troubles, but they reason that if you can't or won't do anything about it, what can they do? You notice that your old friends don't even call anymore just to see how you're doing. They're exhausted by you, and frankly they just don't want to hear any more.

· · ·

Finally you hit bottom in your codependent unwellness. Nobody can predict with accuracy when and where the bottom will come. It could have been years ago over that one embarrassing party, or it may not happen for thirty years, or until the phone rings in the wee hours to tell you that your addict is dead. Bottom is not predictable by length of time or severity of consequences of living with an alcoholic or addict. Bottom comes to each codependent at that moment of truth when you see, with nauseating clarity, that the life you've been living is utterly without joy, peace, or spiritual meaning. Bottom comes when you see that your life is not what your alcoholic or addict has made of it, it's what you've made of it, by acting out your codependent sickness, by trying to control the life of another person, by minding his business and not your own. Bottom comes when you realize that you're no damn good, not in the sense that you have neurotic feelings of low self-esteem, but in the sense that you're of no good to your addicted partner, no good to your children, and no good to yourself.

Hitting bottom is every bit as much of a crisis for you as the alcoholic's bottom is for him. It is an experience of utter and absolute intellectual futility, emotional emptiness, and spiritual desolation. One wants to cry out, "My God, my God, why have you forsaken me?" It is a frightening time at which some codependents, at the end of their resources, commit suicide. Others, in their extremity, are finally able to make a decision to leave their suffering addict, ultimately seeing that it is better to save themselves and the children than to allow everyone to go down with the ship. Some will seek professional help, and of these some are dealt yet another cruel twist by seeking help from a clergyman who advises them to stay and heaps yet more guilt upon them, or from a psychologist who doesn't understand addiction and who insists on interpreting their symptoms as an intrapsychic problem, or worst of all, from a psychiatrist who prescribes medication to mask the symptoms and render them more unable to take effective action for themselves. A fortunate few are directed to qualified codependency treatment and to Al-Anon and enter the community of recovering codependents.

The point of this chapter is to help you to see that codependency, because of its intimate and reciprocal relationship with addiction, is progressive. It goes from bad to worse as the addict's disease progresses, and each new symptom of codependency is a direct response to a change in the condition of the addict. Codependents hang in there year in and year out believing that if they will only try hard enough, pray hard enough, and love hard enough, things will change.

Things will change, all right. Until you begin to work at your own recovery from codependency, things are certain to get worse.

9

AM I

CODEPENDENT?

U nless you're a recovering alcoholic or addict trying to understand your partner who is sick with codependency, it's quite unlikely that you've read this far in this book unless you suffer from codependency. The degree to which your symptoms have developed may depend on many things, and I suppose it's possible to have a mild case of codependency, but if you have seen yourself in the pages of this book, chances are your symptoms are fairly severe and getting worse.

There are a number of populations that are highly at risk— groups of people who are very likely to develop the syndrome. If you . . .

- are recovering from alcoholism or other chemical dependency;

- are the child of an alcoholic or chemically dependent family;

- are the child of a family in which one or both parents were mentally ill or had a long-term serious illness;

- were physically or sexually abused as a child;
- are or have been married to or lived with an alcoholic or an addict, especially if you have been in more than one such relationship;
- work in the field of mental health, counseling, social work, or chemical-dependency treatment.

. . . there is an *extremely* high probability that you have the syndrome, and that your thoughts, attitudes, feelings, and behavior are dominated by a fundamentally codependent view of life. Whether you live with an addict at this time or not, if you fall into one of the groups listed above, chances are that a number of the symptoms of codependency pose recurring and troubling problems in your life. Probably you . . .

- take care of others at the expense of your own well-being;
- have difficulty being assertive and standing up for your rights;
- get depressed;
- become compulsive about gambling, eating, smoking, house-cleaning, or work;
- have trouble expressing or even feeling your feelings;
- lose track of yourself when you love someone else;
- find yourself in relationships with needy, unreliable, dysfunctional, and unsafe people;
- are extremely sensitive to criticism;
- try to do everything perfectly;
- don't do things that have benefit or enjoyment only to yourself;

- frequently feel overwhelmed by your duties and responsibilities;

- have great difficulty communicating directly about your wants, needs, and feelings;

- focus your attention and energy on people other than yourself.

Because of this last item, you get into trouble in your relationships with people because you . . .

- wish that people would change;

- try to change them;

- advise them, lecture them, beg them, bribe them, threaten them, get mad at them;

- try to blackmail them by helping them, meeting their needs, supporting them, pampering them;

- make sure they meet their responsibilities;

- meet their responsibilities for them;

- think you know what's best for them.

Because you do these things, people get angry with you. It always shocks and surprises you when they do, and you . . .

- feel unjustly treated;

- argue;

- try to show them how they're wrong about you;

- apologize when you're not sorry;

- lie to avoid their anger;

- try to pacify them.

These troublesome behaviors spring from a series of mistaken and sometimes contradictory ideas about life that the codependent holds, either consciously or unconsciously as *core beliefs* about life. Many of these beliefs were formed out of the experience of growing up in a chemically dependent or otherwise dysfunctional family. As a general rule, the earlier in life that the codependent was exposed to chemical or psychological dysfunction, the deeper and more persistent the beliefs will be embedded. You may believe that . . .

- you cannot be loved for who you are;

- you must earn the love you get;

- your inner thoughts and feelings are shameful and abnormal;

- you and everything about you are shameful and abnormal, that you are not attractive, that your clothes are not as nice as those of others, that your home is not as clean as that of others, etc.;

- it is wrong and selfish to meet your own needs, especially if this would mean disappointing or angering others;

- if people get angry with you, it means you are wrong;

- if people get angry with you, they will hurt you;

- if people get angry with you, they will desert you;

- it is normal to be hurt and abused;

- other people can't be trusted;
- other people will hurt you;
- other people make your life unhappy;
- you can make the lives of other people happy;
- if you love someone, you can trust them;
- if you do what people want, they will love you for it;
- if you don't do what people want, they won't love you;
- that somewhere out there is a love relationship that will redeem you and make you whole.

Sometimes I ask my patients to troubleshoot their own codependency by playing "Chinese restaurant" with the "menu" items listed above. Following is a format you can use to see how your deeply held core beliefs result in troublesome behaviors that keep you from meeting your own needs and being happy and interfere with your relationships with other people. For instance, you might say

Deep down I believe that <u>I can make the lives of other people happy</u> so I <u>wish other people would change, think I know what is best for them, try to change them, advise them, beg them, bribe them, threaten them, get mad at them.</u> The problem this creates in my life is that <u>I focus my attention and energy on other people and fail to meet my own needs.</u>

You might want to make five or ten photocopies of the following exercise, just so you can construct some clear statements about how your codependent beliefs affect your feelings and behaviors in ways that get you into trouble. Performing this exercise won't cure your codependency, but it may help you understand it a little better.

CODEPENDENCY TROUBLESHOOTER

Deep down, I hold the core belief(s) that _____

_____

_____

_____

_____.

My behavior as a result of this belief is _____

_____

_____

_____

_____.

The problem in my life that is caused by that behavior is _____

_____

_____

_____

_____.

So . . . are you codependent, or are you just a really nice person who is often misunderstood by others and who happened by chance or by accident to get into a relationship with an addict? It's for you to say.

10

MARY'S STORY

I t was three o'clock in the morning, and Mary Williams sat
alone in her kitchen watching a cup of coffee get cold in front
of her. An hour ago, the phone had rung, startling her from the
anxious drowsiness that passed for sleep when John was out
drinking. For a moment her heart hung suspended, wondering
if this was the phone call that would tell her of the car accident
or the medical emergency that would end her marriage and her
husband's life. It was only when she heard John's angry voice that
her feelings settled into the attitude of resigned disgust that she
felt so much of these days. What now?

"You gotta come down here to the police station and get
me," he had demanded. "Some fucking rookie cop decided to
meet his quota of DWIs tonight, and I got picked to be his
victim. Jesus, am I steamed!" His voice had that belligerent,
rasping edge that warned her not to cross him. She could always
tell by his swearing how much he had been drinking, and tonight
he sounded as if he was about medium well-done.

"All right, John, I understand. Try to relax, okay? You know it won't help for you to argue with the police."

"God damn it, Mary, I don't need any of your fucking advice right now! Will you just get down here and get me out!" The phone had clicked off abruptly.

Mary sat unmoving, knowing that she should probably get herself dressed and down to the police station. It had already been an hour since John called. But she just didn't want to see him now, or put up with his ranting and raving. "He could just sit there for a while yet," she thought. "At least I know he's safe, and he can sober up a little so that I don't have to listen to it for hours on end. Either way, there'll be no more sleep for me tonight."

John. The poor, sad, silly, infuriating, frightening man. Where was all this going to end? she wondered. For the past four or five years she had been increasingly worried and preoccupied about his drinking. Although she had never been exposed to heavy drinking before John's drinking had gotten so bad, she'd never thought of his drinking as a problem until the time five years ago when he got so drunk at the dinner with the partners of the firm he was working for. He'd explained later that he was just nervous, and that he'd had a couple too many without really being aware of it. It was strange how even today he didn't seem to understand that it was those drinks that cost him (and her, she supposed) a partnership in the firm.

"Funny how people change," she mused. John didn't even drink at all when she met him in college. She'd been attracted to him because he seemed so serious and sad somehow (*codependents are attracted to needy people*). She remembered that she felt an almost maternal feeling about him, as if he was a kind of diamond in the rough who would only need a little TLC to realize his tremendous potential. If she'd only known then, she thought, that she would have to spend the rest of her life with a man who sometimes acted like a three-year-old in a tantrum and other times acted like a fourteen-year-old carrying on an adolescent rebellion (*codependents feel parental toward their addicts*).

Mary often wondered if she were to blame for John's drinking. She recalled that he had shyly confessed to her on one of their first dates that the bottle of wine they were sharing at dinner was his first taste of alcohol. She'd been amused at how tentative and frightened he had seemed about drinking it, as if he was afraid that he would turn into Mr. Hyde ten seconds after his first sip. Later, when he had told her about his father, she understood. Somewhere she'd read that drinking problems ran in families, and she wondered what might have been different if she hadn't caused John to have his first drink (*codependents feel responsible for things that are wrong*).

Mary shook her head. "I can't blame myself for something I didn't even know about," she thought. Her father's position as minister in their strictly fundamentalist church had forbidden the presence of alcohol in their home, and even if it hadn't, her mother's serious heart condition, which had killed her when Mary was seven, would have precluded the possibility of drinking in the home. She supposed she could be forgiven for being so stupid and not seeing the problem with John sooner; she'd just never been exposed to drinking or drinkers. (*Codependents don't always come from chemically dependent homes. Other family conditions, like chronic illness, can foster codependency. If the family environment places religious or moral principles above the genuine exchange of human thoughts and feelings, the family environment is even more conducive to the development of codependency.*)

Mary's thoughts wandered to her family. "Poor Daddy," she thought. "Such a lost and lonely man." Pastor Jorgenson towered above his congregation like a pillar of moral principle. He had great respect, even awe from them, but no friendship or companionship. Since Mom had taken to her bed when Mary was five, Mary had thought of herself as her father's only friend and confidante (*codependents often felt it was their responsibility to meet the emotional needs of their parents*). That, combined with the fact that her mother's illness made it necessary for her to become "the woman of the house," led the parishioners to jokingly refer to her as "the little woman" and "the pastor's wifelet" (*codependent children often appear to be little adults*). She'd felt proud of her ability to perform these adult functions, but later she wondered if those responsibilities hadn't cost her her childhood. She hadn't had friends, hadn't played after school (there was homework, and Bible study, Daddy's dinner to fix), and besides, she had found it difficult to relate to other little girls because she didn't live a little girl's life (*many codependents feel that they never got to be kids*).

Mary blushed as thoughts about her Awful Secret came unwanted to her mind. They always did if she thought for any length of time about Daddy. After Mom died, it was so natural that she and Daddy should become so much closer. She was, after all, his only friend. And she felt so sorry for him. Far from feeling it was unnatural, she simply accepted that he would hold her on his lap when they read the Bible together, even when she got to be eleven and twelve years old. She couldn't remember the first time she had become aware that his touches and embraces were somehow a little closer than was proper between father and daughter. Later, when she was aware of its significance, part of her felt weird and uncomfortable about it, but part of her also felt sorry for him that he had to live with his need and had no one to give him comfort. These episodes had gone on right through high school, but at no time, even when it was happening, had she or Daddy ever spoken a single word about it, nor had she ever spoken about it to others, even to John. She had always kept those memories in a locked box in her mind labeled My Awful Secret. (*Codependents often have a history of childhood physical or sexual abuse. Because of guilt and shame, and a feeling of obligation to protect the parent, they enter into a conspiracy of silence.*)

She'd read magazine articles and seen TV programs about

things like incest and sexual abuse of children, but she just couldn't relate to them. Incest was such an ugly word, and besides, it wasn't as if she'd had sex with Daddy, it was more as if she had just tried to comfort him in his loneliness. She certainly didn't think she'd been abused (*denial, rationalization*). She had to admit that it certainly wasn't normal, though, and when she thought about it, it made her feel dirty and guilty (*codependents usually feel different and abnormal, and they feel ashamed and guilty about it*). Long ago she'd decided that the best thing was to just not think about it (*repression*).

When she met John in college, his air of seriousness and sadness had aroused in her the same feelings of wanting to take care of him that she had felt toward Daddy (*codependents often unconsciously select partners who help them re-enact the problem situations of their childhoods*). But at least Daddy, she thought with a flash of anger and contempt, was somebody you could be proud of. He may have been rigid, and he may have been silent about his inner thoughts and feelings, but at least he behaved properly (well, with that One Exception . . .) and enjoyed the respect of the community. He hadn't been a drunk like John, bullying his wife, embarrassing his family, and offending his neighbors, his friends, and his associates (*codependents lose respect for their addicted partners*).

She'd decided five years ago, after he lost the partnership opportunity, that she'd figure out how to get him to control his drinking. She believed him when he said he would watch it, but it had been clear that he needed some help. She found he was more careful about his condition when she stopped allowing sex when he was drunk. She controlled his intake somewhat by buying only one bottle of whiskey a week, until she realized that he was conserving the supply by spending more time out in the cocktail lounge. For a long time she'd been able to monitor his drinking by the checks and the credit card receipts from the bars, but for the past several years he had taken to drawing money from the cash machine, so she couldn't tell how much was going toward liquor. She'd given up on pouring his booze down the drain the night he hit her. (*Codependents take responsibility for and try to control the addict's use. These attempts quickly degenerate into power games played by the addict and the codependent.*)

Mary didn't know whether it was crazy to feel this way (*codependents often don't know whether they're crazy or not, and they have little idea of what is normal and what is not*), but the results had almost made getting hit by John worthwhile. He had stopped drinking entirely for almost a month, and he had gone back to being the gentle, loving man she'd first fallen in love with. He was considerate and stopped criticizing her. He felt better, she could tell. He was up earlier, began to work out again, and was generally cheerful and upbeat. It was so disappointing when he went back to drinking after a month, even though he did a pretty good job of not getting drunk for several months after that. Gradually, things had gone back to their normal pattern of bad to worse. (*Codependents want to believe in and take hope from the promises of their addicts. They feel morally superior at the addict's remorse, and they enjoy the special treatment they get because of the addict's guilt.*)

Mary didn't know exactly when it had happened, but it certainly seemed like her life had turned into a dreary chore. Gradually, they had stopped seeing the few friends they had (neither she nor John had ever been terribly social people), and she guessed it had been a year since they had even been out together. She just felt tired all the time. They needed her part-time income as a legal stenographer simply to pay the bills, and between that and taking care of Jennifer, managing the family's finances (which these days meant deciding how to rob Peter to· pay Paul), and coping with John and his critical, unreasonable, and negative manner, it seemed as if all her energy and time were taken. Worse yet, it didn't seem that she was making any progress. All her effort seemed like treading water, just barely keeping them even. It was a dreadful cycle. She knew they weren't getting anywhere financially, socially, or as a family, and yet she knew that if she let up, even a little bit, everything would fall apart. (*Codependents fall with their addicts into a pattern of social isolation. They assume more and more of the family responsibilities as the addict becomes more and more irresponsible. They become chronically depressed as their lives become more joyless and more stressed because of the addict's mistakes, omissions, and failures.*)

What were they going to do now? Mary wasn't sure what this drunk-driving charge would mean to their lives, but she was sure it wasn't good. "Oh God," she thought with sudden panic, "if this gets out, I wonder if he'll lose the partnership again?" They had been counting on the additional income that would result from partnership in the firm. She didn't want to think about what would happen if they lost that. John still hadn't stopped ranting about the senior partner of his previous firm, and she remembered her terror when he had quit the firm without another job lined up, and her six months' pregnant with Jennifer.

For what seemed like the hundredth time, she thought about divorcing John. Even the idea made her want to cry. It would kill Daddy, even though he didn't much like John (he had told her repeatedly that the marriage would come to no good because John wasn't "saved"), because he believed that divorce was wrong no matter what. He might even disown her. And John. He wasn't a bad person, really, and what would happen to him if she left him? She was, after all, the only thing holding his life together. What about Jennifer? Was she to become another statistic among the ranks of children of broken homes? "I don't know, I don't know, I don't know," she sobbed to herself. (*Codependents discount their own suffering. Even in their extremity, they worry about pleasing others and meeting their needs.*)

Maybe in the morning she'd call that woman who came to their church to talk about Al-Anon. Not that she'd go to those meetings; airing her dirty laundry in public was certainly not her style. But perhaps that woman, who had given Mary her phone number after her talk, would have some suggestions about how Mary could save the family from what seemed like certain disaster.

Mary, like John, is at a crossroads in her life; and like John, she is so totally overwhelmed in her codependency that she cannot see it. All she can think about is getting from one crisis to the next.

Mary's thoughts about getting advice so that she could "save the family" indicate that she has not yet "hit bottom" in her codependency, that is, that she has not yet truly glimpsed her absolute and utter powerlessness over the behavior of another human being. She apparently still believes there is a way for her to convince, manipulate, or control John out of his alcoholism. Perhaps her contact with the woman from Al-Anon will start her in a process that will change Mary's way of seeing things. But if she persists in these beliefs, things will continue to get worse for her and the family. She will descend with John into the hell of late-stage alcoholism/codependency. The stress will increase, her arguments with John will become more frequent and more violent, the damage to Jennifer will become more severe, and Mary will begin to develop physical illness to go along with her already chronic depression. The disastrous consequences of John's alcoholism will follow faster now; bankruptcy is looming on the horizon, and if John loses his job, which he must if his drinking continues, Mary will become the family's sole bread-winner. Ultimately, as it always does, the choice for Mary, as for John, will narrow down to one: recovery or death.

IV

GETTING

HELP

Whether you've recognized yourself as the alcoholic/addict or as the codependent or both, by now I hope you've seen that you need help. Addiction and codependency aren't problems that are going to go away. You may try the geographical solution, that is, running away from your addict, or if you're the addict, running away from the home, the job, the wife, the kids, the town, even the country where you've had such "bad luck." The problem with the geographical solution is that wherever you go, as soon as you get there, there you are! Whether your problem is addiction or codependency or both, the problem is in you, not in your spouse or your job or your relatives. Until you accept that the problem is yours, nothing is going to change, except for the worse.

If you've got the misfortune to have addiction or codependency, then in a paradoxical way you're fortunate to live in this day and age. Sixty years ago there would have been no effective help for you, for neither AA nor Al-Anon had yet been born. Even twenty years later, your hope for recovery would have been slight, because addictive disease is very powerful, and the knowledge of what it was, and how to recover from it, was still vague and undeveloped. As recently as twenty years ago, while there were a few isolated treatment resources scattered around the country, they weren't generally known. You would have been lucky to have found one.

The decade of the 1970s saw a boom in the proliferation of competent, appropriate, and effective treatment for addictive disease. Residential treatment centers, staffed for the most part by recovering alcoholics and addicts, sprang up in almost every major metropolitan area in the United States. These facilities varied widely in the quality of staff, quality of environment, and appropriateness of their treatment procedures and practices, but at least they were available. Corporate America began to realize that alcoholism was a growth industry, and several major health-care corporations plowed millions of dollars into the development of treatment-center chains. This was a mixed blessing. The benefit was that treatment services became much more widely available, and the corporations, mindful of their exposure, did their best to improve and standardize the quality of their staffs. The downside was that treatment became big business, with many of the negative implications of that phrase. Aggressive advertising, almost unknown before in the health-care professions, pursued patients on radio, television, in magazines, and even on the sides of buses! Directors of treatment became responsible to corporate superiors, who were sometimes more concerned about profits than patients and whose major interest was often to minimize the cost of care so that the margin of profit was maximized. (This isn't all bad, I hasten to say. In America, a health-care facility must earn a profit in order to continue to exist and deliver care. The built-in tensions between treatment staff and management people is probably, in the end, a good thing, but it can certainly lead to abuses.) However you feel about big business in the health-care field, the fact is that today there are more treatment resources available in more places than ever before.

As recently as the late 1970s, effective care for the codependent was scarce and usually only scratched the surface of the codependent's real problem. Counselors in addictions treatment centers, most of them recovering alcoholics or addicts themselves, addressed the problems of codependents only from the perspective of whether the codependent might present a problem to the addict's recovery, and whether the codependent might him- or herself be addicted. Al-Anon, of course, had existed for many years, and the quality of support and the strength of its time-tested wisdom provided a safe harbor for the codependent who was caught in the storm of his or her addict's illness. But because of the very structure of Al-Anon, the process of confronting the codependents' unhealthy behavior and attitudes was often slow and unclear. It took years of Al-Anon for the codependent to get clear about the real nature of his or her problem, and the codependent's recovery usually lagged far behind that of his or her addict. Participation in a Twelve-Step program like Al-Anon or the much newer Adult Children of Alcoholics and Codependents Anonymous is still an absolutely essential part of recovery for the codependent, but most codependents need more, especially at the beginning of their recovery.

It wasn't until the early 1980s that researchers, theorists, and workers in the field began to see that codependence was a personal emotional and behavioral problem in and of itself, and although it was usually seen in connection with an addiction in another person, it was, in the end, an independent problem. Early writers in the field like Claudia Black, Sharon Wegscheider-Cruse, Dr. Timmen L. Cermak, Stephanie Brown, Robin Norwood, Anne Wilson Schaef, and others contributed seminal work in the field that was as important to our understanding of codependence as the early work of Jellinek and Milam was to our understanding of alcoholism.

Today there is plenty of effective, enlightened help for the codependent. Treatment centers, self-help groups, good literature, and even the counseling and mental-health professionals, who historically have done more harm than good for addicts and their codependents, now offer help that ranges from basic education about codependence to long-term, intensive inpatient treatment for the syndrome.

In this section of the book, we're going to talk about what

kind of help you and your alcoholic need, how to find it, and how to be sure that the help you're getting is the best kind for your particular circumstances. I want to warn you about some wrong directions that can lead you up blind alleys and delay your path to recovery. If you're an alcoholic or addict, we'll talk about how to initiate the process of your recovery even if your codependent isn't supportive or interested, and won't recognize that he or she also has a problem. If you're a codependent, I'll offer some guidelines about how you can start your recovery even if you can't imagine your addict accepting help at this time. Forewarned is forearmed, as they say, so we'll discuss some ways for you to learn about your options for addiction treatment if and when your addict is prepared to accept help. I'll tell you about a process that may get your alcoholic or addict to accept help even if he or she seems totally resistant to the idea now. Finally, I want to share with you some information about the most important tool you can ever have for your long-term recovery—the Twelve-Step programs.

11

TREATMENT
FOR
ADDICTIONS

If you live in any metropolitan area in the United States, chances are that there are a number of inpatient and outpatient treatment facilities near you. You may have seen ads on radio and TV and may even be able to name some of the more prominent treatment agencies. Some areas are better served than others, of course. My own area of western Washington State happens to be among those areas, and I imagine there must be in excess of a hundred treatment centers and agencies within a hundred miles of my own little town of Kirkland. There may be far fewer locally available to you, but, happily, today the problem is usually more one of picking from among the treatments offered than of finding a source of treatment.

This chapter is intended to help you sort out the amazing variety of treatments that are offered, to identify what forms of treatment are not helpful at all, and of those that are, which may best fit your needs and your addict's at this time. If you're an addict or alcoholic considering treatment for yourself, you need to be careful about trying to make this judgment alone, because your denial will lead you, even if you admit that there is a problem, to underestimate your need for treatment. If you are a codependent and trying to identify treatment options for your addict, you need to be careful, because your tendency to try to control and run other people's lives may cause you to use this information to try to batter and browbeat your addict into treatment. You need to know that when the moment comes that your addict is ready to accept help, it will be a great advantage for you to have already researched the kinds of treatment available in your community, but if you try to use this information in the wrong way or prematurely, you can cause your addict to dig in his heels and delay the process of getting help.

TYPES OF HELP YOU DON'T NEED

There are some types of help that don't help at all. In fact, they can cause delays to the beginning of recovery, cost thousands of dollars, and allow your alcoholic to die in the process of "treating" him. It's unfortunate, but even in this day and age, there are still a wide variety of people who hold out moral, psychological, and "alternative" treatments for this very physical disease. These treatments, to be blunt, don't work, except with the most highly motivated of patients, who sometimes get clean and sober in spite of the treatment.

Don't seek a spiritual cure. Addiction is a disease that saps one's sense of spiritual strength, creates feelings of moral guilt and blame, and causes one to feel out of touch with the source of spiritual life. Many addicts first consult a member of the clergy when they feel that they need help. It's wonderful if your family has such a person to turn to, but you need to be aware that most clergy are still uninformed about the real nature of addiction (if you read part I of this book, chances are that you know more about addiction than your minister), and because of their training, most are inclined to offer some form of spiritual help as a "cure" for your addiction. It's fine to get spiritual help and advice, but you must remember that addiction is a physical disease. You wouldn't turn to your priest for a cure for diabetes, would you?

Many of the more "metaphysical" religious organizations can be worse yet on this score. Because many believe that everything that happens to us "on the physical plane" is a "manifestation" of our spiritual ills or struggles, their tendency is to involve you and your addict in spiritual exercises that don't address the fact that you're ill. They'd like you to think about your lives, but they don't realize that because of his addiction and your codependency, your thinking ability is sick. Spiritual growth is wonderful, but you have to be a well person for it to mean anything.

If your clergyperson's attitude isn't one of "Let's see if we can find you some professional help for this problem," you need to seek help elsewhere.

Don't seek a psychiatric or a psychological cure. Psychiatrists are lovely folks, for the most part, but you need to realize that nothing in their training or in their day-to-day work prepares them to deal effectively with your alcoholic's addiction. Psychiatrists are medical doctors who are trained to deal with those chemical diseases of the nervous system that cause abnormalities in thought and behavior. Mostly they treat these diseases with medications, some of them quite strong and powerful. Although your addict's brain may have been damaged as a result of his use, and his nervous system may not be in any great shape, neither his addiction nor your codependency are psychiatric disorders, and the last thing in the world that you need is psychotropic medications.

Many addicts and alcoholics admit themselves to psychiatric

hospitals, making the logical conclusion that their symptoms of irrationality, belligerence, inability to get along with spouse, boss, or coworkers, and indeed their compulsion to use their substance must prove that they're crazy. Logical, but wrong. The mental, emotional, and behavioral symptoms of addiction mimic those of mental illness. But if your loved one is using a psychoactive substance like alcohol or other drugs every day, while you can't be sure that there isn't something wrong with his mind, you can be sure that the first and foremost thing that's wrong is the presence of the drug in his body. A stay in a psychiatric hospital may do him some good in the sense that it cuts off his access to the drug, but any good it may do you is more than offset by the harm caused by the likely prescription of new drugs to mask the symptoms, a psychiatric label to support the denial of what's really wrong, and an excuse to continue drinking or using. It may be that six months or a year into an addict's recovery he may discover that he has some coexisting mental problem requiring the attention of a psychiatrist, but my advice is to avoid seeking a psychiatric cure for addiction.

Psychologists are almost as bad. A few psychologists have had special training in addictions, but they are so few that normally you won't find them unless they are recommended to you by an addiction counselor or by someone you meet in a Twelve-Step program. The training of a psychologist, unless he's had special training in addictive disorders, leads him to see people's emotional and behavioral problems as the product of their past emotional or behavioral experience. I've had a number of patients tell me that they had been in psychotherapy for years, and had even complained to their psychologist or therapist that they felt their drinking had something to do with their problems, only to be told "When we get your emotional problems straightened out, your drinking will either stop or become normal." You need to understand that even though your addict may have had bad experiences, had an unhappy childhood, feel depressed, have poor self-esteem, or any number of other psychological problems, *these problems are for the most part the products of, and not the causes of, his or her drinking.* It may well be that in your recovery you and your alcoholic will need to deal with some of these problems and issues with a psychologist, but now is not the time. If you have seen through reading this book that your partner is an alcoholic or addict, and you are codependent, and your therapist is not paying attention to this and recommending treatment for your addiction and codependency, get out of therapy and start seeking more appropriate help. As it is, you're just wasting time and money, and your therapist is helping you do it.

Don't seek "alternative treatments." In my years in the addictions field, I have heard many claims made by practitioners of "alternative therapies" for their success in treating addictions. I've heard chiropractors, "naturopaths," allergists, hypnotists, and nutritionists claim that they've "cured" alcoholic or addicted patients using their special forms of treatment. I've heard psychological specialists such as gestaltists, bioenergeticists, aversion therapists, and biofeedback specialists claim that their form of treatment is effective with addictions. There is probably a germ of truth in these claims. Some alcoholics and addicts have hit bottom so hard when they finally decide to accept help, and are so motivated to stop drinking or using drugs, that they would probably quit if you got a pygmy witch doctor to do a dance around a pile of chicken bones. You need to remember that there is no "cure" for addiction (and may never be), and that simply stopping drinking or using drugs may stop you from getting sicker, but it alone won't get you well.

Many alcoholics and addicts seek out these treatments because they fit right in with the tendency toward denial. Denial is such that it creates appeal for treatments that don't call upon the alcoholic to admit that he is alcoholic, don't tell him the truth about the fact that his only chance at life is complete and permanent abstinence, don't tell him that he has to participate in a Twelve-Step program if he hopes to stay sober and clean and get well. Accepting a form of treatment that is other than a proven, accepted, and respected type is like playing Russian roulette with your life. Sure, you might get incredibly lucky and get help from one of these sources, but doesn't it make better sense to find a treatment that has a high probability of success?

Don't accept treatments that offer "controlled drinking" as an objective of treatment. There is a small but vocal minority in the field of addictions treatment who claim to restore alcoholic drinkers or addictive drug users to a state of "normal, controlled social drinking." The notion is based on the mistaken idea that addiction is a behavioral disorder. If someone who represents a treatment for your addiction mentions controlled drinking, run in the opposite direction as fast as you can. Your life may be in danger.

The controlled-drinking movement, comprised mostly of psychologists and other mental-health professionals, has an ugly history that involves falsified research findings and unreported deaths of research subjects (not from the treatment itself but from relapses into alcoholism that resulted from the subjects being told that they could now drink normally). I have often wondered what the motivation could be for a few apparently well-intentioned members of my own profession to give this sort of irresponsible and potentially fatal advice to patients. In my opinion, no responsible professional person, in view of the available evidence, should ever create in the mind of an addicted patient the expectation that he or she can ever use alcohol or other drugs in safety. At best it is professional cruelty that has a high probability of extending the patient's misery. At worst it is professional murder.

Of course, the notion that a treatment can produce controlled drinking in an alcoholic patient is wonderfully attractive to the addict or alcoholic. Perhaps to some "professionals," the idea of hordes of patients stampeding to an ineffective and dangerous treatment is more appealing than saving lives. I don't know, but I do know from both professional and personal experience that controlled drinking is an idea that kills.

WHAT KIND OF TREATMENT DOES YOUR ALCOHOLIC OR ADDICT NEED?

There are a variety of effective treatments for addiction. As you will see, they all have certain things in common, and they all work, if they are appropriate to the patient's individual personality and life situation and if they are administered at the right stage in the progression of the addictive disease. Often these treatments are most effective when they are combined, either at the same time or in a carefully planned sequence.

Inpatient Treatment. Inpatient treatment, as the name implies, involves the patient entering the hospital or treatment center (each state defines what is a hospital and what is a treatment center) for a period ranging from two weeks to as much as six months in some cases. Treatment centers vary tremendously in the quality of their staff, the quality of their environment, the cost of their treatment, the size of their patient population, and the demographic characteristics of the patients they tend to treat. There are treatment centers that resemble vacation resorts and treatment centers that resemble prisons. There are treatment centers where all members of the staff hold M.D. or Ph.D. degrees, and treatment centers where none of the staff has a college degree. There are treatment centers where two or three hundred patients may be in residence at any one time, and treatment centers that have a maximum capacity of ten patients. There are treatment centers for the indigent, treatment centers for minorities, treatment centers for women only and for homosexuals only, and very, very private treatment centers for those with very public identities. There are treatment centers where the fee is nominal, and treatment centers where the fee can be as much as fifteen hundred dollars a day. But no matter the size of the program, the cost, or any other special characteristics, I have found that the truly reliable and trustworthy inpatient programs offer quite similar components.

Although your state has its own definition of what constitutes an addictions treatment hospital and what constitutes an addiction treatment center, for our purposes we can understand a hospital as a facility that, in addition to the aspects of treatment we'll discuss later on, is able to provide twenty-four-hour medical and nursing attendance and can take you through the dangerous period of *detoxification* safely. Treatment centers, while they usually have physicians on call for emergencies, generally do not provide detoxification and often require one to three days of abstinence prior to admission. In very general terms, if your addict has been drinking for more than twenty years, if he cannot manage the required period of abstinence, or if he or she has any of the symptoms of *withdrawal,* such as nausea, shakes, sweats, or convulsions anywhere from six to twenty-four hours after his last drink, or if there is some special medical condition such as a heart condition or epilepsy, your alcoholic or addict should start his treatment in a hospital.

During and after the detoxification period, which can last from two to seven days for most alcoholics, and sometimes longer for addicts to other drugs, a comprehensive assessment is made of each patient. Assessment is done mostly by testing and interviewing, usually by several specialists. The patient is seen by a physician to determine his general physical condition and to identify any special medical problems that may be related to his addiction and need to be attended to. A psychologist does testing and interviewing so that the patient's individual situation and personality characteristics can be taken into account when the staff plans the overall treatment program. The addictions counselor will see the patient individually during this period, to begin to get a feel for how best to work with him.

There is an emphasis on fairly intense education in most reliable inpatient treatment programs. After detoxification, when the patient feels better and is able to think more clearly, she is exposed to a variety of lectures and classes, sometimes two or three a day, five or six days a week, that are designed to help her understand the nature of her disease, to comprehend its profound effects on her personality and behavior, and to learn how to stay clean and sober and to go on to a stable and permanent recovery. By the time the average patient completes inpatient treatment at a reputable addictions treatment center, she knows more about chemical dependency than the average graduate of a university master's program in any of the counseling fields.

Individual counseling is a key part of the inpatient treatment program. Addiction counseling is not psychotherapy, and it is not intended to explore with the patient his or her feelings about childhood, or parents, or any other of the issues that are typically dealt with in outpatient psychotherapy. Individual addiction counseling addresses the patient's denial of his or her disease, helps the patient to overcome resistance to treatment, supports the patient as he realizes how utterly powerless he is over his disease, and how much devastation it has caused in his life and in the lives of those he loves. It is a time for clearing up misunderstandings she may have about the lectures or reading materials. It is a process in which the patient can learn about the particular aspects of his or her personality that may pose a problem for recovery, and begin to deal with them. A decent inpatient treatment program should offer at least one hour of individual counseling with a qualified addictions counselor per each week of treatment. A good program will offer more.

Another critical component of a good inpatient program is group counseling. Group counseling is different from classes or lectures in that in group counseling the patients do a lot of the talking. Patients support each other and find that they all have similar fears about staying sober after treatment, resentments and angers toward family, friends, and even the treatment staff, sorrows and remorse about what their addiction has done to their lives. Patients who have been in treatment longer help newcomers to see how their denial and resistance are keeping them from getting well. The group provides important approval for behaviors that are helping the patient to get well and disapproval for behaviors that are blocking recovery.

Not every good treatment program pays a lot of attention to the process of spiritual recovery, but all the best ones do, and any program that ignores entirely the spiritual aspects of the disease of addiction is, in my opinion, not a treatment to be chosen, even if all the other components of treatment are present in impressive array. Unless the addict can be helped to deal with the sense of spiritual barrenness and isolation from any power higher than his own, his recovery will always be unstable and at risk to the "slings and arrows of outrageous fortune" that periodically come our way. In treatment, the addict is taught to meditate (which is not so mysterious and Eastern as it sounds; it just means taking the time to be quiet and think about one's self), to keep a journal of personal thoughts and feelings, and to orient to the inner goals of serenity and well-being.

The most critical aspect of spiritual recovery in inpatient treatment is the patient's introduction to the Twelve-Step programs, which include Alcoholics Anonymous, Narcotics Anonymous, Cocaine Anonymous, Codependents Anonymous, Adult Children of Alcoholics, and perhaps even Gamblers Anonymous and Overeaters Anonymous. I consider these programs so vital that I'm going to devote a whole chapter to them later, but for now I'd advise you not to select a treatment program that treats the Twelve Steps as optional or minimizes their importance to the lifetime process of recovery. Normally, patients are participating in their first in-house Twelve-Step meetings by the second week of treatment, and by the fourth week they are being transported out of the treatment center to participate in meetings in the community.

The last essential component of the good treatment program is aftercare. Inpatient treatment is only the very beginning of recovery, and no one leaves a treatment center after four weeks or even after six months with a stable, rock-solid sobriety. The treatment center should have a program of aftercare meetings extending for at least six months after the patient has completed inpatient treatment, included in the price. There should be an aftercare coordinator, who can help the patient make appropriate arrangements for aftercare if he or she lives too far from the treatment center to attend aftercare sessions there. During the later phases of aftercare, individual psychotherapy with a psychologist or counselor who knows about and understands addiction and recovery may become appropriate.

In addition to the basic components of detoxification, assessment, education, individual and group counseling, spiritual recovery, and aftercare, the better treatment programs offer a wide variety of important, but less than absolutely critical, treatment activities. These may include nutritional education, exercise programs, art therapy, anger-management training, stress-management training, and many other therapeutic activities. It's not always true that more is better, however, and you need to be sure that the program you select for yourself or for your addict is not so full of these secondary activities that the main components of treatment just listed don't suffer.

Once you've satisfied yourself that the treatment center's

program contains all the necessary elements to predict good success, you need to take a look at the quality of the center's staff. Historically, the best qualification for treating others suffering from an addiction was to be recovering from an addiction oneself. There was a time when professionals, that is, doctors, psychologists, social workers, counselors, and the like were the enemies of alcoholics and addicts, offering them treatment that not only didn't help but often harmed. This state of affairs has not entirely changed. But there are today a number of well-qualified professionals with master's or doctoral-level training in the fields of psychology, counseling, medicine, nursing, and social work who understand addiction and who themselves may be recovering from addiction, codependency, or both.

The ideal treatment center, in my opinion, would have no counselor's aides without a bachelor's (college) degree, no counselors without a master's degree, at least one Ph.D. psychologist on staff (not on call or consulting), a Ph.D. or M.D. as director of clinical treatment, and at least one M.D. on staff (not on call or consulting). No less than 60 percent of the staff would be recovering from an addiction (and no more than 75 percent), and at least 35 percent would identify themselves as recovering from codependency (no more than 50 percent). When there are too few recovering staff, there exist the dangers of misunderstanding the nature of the disease and of failing to confront denial and rationalizations. The nonrecovering staff person is liable to enabling the addicted patient, but if there are enough recovering staff people around to consult with, this can be avoided. If there are too few nonrecovering staff people, the unhealthy personality and behavioral dynamics of alcoholics and codependents (even recovering ones!) can disrupt or negate the treatment program and generally make a mess of things. There should be a ratio of treatment staff to patients of no more than one to eight (that is, if there are forty patients, there should be at least five full-time treatment staff, not including night staff), and one to six or even one to four is better still. If, after you've conducted your search, you find that you can't get near the kind of staff that I've been describing, you are best off to pick the ones with imbalances in favor of recovering people rather than non-, and in most cases, in favor of nonprofessionals rather than, say, all doctors on the treatment staff.

The quality of the treatment center's environment is more important than is immediately apparent in shaping your attitudes about your recovery, and you should, if possible, conduct a physical inspection of the center before admitting yourself or recommending it to your addict. Most treatment centers are happy to arrange a tour for you, and to answer all your questions about treatment in person. If they're not, cross them off your list of possible treatment alternatives.

The treatment center should be a cheery and comfortable-feeling place, even if it's a hospital. It should be clear to you that someone has spent some time trying to make the place as livable, as clean, as uplifting, and as dignified as possible within the financial limits of the program's ability to do so (it makes sense that a program that costs $25,000 should be housed in a nicer and more elegant facility than one that costs $5,000). Meals should be tasty and nutritious, sparing in sugar, and not loaded down with pounds of starch (hospital food doesn't *have* to be bad; it's just kind of a tradition!), and should be taken seated family style, if possible, in a clean, light, and cheery dining room. Except in detox, meals should not be served in the rooms, since addicted patients tend to isolate and must learn to be open and comfortable with others. In the good treatment centers there is an atmosphere that you feel more than observe, that just tells you that this is a place in which to get well. Everything about the environment should remind the patient that he or she is a person of dignity and worth, and that he or she is loved.

The cost of effective inpatient treatment on a per-day basis varies enormously and can be greater or lesser depending on your length of stay. The costs I quote here are based on the assumption of a four-week, or twenty-eight-day, stay. A basic, no-frills treatment with minimal staff and environmental quality (but enough to do the job) can be had for as little as $4,000. You need to understand that at that price, staff are probably underpaid, overworked, and underqualified, but that doesn't mean that if the program fills the bill in other ways you can't get well there.

The price goes up, naturally, as the quality of the staff and environment go up. A four-week stay at a treatment center with a staff like the one I described earlier, even without the ability to provide medical detoxification, probably can't be had for under around $8,000. When you add medical detox to the range of services, you should be in the $10,000–$12,000 range. If you're being promised the moon at a suspiciously low price, something's wrong.

When you start adding in quality-of-environment considerations, the sky is almost the limit in cost. There are a few treatment programs that cost in excess of $50,000 for a four-week stay, and they're a little bit like spending a month in Acapulco. You have to be careful here. There is certainly nothing wrong about having treatment in a lovely and elegant setting, and it's nice to have some pleasant things to do in the free times, but a treatment center that is more like a vacation resort tends to provide too much in the way of amenities that constitutes a distraction from the real business of being there—getting well.

I personally prefer to refer most of my patients to treatment centers in the $300–$500 per-day fee range (since prices invariably rise over time, I should tell you that I write this in 1988). I can, at that price range, be more-or-less assured that the program is profitable enough to hire professionally trained staff in sufficient numbers to provide enough individual attention to a patient, that a patient will be treated with dignity, that the environment will be pleasant and well kept, and that all the necessary support services will be efficient and effective. There are exceptions, of course. I know of a treatment center for women founded by the late Marian Hutton Schoen, the well-known singer of the 1940s, that provides a wonderful program of treatment, and it is offered for under $5,000 for the four-week stay. The famous Betty Ford Center in Palm Springs, which provides excellent care, is so heavily endowed with funds that it is also able to provide its program for under $5,000. But in addiction treatment, as with most other things in America, the old adage that "you get what you pay for" applies—up to a point. On the other end of the scale, I would be reluctant to refer my patient to a program costing in excess of $25,000 for the four-week stay because of the tendency to cater to patients who can pay such sums. In addiction, catering often means enabling.

Most group and many private insurances provide benefits to help with the costs of addiction treatment. Many companies and labor unions maintain funds to help with the copayment (the part of the fee that you must pay), recognizing that by the time the decision to seek treatment comes, the addict and his family have often exhausted their funds. You can get help from your insurance agent, from your company's Employee Assistance Program office or personnel office, or even from the treatment center itself for determining how much health-insurance assistance you may have.

I do in many cases refer patients to treatment programs costing less than I would consider minimum for the provision of ideal treatment services, especially when there are no money and no insurance benefits, because I believe that if you are truly ready to get well, you can do it by the grace of God in any treatment environment that offers you protection from the substance to which you are addicted, and that subscribes to the principles of the Twelve-Step programs.

Outpatient Treatment. Recent years have seen the proliferation of a tremendous number of outpatient treatment programs, which, as the name implies, do not involve a stay in the hospital or treatment center. These programs have such a close relation-ship with the legal system and the nation's recent and laudably strict enforcement of drunk-driving laws that outpatient treat-ment can almost be seen as a court-created industry. If the patient is not too far advanced in his or her addiction, and his life is not in total chaos as a result, the intervention of the legal system in the form of outpatient treatment can be wonderfully effective.

Outpatient treatments vary in their duration from eighteen months to as much as three years, as opposed to the four weeks to six months for inpatient treatment. Typically, outpatient pro-grams are structured in phases, with the first phase being quite intense and involving up to four hours a day, five days a week, for the first month or two. The second phase may involve one or two group sessions a week, with periodic individual counsel-ing. The phases of treatment taper off in intensity, until in the final phase of treatment one may be attending only one group session per month and an individual counseling session every three months. Sometimes the duration of these treatment pro-grams coincides exactly with the period of suspended sentence or deferred prosecution of DWI (Driving While Intoxicated) or DUI (Driving Under the Influence) offenses.

The components of a good outpatient program are quite similar to those of a good inpatient program. Typically, outpa-tient programs do not offer detoxification services and assume that your addict has not yet reached the stage of physical depen-dence on his drug. Some outpatient programs require the use of disulfiram, or Antabuse, during the first phases of treatment, just so your alcoholic won't be tempted to use alcohol. Otherwise, good outpatient programs offer most of the same services that inpatient programs do, including addiction education, group and individual counseling, and spiritual recovery. Aftercare is in-cluded in the two-year model. The major difference between the two types of programs is that outpatient treatment unfolds much

COMPARISON SHEET FOR PROSPECTIVE TREATMENT PROGRAM

You can make a number of copies of this form. Use it to gather information on a specific treatment center or program, so that when the time comes for you or your addict to accept treatment, you'll be able to make an informed choice.

Name of treatment center: _____

Location: _____ Phone: _____
_____ Contact: _____
_____ Inpatient _____ Outpatient
Length of stay: _____ Cost: _____ Per day _____ Total
Insurance benefits: _____
Recommended by: _____ JCAH (Joint Commission on the Accreditation of Hospitals) approved? _____

Program
Is medical detoxification offered? _____
Are formal medical, psychological, and addiction assessments performed? _____
How many hours of lecture/instruction are provided? _____
How many hours of individual counseling are provided? _____
How many hours of group counseling are provided? _____
Is there an aftercare program? Is it included in the price? _____
How is spiritual recovery addressed? AA Twelve Steps included? _____
_____

Staff
How many treatment staff (do not count management or support staff)? _____
Maximum number of patients: _____
Treatment staff–patient ratio: _____
Qualifications of Director of Treatment: _____
Number of counselors with Master's Degree: _____
Total number of counselors: _____
Ph.D. Psychologist: _____ On Staff _____ On Call
M.D.: _____ On staff _____ On call
If detoxification is offered, is there twenty-four-hour nursing? _____

Environment

Circle the numbers that describe your impressions:

clean	5	4	3	2	1	dirty
homey	5	4	3	2	1	institutional
bright	5	4	3	2	1	dark
well	5	4	3	2	1	sick
upbeat	5	4	3	2	1	depressing
lovely	5	4	3	2	1	awful
caring	5	4	3	2	1	uncaring

Food

tasty	5	4	3	2	1	unappealing
nutritious	5	4	3	2	1	poor nutrition

Seating

family style	5	4	3	2	1	isolated

Patients

laugh, smile	5	4	3	2	1	deadpan, sad looking

Staff

look relaxed	5	4	3	2	1	harried, stressed

Total _____ (Maximum = 60)

Are there adequate grounds for walking or jogging? _____
Is there an exercise facility? _____
Pool? _____ Tennis court? _____ Other _____
Comments about the environment: _____
_____

Your notes and comments: _____
_____
_____
_____
_____

more slowly. There are important advantages and disadvantages to outpatient treatment, and you should consider them carefully before choosing it. Remember, your denial, whether you are the addict or the codependent, will lead you to consistently underestimate the seriousness of the illness, overestimate your ability to deal with it on your own, and underestimate the need for treatment.

INPATIENT TREATMENT . . .

- offers a protected environment;

- provides medical attention (often);

- is an intense, concentrated experience that gets you off to a solid recovery;

- offers four weeks of stability when your life is in chaos;

- eliminates the distractions and troubles of everyday life while you get well;

- will change your life in an immediate and dramatic fashion.

OUTPATIENT TREATMENT . . .

- is often more convenient to work and family life;

- provides gradual and steady change in one's life as sobriety progresses;

- is often less expensive, and fees often may be paid in stages.

You should *definitely* choose inpatient treatment if . . .

- you have any symptoms of withdrawal;

- you have been drinking for more than twenty years, or using other drugs for more than five years;

- you live alone, or have recently been divorced because of your addiction;

- you are unemployed, or have recently been terminated because of your addiction;

- you have any serious heart, lung, metabolic, or nervous-system disorders.

Private counseling or therapy for addiction. Many psychologists, psychiatrists, and other types of counselors will accept patients for private individual or group treatment for addiction. Most have no business doing so but think they do. If they are wedded to a particular theory of treatment, they will tend to see addiction in terms of that framework, ignoring the research and knowledge that exist in the field. These types of therapists do a steady business ineffectively treating alcoholics and addicts whose codependent spouses are demanding that they get some kind of treatment. The alcoholic or addict can "get treatment" on a weekly or biweekly basis while not interrupting his or her drinking schedule. This appeals greatly to those addicts who are not yet really serious about recovery. If you are the alcoholic or addict in your relationship and have read this far, we'll assume that you are very serious and don't wish to delay your recovery by seeking ineffective treatment.

There are exceptions to the rule, but they're few and far between. Don't plan on finding such a therapist out of the phone book. If a psychologist or counselor is responsible and reputable, your doctor or people in the addictions treatment field will probably know his or her name. Even if you get to such a person, he or she will probably recommend that you get either in- or outpatient treatment at a recognized addictions treatment center. Only very occasionally will a reputable and responsible psychologist judge that a particular patient may be a good candidate for private addiction treatment.

My own requirements for taking a patient for office treatment of an addictive disorder are quite stringent:

- The patient comes voluntarily and is under no pressure from his spouse, employer, or the legal system to receive treatment.

- The patient is treated by me twice weekly for three months.

- The patient is willing and able to be abstinent starting immediately.

- The patient is willing and able to do "ninety in ninety," that is, ninety Twelve-Step meetings in the first ninety days.

- The patient has a stable marriage with a partner who is not too sick with codependency.

- The patient has stable employment.

- The patient is willing to allow me to confer with his spouse or employer.

- If alcoholic, the patient is willing to take supervised Antabuse for six months.

- The patient is willing to agree with me and with his spouse that upon violating any of these conditions, he or she will immediately enter inpatient treatment.

The patient who meets all of these conditions is rare indeed; although I have worked with many, many addicts and their families, I have only accepted five or six for office treatment of their chemical dependency. Of these, all are clean and sober so far as I know. However, I don't recommend that you seek this form of treatment. The odds are too great that you'll be undertreated or treated inappropriately.

Twelve-Step program only. Alcoholics Anonymous, Narcotics Anonymous, and the other Twelve-Step programs have existed for more than fifty years, and they are the most proven, reliable, and straightforward sources of help for the alcoholic/addict. Most workers in the field, including myself, feel strongly that participation in the Twelve-Step programs is absolutely necessary for permanent and meaningful recovery from addiction. Tens of thousands of alcoholics and addicts have gotten and stayed clean and sober through participation in the Twelve-Step programs alone.

Nevertheless, Twelve-Step participation by itself is not treatment. If your addict is physically dependent on his drug, in the Twelve-Step programs he or she simply suffers through withdrawal, often with the company and support of other members, but without medical attention and support. This can be dangerous.

Twelve-Step participation also does not provide adequate information about addiction. It's easy to make mistakes that result in relapse, and if you're not given enough information about what addiction is, how it works, and what you must do to avoid relapse, you may fail. AA wisdom recognizes that often "relapse is part of recovery," but relapse can also result in discouragement that causes you to give up. And if you're an addict, giving up is fatal.

The Twelve-Step programs are not counseling either. The process of talking and sharing that is the hallmark of the programs is enlightening, supportive, and very helpful, but it does not, by design, provide the kind of confrontation and interaction that you need to deal with your denial and resistance.

The Twelve-Step programs are the most powerful tool for emotional and spiritual growth you and your alcoholic will ever find in your recovery. They are your lifeline to serenity and your path to a life of normality and happiness. They are absolutely necessary to your recovery from addiction and codependence. But I do not recommend that you rely on the programs as your only method of treatment.

Where to get information about treatment options. The array of treatment services that are now available in most major cities can be bewildering. And you are not in the best of shape to do research, unless it's research about what will happen to you if you keep drinking or using drugs, or keep living in your codependency. Here are some ways that you can shortcut the research process and find the right treatment option for you and your addict in the most direct and efficient manner.

1. Photocopy the "Alcoholism" and "Addiction" or "Drug Abuse" sections of your Yellow Pages. These can serve as your research directory. Cross out entries as you eliminate them from your choices.

2. Call your local AA headquarters. Get a recommendation for a meeting location and time for every night of the week. Keep these on standby. Even if you're not the alcoholic or addict in your relationship, attend one or two "open" meetings so you can get an idea of what they're like. AA will not recommend treatment programs; they have a policy of nonpromotion.

3. Call a local inpatient treatment center. Get the names of two or three independent psychologists or counselors who specialize in addictive disorders. Schedule an appointment with one to describe your situation and get recommendations for your treatment. If the first recommendation is to the treatment center that

referred you, ask about the nature of the relationship between this person and the center.

4. Call the other two or three psychologists, physicians, or counselors and ask for a five-minute chat. Ask which treatment programs they recommend and why. Most often you will not be charged for this brief consultation, but you should volunteer your name and address for billing.

5. If your city has a "Drug and Alcohol Helpline" or a "Crisis Clinic" telephone service, call it. Briefly describe your situation, and ask for recommendations to specific treatment programs. Inquire about whether their recommendations are limited to subscribers of the service.

6. Call or visit your company's Employee Assistance officer, who should be able to make recommendations (if he or she tells you that the company will only pay for one program, don't accept the answer) and to clarify for you the extent of your insurance coverage.

7. Call the three most-recommended treatment programs and arrange for a personal visit. Be sure there is no charge for the visit. If the staff of a facility is unwilling to show you around or discuss the treatment philosophy and program, cross it off your list. On the other hand, don't expect the treatment center to provide you with a day-long seminar. Your visit should take forty-five minutes to an hour. While you're there, the center or treatment program should be able to determine for you what insurance benefits you have, if any.

If you are the alcoholic or addict in your relationship and have made or are making the decision to seek treatment for your illness, congratulations! Please remember that even though you have pierced through your denial sufficiently to see that you have a problem and must deal with it, denial will certainly lead you to underestimate your need for treatment, and to see all kinds of reasons why you can't afford the time, the money, or the effort to receive the treatment you really need. Remember that addiction is a fatal illness, and your life depends on your receiving the correct form of treatment in the correct amount. Fortunately, it's not possible to overtreat addiction. You should have very strong reasons that don't have to do with time or money for choosing less than the strongest treatment, inpatient treatment. If you do choose a less concentrated form of treatment, be sure that the consultants you've talked with agree with you and support your decision. If they don't, you need to carefully examine your motives for your choice.

If you are the codependent in your relationship, you'll need to check yourself at every turn to make sure the research you're doing on treatment options doesn't degenerate into another codependent attempt to change your addict. The best and safest way to do this is to *keep your research to yourself* until and unless your addict requests your advice or suggestions. Don't leave treatment center brochures lying around. Don't get into futile pleading/haranguing sessions with your addict about his or her need to get treatment. Don't make ultimatums about getting treatment unless you're absolutely prepared to back up the "or else" part. This doesn't mean that doing this research is a pointless activity. When the time comes, having all this information readily available will be a great help. It will also yield the added benefit of getting you acquainted with the world of recovery, and make it easier for you to get started on your own recovery.

12

INTERVENTION: HELPING THE ADDICT WHO DOESN'T WANT HELP

Okay, let's say that things have gotten really bad in your family. Your addict seems utterly out of control. There may have been fights between you, job losses, DWIs, bankruptcy, extramarital affairs, and any number of other crises. Your addict shows no signs of hitting bottom, but either you've hit yours or you see it coming. What are you going to do?

You can leave, of course. That's been an option all along, and you may have been thinking about it for months or years now. But the fact is, whether out of your own codependency or legitimate human feeling, you care for this person. It may be that you really don't want to leave if there could just be a way for things to turn around. Or it may be that you've finally made a firm decision to leave, but you don't want to do it without being sure that you've done everything you can to restore this person you care for to health and well-being.

The common wisdom has always been that the only time an alcoholic will stop drinking or an addict will stop using drugs is when he or she hits bottom, that is to say, when the addict, blinded by his addiction and the denial that comes with it, races headlong down the course of his disease progression and runs smack into the brick wall of reality in the form of a DWI, or a spouse who leaves him, or the loss of a job, or the child whom she kills while driving under the influence. And it's true. The addict can't get well until he or she begins to deal with the reality of the situation, and the nature of addiction being what it is, the addicted mind can be relied upon to avoid facing reality unless and until there is no choice.

But that doesn't mean you have to stand idly by and twiddle your codependent thumbs while your addict finishes his power dive toward destruction. There is a strategy that treatment professionals have evolved over the years to "raise the bottom" to come up to hit your addict long before he might have found it on his own. The strategy is called *intervention*, and while professionals in the field have been using the technique for many years, the real pioneer in the development and refinement of the technique is Dr. Vernon E. Johnson, founder of the Johnson Institute in Minneapolis, Minnesota. Dr. Johnson was another early writer about the true nature of alcoholism and addiction, and his book *I'll Quit Tomorrow* (New York: Harper & Row, 1973) helped thousands of people to understand for the first time what was really happening to them and to their families. In his newer book, *Intervention* (Minneapolis: Johnson Institute, 1986), Dr. Johnson gives step-by-step instructions on how codependents can use the process of intervention to break through their addict's wall of denial.

Simply, an intervention is a gathering of spouse, children, friends, employer, and often a professional person retained specifically for the purpose of conducting the intervention, during which the addict is calmly and lovingly presented with eyewitness accounts of his or her behavior, its effects on those he cares for, and in some cases, the consequences if the behavior continues. When an intervention is successful, it renders the addict unable to maintain his denials and excuses, his anger and blaming of everyone but himself for his behavior, and leaves him no real choice but to take constructive action. If successful, the intervention may lead directly to the addict accepting treatment for his or her chemical dependency.

How does this miracle come about? Johnson describes five steps for organizing an intervention:

1. Conquering your own reluctance.

2. Gathering the intervention team.

3. Gathering the data.

4. Rehearsing the intervention.

5. Finalizing the details.

He describes these steps in an enlightening and understandable way, and I would urge you to read his second book as a part of your research on getting help for your addict. However, I want to summarize his advice and add some of my own right now.

CONQUERING YOUR OWN RELUCTANCE

Dr. Johnson lists a few of the major feelings of reluctance that people feel when they think of doing an intervention. The short form of those feelings, and Johnson's answers to them are these:

Q: *Why me?*

A: Because you're there. Because the addict is sick and needs help. Because you've gained the knowledge about addiction.

Q: *Why now?*

A: Because no one knows when an addict will die. Because the sooner you intervene with the addict before he hits absolute bottom, the better the chances for permanent recovery.

Q: *Isn't it meddling?*

A: Is it meddling to help a sick person if she's disabled by her illness?

Q: *Isn't it sneaky?*

A: Just the opposite. The point of the intervention is to bring the addict out of the closet of his denial and excuse making. To go along with that denial is sneaky and dishonest.

Q: *Isn't it manipulative?*

A: Yes. Only you can decide if the end of getting your addict to accept help justifies the means of manipulating the bottom stage of his illness.

   You have a good deal more work to do with yourself than just conquering your own reluctance, however. Remember, you're a codependent, and while part of you may be reluctant, or afraid, to confront your addict with reality, there are other parts of you that need your attention before you plunge ahead with an intervention. There's the part that loves to control, for instance. You know, the one who has such a desperate and compulsive need to take over people and situations and make them come out all right? Before you even think to take on an intervention, you need to spend some time with your Al-Anon friends, your Al-Anon sponsor, and with your God to make sure your motives are clean and your concerns are truly for your addict. If you're trying to get your addict to accept treatment because you think, deep down, that his stopping drinking or using will fix what's wrong in *your* life, or if you think that your addict's getting well depends on your actions, you'll only succeed in putting off your addict with more of your codependency.

And what about the part of you that's madder than hell, and won't take it any longer? That part would just love to see your addict "get hers" by staging some kind of emotional ganging up in which she has to admit how much she's hurt you and everyone else. That part would like everyone else to know how much you've suffered with her and how hard you've tried. If it could, that part of you would try to hold a canonization party for yourself, with illumination provided by your addict burning at the stake! You can't engage in an intervention until you've purified your heart of the rage and resentment and truly let your addict off the hook with forgiveness. If you don't, your rage will leak out and toxify the environment of the intervention, forcing your addict to react with similar rage and resistance.

Don't forget the part of you that is full of phony pride, the part that doesn't want to "air our dirty laundry in public," the part that's been conditioned to cover up, make excuses, do anything but spill the family secrets. If there's so much as a shred of that left in you, your addict will draw you into a conspiracy not to see or admit the truth, and this will drain all the power from the intervention.

GATHERING THE INTERVENTION TEAM

The process of defining and enlisting a group of people to present your addict with the reality of his behavior is a delicate one. They need to be people whom your addict cares about. They need to be people who aren't themselves afraid to tell the truth. They need to be people who aren't chemically dependent themselves, or they'll end up protecting your addict every time reality gets a little too close to home. They need to be people who aren't so consumed with codependency that they'll sabotage the intervention in the ways I just described. And they need to be people who have direct experience with your addict's behavior, not just hearsay.

You'll need to identify who these people are, contact them, explain the problem, explain what an intervention is, and ask them if they'll take part. If they agree, you'll need to set up a meeting of all the players except the addict and train them in how their feedback should be communicated.

All these tasks are not easy. They require clarity of mind and clarity of communication. There is considerable professional disagreement about whether it may be wiser to retain a professional to coordinate and conduct all the aspects of an intervention. Dr. Johnson says you don't need a professional, and I don't like to disagree with the man who practically invented intervention. But I think it deserves to be noted that to do an intervention properly is a delicate, precision task that you normally don't get the opportunity to attempt twice. Although I have a Ph.D. in psychology and have conducted numerous successful interventions, about four years ago I conducted one with a member of my own family, and it scared me half to death. Johnson says that "if you feel the need for such [professional] assistance, you should seek it." I would say that you should seek professional assistance with the intervention process unless you feel very sure you don't need it.

GATHERING THE DATA

Once you've identified the intervention team and enlisted their help, you'll need to gather them together and do some education on how and how not to present their feedback to the addict. You can use the following statements to explain the how and why of the process:

> *"You all know that we're going to get together with Joanie to help her to see more clearly how she's been behaving, and how her behavior has had an effect on those of us who love and care for her. We are not interested in punishing her, or making her feel bad, or in forcing her to admit her mistakes. We do hope to help her admit that she has a problem, and to see that we support her in deciding to do something about it.*
>
> *"It would be very helpful if each of you would recall and write down one or two experiences you've had with Joanie when she's been drinking. Please be as factual as possible. Give the date if you know it, and describe the place, the time, and the situation. Describe her behavior, including the things she said, as accurately as you can. Please avoid giving your opinions or conclusions. Please also describe how you felt, that is, whether you were hurt, or angry, or ashamed of her, or lost your trust in her. Conclude your statement with how you feel about Joanie, and explain that you're here because you care about her.*

> *"If you feel you can or must give Joanie an ultima-*
> *tum about what will happen if her drinking continues,*
> *please be sure you mean it, and give it with love. I plan*
> *to tell her that if she will not accept help with her drink-*
> *ing problem, I'm going to leave her. I also plan to tell her*
> *that I love her very much, and that I hope it won't come*
> *to that.*
>
> *"Please try to be brief in your feedback. It would be*
> *best if you can keep each item to two or three minutes*
> *or less. Remember that there are _____ of us here, and*
> *if we each gave Joanie only two items of feedback at four*
> *minutes each it would take _____."*

Once everyone understands what the process is, what it's supposed to accomplish, and what you're asking them to do, they can begin to write down on index cards the anecdotes they want to share with your addict about his or her behavior. These anecdotes should be given with love and without humor. (Obviously, we're not interested in telling the addict that he was funny or cute or entertaining.) They should be specific, and they should be brief. They should not contain moral judgments, psychological analyses (I think you drink so much because you feel insecure), nor should they indicate your opinions about whether the person is or is not an addict or alcoholic. They should explain how the incident made them feel, and each statement should close with an expression of caring and support.

The second step of the data-gathering process that Dr. Johnson recommends is that you identify the one or two best options for treatment available to you. We've discussed how to do that in the previous chapter. Many interventions end with the addict getting in the car and heading straight for the treatment center. If you're not prepared with the information you will need, the resulting delay may give the addict time to reform his defenses and rethink his agreement to accept help. By the time of the intervention, you should have a definite arrangement with a treatment specialist or with the intake team at the treatment center you have identified. The appointment should be set for approximately two hours after the intervention is scheduled to begin.

SAMPLES OF ANECDOTAL FEEDBACK IN AN INTERVENTION

"Daddy, last week when you came home, I was real excited to show you the model ship I built. It took me two weeks to build it. You said you would help me, but you never did. When you came home, you had been drinking. I know, 'cause I smelled it. I showed you my model and you said you'd look at it later and you never did. I was so proud of it. I felt real bad. I worked on it *two weeks,* Daddy! Mommy says there's places you can get help to stop drinking. Please, Daddy, I love you, and I want us to be happy."

·   ·   ·

"Fern, when you got drunk and hit me last week with the frying pan, it was the last straw for me. I was hurt and angry then, but I respected and accepted your apology the next day. But that doesn't change the fact that it happened. I'm afraid that I've decided that if you won't accept help for your drinking, I have to leave. I love you so much, but I can't and I won't live like this anymore. I love you more than anything else in my life except myself. I don't want to leave you, and I won't if you'll accept help."

·   ·   ·

If you wish, provide your team with the guidelines and sample statements from the following chart:

SAMPLES OF ANECDOTAL FEEDBACK IN AN INTERVENTION	
Be specific; describe the behavior.	Ralph, last week at the office Christmas party you were drinking and you told the dirtiest joke I've ever heard to our firm's biggest client, with his wife standing right next to him. You were none too quiet about it either, and several of the women left the party right away. The next day the guy called, and I had a hell of a time keeping his account. He finally agreed, but only after I guaranteed him that you would not have anything to do with his account.
Describe your feelings.	I felt embarrassed and ashamed for you, and hurt that my partner would jeopardize my business in that way. And I was madder than hell!
Request that he accept help.	I think there's a problem here, and I want you to get some help. It's clear to me that the problem is your drinking.
If ultimatum, be specific, and mean it!	This is not the first time this sort of thing has happened, Ralph. I have to protect myself and my business. I'm sorry, but if you won't accept help, I'll have to dissolve our partnership and cut you loose.
Express caring and support.	I certainly don't want to do that, but I will. Ralph, you've been my partner and my friend for fifteen years. I care about you, and I value your ability. Hell, when you're sober you're a better architect than I am, by far. I want our relationship to continue, and I care about you. But for us to stay partners, you're going to have to get help.

REHEARSING THE INTERVENTION

When your team has finished writing down their anecdotes and reading each one aloud to the group, and when the group has finished editing them to be sure they are specific, brief, nonjudgmental, feeling, and express caring and support, you can begin rehearsing for the intervention. Don't skip this step! It's easy to feel silly playacting, particularly when the subject is so serious, but this step is very important. Most people are not used to speaking in front of a group, and the intervention itself is likely to be very scary. It's a great help to have rehearsed beforehand. You should have someone who knows the addict well play him or her during the rehearsal, so that the whole group can have the feeling of really addressing someone.

FINALIZING THE DETAILS

The fifth and final step in Dr. Johnson's model for planning and conducting an intervention is agreeing on the details of date, time, and place for the intervention to take place, and on the specific roles the team will assume.

There is no prettier way to say it than that you need to plan an ambush. The nature of addictive defensiveness and denial is such that you just can't invite the alcoholic or addict to a conference where his friends and associates want to discuss his drinking or drug use with him. He will either not show up, or he will show up with all his defenses, excuses, rationalizations, and denials well rehearsed and in place. Your intervention team members need to be made to understand this. Many interventions have been blown because a team member decided on his or her own to spare the addict the embarrassment of being caught by surprise.

You need to agree on a place where the intervention will be held. It should be large enough to seat all of you, small enough to be intimate, comfortable enough, and private enough to avoid distraction or the unwanted entry of people not involved. The date should be one that you can be quite certain of (there are a number of people adjusting their schedules), and the time of day should be one when you can be fairly certain that your addict will not have been drinking or using drugs (the probability of success for the intervention plummets when the alcoholic has been drinking).

You need to designate someone who will be responsible for getting the addict to the appointed place and time, on a pretext if necessary. It's better still if the place and time fall within the addict's natural pattern of activity (if you can be pretty sure he'll be home and sober at 10:00 A.M. on Saturday, set the time and place that way).

If you're not using a professional to conduct the intervention, you also need to designate who will chair or moderate the intervention. The chairperson's role is to open the meeting by addressing the addict, telling him or her what the purpose of the meeting is, and setting the ground rules. The chairperson also enforces those rules during the intervention, stops the addict from arguing or defending himself, and, if necessary, cuts off members of the team if they're becoming judgmental, argumentative, lengthy, or otherwise unhelpful. The chairperson should be the one who carries the most authority with the addict, and should not be the spouse of the addict (the spouse can be intimidated and manipulated, and may be too sick with codependency to be effective in the role).

The chairperson's job is probably the hardest in the intervention. He or she introduces the meeting to the addict, who is already restless, defensive, anxious, and clearly knows something is up. The chairperson starts the intervention something like this:

> *"Doris, we all came together today because we love you and care about your well-being. We think there are some things you don't know about how we're feeling about you, and we want to share them with you. It's not going to be easy, and we're all a little nervous. We want you to know that we're not here to accuse you, or punish you, or be angry with you. Everything that's said here today is said because we love you.*
>
> *"We'd appreciate it if you would just hear what we have to say. We don't want to argue or debate or discuss it with you; we want to tell you. Please just listen to what each of us has to say."*

Periodically, the addict will start to get angry or want to defend him- or herself by giving rationalizations and excuses for the incidents that are shared. The chairperson's job at these times is to interrupt the addict by saying . . .

> *"Doris, we're not attacking you, and we don't want you to defend yourself. Now is the time for you to listen to what we have to say. You can make your own decisions about what we've said after you've heard us out."*

Even though you've rehearsed, some of the team members may get lengthy, angry, or judgmental. If this happens it's the chairperson's job to interrupt and say,

> *"Charlie, I know you have a lot of feelings about this, and we all know how tough it's been for you to say these things, but I think Doris gets your point."*

It's also the chairperson's job to present the plan of action in a clear and forceful way after the sharing is done. He or she needs to accomplish this simply, directly, and in a way that makes it difficult for the addict to say no. The assumption should be that any sane person, after having heard the things that have been said, would accept the recommendation without question, and since the addict is sane (though his or her behavior may have been crazy), he will certainly do so. The chairperson should close the intervention by saying . . .

> *"Dominick, we've made an appointment for you with Dr. MacKenzie, a well-known specialist who helps people with drinking problems, at the Wildwood Treatment Center in an hour. Why don't I wait while you get dressed, and I'll drive you there."*

The chairperson should not go into detail about what's to happen at the appointment or what will happen next. Best to leave that to the professionals.

FINDING A PROFESSIONAL INTERVENTIONIST

When they are planned and managed properly, interventions are a powerful and remarkably effective way to force the issue of treatment for the alcoholic or addict. When they're not properly planned or executed, interventions can turn into an ugly mess. If you have any doubt at all about your ability to manage the intervention, use a professional.

The are several good ways to go about finding a professional interventionist. You can call the following:

- your local office of the National (or State) Council on Alcoholism;
- your local drug and/or alcohol helpline;
- a local treatment center (be aware that they may recommend their own interventionist, which would result in a probable recommendation that your addict be treated there);
- your company's Employee Assistance Program officer.

You should be sure that the interventionist has had experience (it's still a fairly new field), that he or she has appropriate general counseling credentials, and that he or she is free of affiliation with any specific treatment center or program.

There are now thousands of recovering people who have the process of intervention, initiated by caring friends or a loving spouse, to thank for literally saving their lives. Good luck!

13

TREATMENT
FOR
CODEPENDENCY

I f you've learned one thing from reading this book, let it be that you, the codependent, have gotten very, very sick from the disease of addiction. You need help to get well, just as your addict does. You need help to get over the chronic depression that has dominated your emotional life. You need help to deal with the grief you have experienced over the numerous losses and traumas associated with your partner's disease. You need help to learn to mind your own business, to stop trying to control other people's lives, and to learn to take care of yourself. You need help to learn to be responsible for yourself and to yourself, and to stop taking responsibility for the problems and feelings of everyone else in your life.

Fortunately for you, there is now effective help available. As recently as five years ago, the understanding of codependency was very primitive, even among the professional community. The average treatment professional could not have defined the primary issues of the codependent, nor could he have been very specific about how to treat the codependent. Many would have been surprised at the idea that most codependents even needed some form of treatment. It was generally understood that the spouse of an alcoholic in treatment needed to be seen during the treatment. The spouse needed to be checked out with regard to his or her drinking, to be sure that the newly recovering addict would not be leaving the treatment center to return to an alcohol or drug environment in the home. It was also recognized, but not generally well understood, that the spouse of the alcoholic or addict was a rather unhappy person, but it was assumed that he or she would return to normal as the alcoholic recovered. "Things get better as you get better" was the general wisdom of AA (and it's true), and the codependent was assumed to be one of those "things" that would naturally get better with time.

Professionals observed that it was quite a common phenomenon to see the alcoholic or addicted couple get a divorce after six months or a year of the alcoholic's recovery. We didn't always know why. When it was the recovering alcoholic who initiated the divorce, we assumed that since he was now sober and clear-headed, he realized what a pain in the assorted anatomical parts his spouse was, and that the decision to divorce was a step in his recovery. When it was the spouse who sought the divorce, we shrugged our shoulders and said, "Some alcoholics drink and then act like jerks; others are jerks, whether they drink or not,"—the idea being that the disappointed spouse had stuck with the alcoholic all through his drinking career, hoping that when he got sober he would become a wonderful person, and instead, when he got sober, he was still an awful person.

The fundamental truth that until recently few people recognized is that codependents are psychologically sick, and that recovering alcoholics or addicts, as they become healthier and happier, become less tolerant of living with a person who is emotionally and behaviorally sick. Codependents, as their addicts become healthier and happier, are less able to exercise their controlling behavior and can't be comfortable anymore in their cocoon of martyred self-righteousness, and if they won't get involved in their own recovery, they often divorce so that they can go find someone else to be codependent with.

Many codependents feel that it's unfair, after suffering for all those years with their addicts' abuses and excesses, that they are now confronted with the need for them to work at recovery, too. "After all I've been through, I just want to rest," they say. They're angry, and they feel that since they bore all the family's burdens throughout the course of the addiction, the recovering alcoholic now ought to pick up the burden, behave normally, be more responsible, and take care of them for a change.

Well, fair or not, if you want to have any hope for personal happiness and for your relationship staying together once your addict begins to recover, you're going to have to recognize that your recovery is your responsibility. If you don't, *you'll* become the sick and dysfunctional member of your relationship as your addict recovers, and if he has any sense at all, he'll leave you eventually. And if he does, you won't find happiness with someone else, because your codependency will cause you to behave in the same sick and dysfunctional ways with the new person.

Treatments for codependency are similar in structure to treatments for addiction, in that the primary components are *education, group and individual counseling, and Twelve-Step program participation.* Effective treatment is becoming more available every day, with outpatient treatment centers opening in most major cities, psychologists and counselors (some of them, that is) becoming more aware of and more experienced at treating codependents, and the new Al-Anon, Adult Children of Alcoholics, and Codependents Anonymous Twelve-Step groups forming every day. There are even a few inpatient treatments for those codependents who are so weary and sick at heart that they are having difficulty functioning at all in their day-to-day lives.

EDUCATION

Education for codependents consists of classes, lectures, and readings that will help you to understand what codependency is, where it comes from, and what you need to do to get well. In most major cities, there are groups of addictions counselors, psychotherapists, and psychologists who have formed treatment programs for codependents. You can often find them listed in the Alcoholism section of your Yellow Pages under names like "The Center for Codependents" or "The Center for Adult Children of Alcoholics" (even if you are not the child of an alcoholic or addict, programs oriented to them will be of great help to you if you see that you are codependent). Your local treatment centers for addiction will normally be able to recommend to you other sources of treatment for codependency.

These treatment groups usually offer lectures and classes on codependency, where you can learn in a person-to-person setting how to stop trying to control others and start taking care of yourself.

Reading is also an important step in getting well. Codependency can be hard to understand at first (we have our own denial to deal with), and it helps to read the concept explored in a number of different ways. You have probably read the chapters on codependency in this book, so let me recommend a few other books to get you started. You'll find complete bibliographic listings of these and other books in Appendix C of this book. You would do well to read Melody Beattie's *Codependent No More* (New York: Harper & Row, 1987), Claudia Black's *It Will Never Happen to Me* (Denver, M.A.C., 1981), Janet Woititz's *Adult*

Children of Alcoholics (Pompano Beach, Fla.: Health Communications, 1983), and Robin Norwood's *Women Who Love Too Much* (New York: Pocket Books, 1985).

GROUP AND INDIVIDUAL COUNSELING

Group and individual counseling are key parts of codependent recovery. If you think you're codependent, you can be almost certain that you will need counseling to build a meaningful recovery. Whether it's conducted in a group or individual setting, counseling for codependents must deal with a number of issues that almost all codependents have in common:

Dealing with grief and loss in childhood. Codependents, almost by definition, grew up in families that, one way or another, were dysfunctional. It may have been that there was alcoholism or addiction in the family. It may have been that one or both parents suffered from a serious mental or emotional disorder. Maybe the parent was ill with a long-term, chronic disease.

In any case, the family didn't work right, and being a child in that family *hurt.* Many codependents have blanked out the memories of childhood as a way of stopping the pain. They may tell themselves that their childhood was quite normal and happy, and they may even believe it. In my early years as a psychologist, I accepted at face value these kinds of statements from codependents, but I could never for the life of me figure out why they seemed so hurt and sad.

Dealing with the grief, trauma, and loss of childhood is a major task of psychotherapy for the codependent. There are memories to be uncovered, tears to be shed, and unpleasant truths to come to terms with. It's not fun, but it's a necessary part of recovery.

Dealing with physical and sexual abuse in childhood. Not all codependents, but remarkably many, were either physically or sexually abused as children. They may consciously remember it, or they may have repressed the memories because they are too painful. Nevertheless, the picture of themselves and the behaviors they adopted as a result of being abused children continue to infect and influence their behavior as adults.

Abuse survivors suffer from terribly low self-esteem. They blame themselves for the abuse they suffered. They are fearful and tentative about taking on new things and doubtful about their ability to function successfully. They are frightened by anger, both their own and that of other people. If the abuse was sexual, they feel dirty and ashamed, and often have difficulty relating to their partners sexually. They are filled with repressed feelings of pain and terror with which they cannot deal without help.

Uncovering the memories of abuse, reexperiencing the feelings in the safety of the psychotherapy relationship, and putting the experience into proper perspective of adulthood are critical to the process of getting well.

Learning boundaries and appropriate interpersonal behavior. Codependents are always getting mixed up about boundaries, that is, they have a great deal of trouble seeing where they end and another person begins. They spend inordinate amounts of time taking care of others, trying to control the behavior of others, worrying about others, assuming the responsibilities of others, and taking on the feelings of others. It's this collection of tendencies that leads so many codependents into the counseling fields. It's also these behaviors that lead codependents to behave in bizarre and inappropriate ways toward other people.

Codependents literally don't know how to behave around others. Their ways of dealing with interpersonal situations usually don't make sense. An important function of the counselor or psychotherapist is to act as a kind of Dutch uncle (or aunt), who often must patiently teach the codependent basic interpersonal and relationship skills. At other times the therapist has to function as a limit setter, reminding the codependent with firm kindness that "that's none of your business."

Learning self-care. Codependents don't take care of themselves. They run themselves into the ground taking on other people's responsibilities and generally overcommitting themselves. They are chronically tired and often seriously damage their health. They don't spend time or money on themselves, and they won't plan or do things just for fun.

Usually they are quite attached to the role of someone who is so busy and put upon that they don't have the time or energy to take care of themselves. They see themselves as beleaguered heros and heroines. This self-concept is often reinforced by relatives and friends ("That woman is a saint!"), and the codependent is secretly enjoying the admiration and sympathy of others.

It often takes a firm and directive approach to therapy with the codependent to separate him from his role of the suffering servant, and to persuade him that it is his responsibility to take care of his physical and emotional health. I have often had to *require* codependent patients to take themselves out to lunch, or go skiing, or to perform some other self-caring and pleasurable activity.

Correcting the secondary psychological problems of codependency. As a result of the codependency syndrome, many codependents develop psychological and behavioral symptoms that themselves become major psychological problems. Anxiety, depression, compulsive disorders, such as overeating, anorexia, bulimia, gambling, sexual compulsions, and overspending, and other serious psychological and behavioral problems are commonly seen in codependent patients. Although these problems may have developed as a result of the codependency, in many cases they won't disappear or correct themselves just by treating the codependency.

A good counselor or psychologist will address these problems directly and clearly in the context of the larger issues of codependency. While the counselor may recognize that the issues of childhood must be dealt with in the course of therapy, these secondary psychological and behavioral problems of codependency must be met with appropriate treatment interventions without delay.

Finding a good counselor to help you with individual therapy for your recovery from codependency can be just as tricky as finding one to help with recovery from addiction. Often local treatment centers maintain listings of private psychologists and counselors who understand addiction and codependency. Some Yellow Pages listings may indicate a specialty in working with codependents. Codependency education centers usually are able to refer you to qualified, ethical counselors. Your Twelve-Step sponsor may know of a good therapist. The therapist you select should be qualified (at least a master's degree in social work, psychology, or counseling), ethical (you can and should inquire of the state or local licensing board whether there have been complaints lodged against him or her), and professional (many counselors are themselves raving codependents whose quality of recovery is questionable; for codependents in particular, you should be very careful about counselors who see patients in their home, who volunteer their home phone number and tell you that you can call anytime, or who are willing to interact with you in any other way than as your therapist).

Counseling or psychotherapy for codependency is not a quick-fix process. In this day and age of health-maintenance organizations (HMOs) and Preferred Provider Organization (PPO) management of insurance benefits, many people have experienced drastic reductions in the amount of psychological treatment that their insurance will cover. Even if your insurance will only pay for ten or twenty counseling visits, you need to plan to be in counseling for a minimum of a year and for possibly as long as three years.

TWELVE-STEP PROGRAMS

There are several *Twelve-Step programs* available to codependents, and depending on your situation, they can all be immensely helpful. *Al-Anon* is the oldest of them and probably the most widely available. The focus in Al-Anon is on the codependent who is living with an alcoholic or addict, whether he or she is in recovery or not. Just as is the case with AA, there are Al-Anon meetings in almost every city and town in the country, with meetings on every day of the week. *Adult Children of Alcoholics* focuses, as the name implies, on the issues faced by children who grew up in alcoholic (or otherwise dysfunctional) families. ACOA is an organization that is only five or six years old, but the response to it has been enormous, and there are now meetings available in most cities. *Codependents Anonymous* is a brand-new organization that is the logical outgrowth of Al-Anon and ACOA, and it is for those codependents who are not necessarily married to alcoholics or addicts, or who did not necessarily grow up in chemically dependent homes, but who nevertheless have come to realize that they suffer from the syndrome of codependency.

We'll talk more about the Twelve-Step programs in the next chapter, but for now I cannot say too strongly that participation in them is *absolutely necessary* for most codependents who are serious about recovering. You need the structure of the Twelve

Steps, which have proven themselves over decades and thousands of lives to be a reliable road map to recovery. You need the support and experience of your brothers and sisters in codependence. You need the special relationship with a sponsor (a sort of older brother or sister in the program) for those times when you feel low, or feel you're becoming codependent in a particular situation, or when you just need some friendly advice. And you need a way to remind yourself that you are codependent, and that every day you need to focus upon and pursue your own recovery. While most codependents need more help than the programs can provide alone, no amount of education about codependency or private therapy for codependency can replace or substitute for your participation in one of the Twelve-Step programs.

Whether your alcoholic has stopped drinking or not, you need to do something about the business of your own recovery, *and you need to start now.* If you think you might as well wait until your addict stops, you're making the mistake of thinking that he or she is what's wrong with your life. Thousands of codependents have begun to work their own program of recovery and have found that their growing health has had such an impact on their addicts that they have entered treatment themselves. If it's true that codependents get sick by being with addicts, it's equally true that addicts sometimes get well by being motivated to treatment by the growing health of their codependents. This book has discussed many ways for you to help your addict to get well, including learning about the disease, researching treatment options, and conducting interventions. But the most powerful thing by far that you can do for your alcoholic and your family is to work on your own recovery by getting appropriate counseling and involving yourself in a Twelve-Step program.

If you are the alcoholic or addict in your relationship and you're now recovering, you may be concerned that your codependent is not pursuing his recovery actively enough, or at all.

You might show him this chapter and invite him to talk about it with you. If your codependent is really out of control with his controlling and manipulating, you might tell him that you feel that your marriage is suffering for reasons you don't really understand (don't accuse him or label him codependent if he hasn't seen the problem for what it is) and suggest an appointment for marriage counseling with a therapist who understands codependence and recovery.

However deep you may have sunk in your codependency, however sick and out of control your thoughts, feelings, and behavior may be, however awful your relationship may have become because of addiction, there is help and hope out there for you. Reach out and take it.

14

THE
TWELVE STEPS:
THE HEART
OF RECOVERY

More than fifty years ago, a sick and frightened alcoholic named Bill Wilson gave up. After years of struggling with his craving and dozens of attempts to control his drinking, or stop drinking altogether, he finally acknowledged that he was utterly powerless to do anything about his enslavement to alcohol. Once a successful and brilliant stockbroker, his life had long since become a complete shambles because of his drinking. He supposed that he was insane, or a moral degenerate, for no one who was sane, he thought, would abuse himself and those he cared for the way he had done with his compulsion to drink. Finally, he admitted that he had no power over his drinking and surrendered himself to his fate. He assumed that his death would follow soon.

Fortunately for Bill Wilson and for the rest of the world, an old drinking buddy visited him in his hour of dark despair. The friend was healthy and well, not at all as Bill remembered him. The friend explained to Bill that certain ideas, partly religious, partly philosophical, and mostly very practical, had changed his life. Turning himself and his life over to God had somehow relieved him of the compulsion to drink, which had destroyed his life as completely as it had Bill's.

Bill was powerfully attracted to his friend's new-found freedom from drink, but somewhat put off by the religious aspect of his new philosophy. Like many people, his early life experiences with religion had not been positive, and like many thinking people, he attributed many of mankind's ills to organized religion.

His friend urged Bill to think of a Higher Power in any way that suited him. The point was that whoever it was who ran the show in the universe, it wasn't Bill. And whoever or whatever could save Bill from the compulsion to destroy himself and his life with alcohol, it wasn't Bill.

After numerous discussions with his friend, Bill decided to try basing his life on the principles and philosophy his friend had shared with him. And it worked! His doctor, his friends, and his family watched with wonder as this helpless and hopeless alcoholic went, from one day to another, for the rest of his life, until he died in 1971, without taking another drink. Bill steadfastly maintained throughout his life that he had not accomplished this by willpower. Much the opposite, since every effort of his will had resulted in complete and total failure to prevent him from drinking. Bill attributed his sobriety to the mercy and goodness of a Power far greater than his own and credited himself only with the willingness to allow that Power to do with him what it would.

Very early in his new sobriety, Bill was sorely tested, and there were times when he almost drank again. He found that the only thing that helped him at these times was for him to share his own story of alcoholism and recovery with others who were suffering with the same problems. In June 1935, Bill had traveled to Akron, Ohio, to put together a major business deal, which fell through. Frustrated and disappointed, his thoughts again turned to drinking. He resorted to the only way he knew to keep himself sober, which was to visit another alcoholic in trouble and to share with him the story of his own alcoholism and sobriety.

The alcoholic he found was an Akron physician, who is known affectionately today as Dr. Bob. Bob had been briefly exposed to some of the same ideas that Bill had adopted some six months before, but he had not as yet put them into practice and was still lost in the hopelessness and despair of his alcoholism. The two talked extensively, and Dr. Bob agreed to adopt the program of spiritual recovery that Bill Wilson shared, and he never had another drink in his life.

It was the recognition on Bill Wilson's and Dr. Bob's part that they could remain sober only by sharing their recovery with other alcoholics that gave birth to the phenomenon of Alcoholics Anonymous, as it came to be called. By the end of 1941, an estimated eight thousand alcoholics were meeting together regularly to discuss their affliction, to support each other in sobriety, and most important, to encourage each other in the process of spiritual and emotional recovery using the principles of the Twelve Steps. By 1980, more than a million alcoholics were meeting in thirty-three thousand regularly scheduled groups to "work their program" for recovery. There are a great many more who meet to use the Twelve Steps to deal with other problems of addiction and compulsion. Al-Anon, founded by Lois Wilson not long after AA was established, is the group for spouses of alcoholics. Narcotics Anonymous addresses the particular problems of addicts to drugs other than alcohol. Adult Children of Alcoholics and Codependents Anonymous are groups who specifically use the Twelve-Step programs to deal with their codependency. Gamblers Anonymous, Overeaters Anonymous, and a number of other groups have sprung up around specific problems that members share. The Twelve-Step programs have quite literally changed the history of the United States and have dramatically changed the personal histories of thousands by saving their lives.

WHAT IS THE TWELVE-STEP PROGRAM?

In 1939 the first edition of the basic text for AA, entitled *Alcoholics Anonymous* and known as "The Big Book," was published. It articulated the Twelve Steps, which are the foundation of the AA program of recovery. They represent the philosophy that Bill Wilson and Dr. Bob began to define for themselves in 1935, articulated and informed by the stories and thoughts of the more than a thousand recovering alcoholics and addicts who had joined them by 1938. Each of the Twelve-Step programs has its own, slightly modified version of the Twelve Steps. The meaning of each of the steps is defined by each person who puts them into practice in his or her life. I offer my comments on the steps more as an account of what recovery means to me than as advice about what it should mean to you.

The Twelve Steps

1. We admitted we were powerless over alcohol—that our lives had become unmanageable.

2. Came to believe that a Power greater than ourselves could restore us to sanity.

3. Made a decision to turn our will and our lives over to the care of God *as we understood Him.*

4. Made a searching and fearless moral inventory of ourselves.

5. Admitted to God, to ourselves, and to another human being the exact nature of our wrongs.

6. Were entirely ready to have God remove all these defects of character.

7. Humbly asked Him to remove our shortcomings.

8. Made a list of all persons we had harmed, and became willing to make amends to them all.

9. Made direct amends to such people wherever possible, except when to do so would injure them or others.

10. Continued to take personal inventory and when we were wrong promptly admitted it.

11. Sought through prayer and meditation to improve our conscious contact with God *as we understood Him,* praying only for knowledge of His will for us and the power to carry that out.

12. Having had a spiritual awakening as the result of these steps, we tried to carry this message to alcoholics, and to practice these principles in all our affairs.*

Step One. It is one of life's great paradoxes that recovery begins with an admission of powerlessness. It is our assertion of power, that is, our insistence that we can "quit anytime" our drinking, drugging, codependent behavior, gambling, or overeating that gives us our own permission to keep doing it. It is our insistence that there is no problem that perpetuates the problem. Perhaps a good way to understand this paradox is to realize that if Wilbur and Orville Wright insisted that they could fly by flapping their arms, they would never have gotten at all serious about inventing airplanes.

*Source: Alcoholics Anonymous World Services, Inc.; New York. Reprinted by permission.

It is only when we come to a realistic assessment of our situation and admit that the fact is that our problem is bigger than we are that we put ourselves in a position to accept the help from another source that will save our lives. The alcoholic or codependent who has not yet gotten to Step One is like the shipwreck victim who, treading water five hundred miles from the nearest land, steadfastly maintains that he is in the water for a refreshing dip, and who declines offers of rescue from passing ships.

The beginning of recovery is giving up and admitting your powerlessness. They say that we don't give up until we hit bottom, but each individual addict, codependent, or compulsive defines where the bottom is for him or for her. You have the choice to admit now that you're licked, or you can persist in your addiction or compulsion until the law, your spouse, your doctor, or death itself forces the issue.

Step Two. When I am finally broken under the burden of my addiction or codependency, I can now see that only a power greater than my own can help me. It doesn't mean that I know that there is such a power, or what it might be, or how it might help me. It simply means that since I realized that all of my power is futile, it follows that only a power greater than mine offers any hope for rescue.

Many people, like Bill Wilson, have a great deal of trouble with Step Two and with the other steps that mention God, even when the qualifying phrase *as we understood Him* is thrown in. So did I. It's okay. Fortunately for the rest of the world, God (or Fate or Destiny or Reality or the Universe, or whoever or whatever keeps the machinery of time and history running) doesn't depend on you or me to believe in Him (It) in order to exist.

All that is required by Step Two is our suspension of disbelief. Many more alcoholics or codependents than you or I have come to Step Two saying, "If there's anyone out there, if anyone can hear me, will you please help?"

Step Three. Having taken Steps One and Two, no sane person (and you are sane, no matter how crazy your addiction or your codependency have made you seem) could turn down the opportunity to conduct a simple experiment that could save his life. Both Bill Wilson and Dr. Bob made a decision to turn their will and their lives over to the care of God as they understood Him, not because they knew that God existed, or had undergone a conversion experience, or had any idea of what that decision would mean in their lives, but in the sincere hope that if they did so, that care would save their lives.

Notice that Step Three calls for a decision to turn our will and our life over to the *care* of God as we understood him, and not the *will* of God. The idea of the will of God is assumed, of course, but if you meet anybody who tells you they know what the will of God is, run as fast as you can in the opposite direction. In fact, if *you* ever start thinking that you know what the will of God is, you probably need to sit down and have another think! Nobody in the Twelve-Step programs tells you what to do or how to run your life. That's between you and your Higher Power.

Imagine that you have been entrusted with the helmsman's duties on a ship. The complexities of navigation are beyond you, really, but there you are, charged with the responsibility of piloting this craft through the dangers of the sea. The storm begins to come up, and it's gotten beyond your control. Other crew members have offered to help, but up until now, you've put a brave smile on your face and insisted that you can handle it, that everything's under control. But now the wind has reached a fever pitch, and the waves are washing over your bows. You know you've lost control for sure, and that the next wave may capsize you entirely. Just as you've reached the end of your resources, and have lost the strength to even hold the wheel any longer, a kind and merciful captain comes to you and says, "It's all right now. I'll take over. I can see that you're suffering, afraid, and tired. Go below now and rest, and get warm. I know the ship, and I know the sea, and if you'll just turn the wheel over to me, I'll get you to harbor safely." That's Step Three.

Step Four. If we are to get well, we need to come to terms with who we are. We need to stop denying and start calling a spade a spade. We need to stop blaming others and acknowledge our responsibility for how we behave, what we think, how we feel, the attitudes we hold, and the effects we exert on others. We need to stop blaming the pressures of life, the wife, the kids, money worries, the boss, or the tragedies on the five o'clock news for our drinking and drugging. We need to stop blaming our alcoholic or addict for our crazy behavior, our spiritual and emotional exhaustion, and the chaos in our lives. We need to get honest.

We also need to stop blaming ourselves and indulging our selfish habits of self-deprecation. We need to learn to appreciate ourselves for the dignified and worthwhile beings we are, no matter what our behavior has been.

And, finally, we need to understand the person we are charged to care for and nurture for the rest of our lives. We need to learn about our needs, to learn to take care of ourselves. No one can be a good parent if they don't know or understand their child, and if we are to grow up, to become healthy and mature individuals, we need to know and understand ourselves.

To get to this self-knowledge, we engage in a "fearless and searching" inventory of who we are, the strong parts and the weak, the lovely and the unlovely, the praiseworthy and the despicable. It's a hard process, and you almost can't do it alone. Many recovering people carry out this activity with their sponsors (a sort of counselor/big brother or sister in the program). Many others do it with an addictions counselor or a psychotherapist who understands the program and recovery.

Step Five. The impact of the fifth step is to morally disarm ourselves. Having seen ourselves for who we are in Step Four, in Step Five we show all our cards to our Higher Power (who knew about them anyway) and to at least one other human being (who probably knew about them anyway!). The implication of this sort of "confession" is to say we're sorry for what we may have done imperfectly, we feel bad about the way we may have caused others pain, and that we don't want to be that way anymore. Psychologically, it separates us from our destructive and dysfunctional ways and helps us to define a new way of being as necessary and desirable.

The language of the 1930s characterizes our "wrongs" as if we were malicious evildoers. This kind of moral language is hard for some people to identify with, particularly codependents, who are often inclined to see themselves as martyred victims. It helps to think of "wrongs" as ways of behaving that are not right, that is, that are not proper or appropriate to functional living. Whether we are addicted or codependent or otherwise compulsive, we will inevitably find that we have lied, cheated, manipulated, stolen time or energy if not money from others, even if we have done so with what we believed were the best of motives. We have held resentments and false pride. We have been irrational and out of control. Step Five does not ask of us that we condemn ourselves, nor should we. But we need to admit the stupidity, the dysfunctionality, and the fundamental *wrongness* of our behavior if we are to get well.

Step Six. As we perform Step Five, the natural progress of psychological evolution brings us to a point where we don't want our sickness of thought or dysfunctionality of behavior anymore. It seems strange to think that we ever did want it, but to our sick minds, our dysfunctionality seemed to have a function. We wanted the ability to deceive others because it allowed us to continue to drink or use drugs. As a codependent, we wanted the ability to control or manipulate others, because we thought it was the thing that was going to stop our addict from drinking or using. We wanted our resentment, because it allowed us to keep thinking that others were the cause of our problems. We wanted to focus our attention on our addict because it allowed us not to look at ourselves.

In Step Six we express our willingness to give up our sick and dysfunctional ways of being. Again, the language of the 1930s presents a stumbling block. It is often best to understand "defects of character" as "defective behavior." When we conduct a business inventory, we may discover defective merchandise, and when we do, we certainly are willing to have the manufacturer remove it from our stores. When we discover defective behavior in ourselves, it is just as natural to become willing to have those unworkable ways of being removed from our behavioral inventory.

Step Seven. We don't "go to work on ourselves," trying to "reform" or "become better people." The Twelve Steps are not a program of "self-improvement." We have always been the best people we could be, even when that's not been very good, and trying to be better isn't going to make us any better. In Step Seven, we give our assent and permission for the process of getting well to take place within us. We don't resolve to do it, we just agree to let it happen. We agree to be in the right place at the right time (usually when and where a meeting takes place) and allow ourselves to get well.

In Step Seven we recapitulate Steps One, Two, and Three. We acknowledge our powerlessness to overcome our dysfunctional ways of thought, feeling, and behavior, we accept that while we can't change ourselves by force of will, we can *be* changed, and we make a decision to let go of our vain attempts at control long enough to allow the change to occur.

Step Eight. We accept the responsibility to make right what we have hurt or damaged whenever it is we can, and we compile a list of those injuries to the best of our ability.

Step Nine. We put our willingness to make things right into action by repairing the damage as best we can, if we can see a way to do it without doing more damage. Sometimes this simply means saying, "I'm sorry." Sometimes it means the repayment of debts. Sometimes it means fessing up to a sneaky or deceptive manipulation, and sometimes it means confessing to a crime.

And sometimes it means just leaving someone alone. There are times when we've just hurt people too much, and they've made a personal decision that they're through with us. Insisting that these people see us, or hear our apology when they feel that way, is just hurting them all over again. We don't make amends for the purposes of exculpating ourselves or making ourselves feel better.

Step Ten. We recognize that recovery is a lifelong process, and that we will need to continue to "work a program" for the rest of our lives. We see that the road to recovery is circular rather than linear, and that we will continue to face our powerlessness, our need to surrender, our dysfunctions of thought and behavior, and our need to correct ourselves at point after point in our lives. We see that working a program isn't going to make us perfect or cured, but we're willing to settle for continuing to recover.

Step Eleven. We accept that to continue to recover, we'll need to make a conscious habit of paying attention to ourselves. This doesn't mean that we become our own sideline coach, constantly advising, criticizing, and correcting ourselves. It does mean that we accept the discipline of making quiet time to be with ourselves and with our God, to renew each day our commitment to health and sanity, and to listen to the quiet inner voice that prompts us toward our own recovery.

Step Twelve. We don't become self-righteous, self-appointed missionaries to the unrecovering. We don't control others, and it's not important that others believe or feel the way we do. We don't preach and we don't lecture. But we do hold ourselves ready to be of whatever help we can to our fellow sufferers by sharing with them, when they ask for it, the path of recovery that we have found.

WHAT HAPPENS AT A TWELVE-STEP MEETING?

Many people are shy, and fearful of new or different situations. And going to your first Twelve-Step meeting is scary, at least before you get there. Let me describe for you what a meeting is like and hopefully ease your fears a little.

You can get the time and location of meetings near you by calling the program's offices in your area. Normally their phone numbers will be listed in your phone book. Failing that, you can often learn about meetings by calling a local treatment center. Even if the treatment center is a alcoholism treatment specialty center, they will usually be able to suggest Al-Anon, ACOA, Codependents Anonymous, NA, Nar-Anon, and other Twelve-Step meetings.

Twelve-Step meetings usually start on time and end on time. If you want to be inconspicuous, arrive five or ten minutes before the meeting is scheduled to begin. Most meetings are scheduled for sixty or ninety minutes. Many are held in churches, schools, or other public buildings, but if you don't know the location, it makes sense to make a trial run to the meeting place well in advance of the scheduled time. If you're shaky about driving or simply need some moral support, often arrangements can be made for someone to pick you up and escort you to the meeting. Ask about this when you call the program's office about a meeting near you.

There is a chairperson for each meeting who will get things started by welcoming everyone and inviting them to recite with him the "Serenity Prayer," which is a little poem translated into English by Reinhold Niebuhr, the famous Protestant theologian. Word for word, it may contain more wisdom than any other words uttered by man:

> *God grant me serenity*
> *To accept the things I cannot change,*
> *Courage to change the things I can,*
> *And wisdom to know the difference.*

The chairperson will then ask someone to read the Twelve Steps. Don't worry, he or she won't ask you. AA members know that any new face may be someone who is sick or frightened or shy or just uneasy with first-time jitters. The person who is called upon to read the Twelve Steps will be someone who is known to the chair.

Someone else then reads the Twelve Traditions, which lay down the only official rules for the Twelve-Step programs. These have to do with confidentiality (that's the "anonymous" part), nonpromotion, nonaffiliation, and public relations. These traditions have stood the test of time, and they make real sense for ensuring the continued effectiveness of the program.

A third volunteer will read a passage from "The Big Book" (each of the programs has its own big book, based on the AA model but with specific application to the central focus of the particular program) called How It Works. In my comments above, I've given you my version of how it works, but you're best off to hear it from "The Big Book" itself.

When all this reading and reciting is done, the chair may introduce a subject for discussion, he may introduce a person who will give a talk, or he may just throw open the floor for people to talk about whatever subject they care to relating to their recovery. Sometimes in large meetings the larger group breaks up into smaller groups depending on the particular steps or subjects they need to focus on that night. There's usually a group for newcomers, and you'll be told where it is.

From this point onward, Twelve-Step meetings work a bit like a Quaker meeting, only not nearly as quiet! People are usually amazed that there is a great deal of laughter, and not just the rueful kind but great, deep, joyful belly laughter, from people who are self-identified alcoholics, addicts, and codependents. It's surprising until you discover how good recovery really is. There are a lot of feelings expressed during a meeting: sadness, anger, joy, humor, rage, despair, hope, and frustration. One at a time, people talk about their recovery. Some make what are almost prepared speeches, often quite funny. Others simply comment on what's going on in their lives and in their recovery. In open meetings (those that are open to "outsiders," though I've never heard of anyone who's been shut out of a meeting because he or she is not an alcoholic or codependent) many will give their "drunk-alogue," that is, their story of alcoholism, addiction, or codependency. Someone may be called upon to get things started, but don't worry, it won't be you. Program people are sensitive and don't want to put you on the spot, and besides, until you have some recovery under your belt, there is a danger that your comments won't be that helpful anyway. If the chairperson should make a mistake and call on you, all you need to do is decline with a polite comment like "Thanks, but I'd rather just listen for now."

People who think of the Twelve Steps as "getting religion" won't be disappointed; you will hear the words "God" and "Higher Power" used with some frequency. But you'll also hear words that you never heard in church, and you need to be prepared for them. The Twelve-Step programs are about real life, and sometimes the good old Anglo-Saxon four-letter words catch the flavor and feeling of real life like no others. The other similarity to church is that at some point in the meeting, a plate is passed. Each Twelve-Step group is self-supporting, and the coffee, the doughnuts, and the meeting room generally need to be paid for. If you are a first-timer, not only are you not expected to contribute, you will be asked not to.

At the end of each meeting, the chair invites everyone to join hands and recite the Lord's Prayer. You are free to participate or not to participate as you wish, and no one thinks the less of you if you don't. When the recitation is finished, the people usually say in chorus, "Keep coming back!" This may be the only direct advice you'll receive at a program meeting, and it's good advice, because if you do keep coming back, you'll get well. You can't help it.

There are groups for every subpopulation and interest group. There are meetings for doctors, lawyers, nurses, and other occupational groups. There are groups that meet at lunchtime on job sites. There are women-only groups and men-only groups. There are smoking and nonsmoking groups. There are groups for gays and groups for ethnic minorities, conducted in foreign languages. Many foreign countries have groups which you can visit while on vacation. There are even groups for atheists! If a particular group doesn't suit you, don't quit the program—find another group.

I have known thousands of people who are recovering from alcoholism, addiction, and codependency. Some have been patients, some have been colleagues, many have been friends, and all but one or two have had one thing in common—their involvement in the Twelve-Step programs. In my experience the percentage of people who get sober and stay sober (or free from codependent behavior) and develop some degree of emotional health without the programs is so small—far less than 1 percent—that betting that you can do it alone is like gambling with your life that the sun won't rise tomorrow. You don't have to like the program (though you will come to in time), but you do need to participate if you're at all serious about getting well.

These gentle, simple Twelve Steps have helped hundreds of thousands of people whose lives were lost in addiction, codependence, and other compulsions to a place in their lives of health, sanity, and serenity. I recommend them to you with all my heart.

V

GETTING

WELL

15

RECOVERY

In one sense, the only good news I've given you in this book is that you may live through your addiction or codependency—if you do the right things. In this chapter, I want to give you a sense of what recovery is like, of what will change and what probably won't, of what you need to do at each stage of recovery, and, although there is no schedule for recovery, of where you should be, depending on how long since you began your recovery and how hard you've worked at it. Most of all, however, I want to try to convey to you some small sense of how very joyful the process of recovery is.

RECOVERY FROM ADDICTION

As we learned in the previous chapter, recovery from addiction begins with giving up. Only when the denial of the alcoholic or addict is shattered in the face of reality, whether that reality comes in the form of a legal, medical, marital, or social catastrophe, or in the kinder form of intervention, either the addict must hit bottom or bottom must hit him before the addicted mind will give up the idea that the alcoholic can continue to drink in control and without negative consequences.

These first days and weeks of recovery are anything but joyful. There occurs a general implosion of the personality that feels to the addict like a black hole has opened up within her, swallowing up all hope and all self-respect. It is not unusual to see a fairly deep depression set in, partly the result of feeling ill (the body has, through the entire course of the addictive disease, been developing a dependent relationship with the substance, and when it is withdrawn, the body suffers) and partly the result of the tremendous sense of spiritual and emotional collapse that comes when the end of denial is reached. The alcoholic in the first days and weeks of sobriety may become withdrawn, remorseful, and defensive about abstinence in the same way she was about drinking.

There is often also a grief reaction to the loss of the substance that had become a best friend, a primary means of coping with life and, indeed, a way of life. For many addicts, the door to the treatment center may as well have the inscription ALL HOPE ABANDON, YE WHO ENTER HERE written over the door.

Early recovery is a hard but mercifully short period. Often, the first ray of hope comes when the addict begins to get the idea that his addiction is a disease. He learns in treatment that he hasn't been crazy, he's been ill. She hasn't been a bad mother, she's been an alcoholic mother. He hasn't been a moral reprobate, he's been sick. He hasn't been a flake who can't manage the normal responsibilities of life, instead he's been remarkably effective and responsible, if you include in the equation how terribly sick he's been. As he gradually absorbs the disease concept of addiction, the addict can gradually begin to separate himself from his addiction, and to think of it as an *it*, and not as *me*. In the chapter on the psychological aspects of addiction, we described how, over time, the addiction gradually takes over the addict's personality, until it's hard to distinguish which is addiction and which is the addict. Now the addict begins to see that all the behaviors about which he has felt so guilty are really artifacts of his disease, and he can forgive himself and remove himself from the hook.

Things start to get better also as the physical symptoms of withdrawal subside and as the addict receives medical attention to the damage that her addiction has caused. For all the time I have worked in this field, I am still startled by the dramatic physical changes that occur in early sobriety. Color comes back to the skin (or fades to normal if the skin has been florid), and light returns to the eyes. Substantial weight loss often occurs if there has been bloat, or if food has been neglected in the addiction, healthy weight gain occurs. Blood pressure normalizes, bruising and skin lesions clear up, and motor functions steady. Sleep returns to normal patterns, and the quality of the addict's rest is better than in years, resulting in clearer thought and greater emotional stability. The most common comment I hear from newly recovering alcoholics and addicts is "I'd forgotten how it felt to feel good." From their spouses I hear "I'm shocked. I guess it happened so gradually, I just didn't realize how terrible he looked."

Emotional recovery starts with the treatment program. The addict looks around at his fellow patients and sees that he is not alone in the universe; other people have suffered as he has. Other people have to combat the same sense of shame, the same capacity for denial, the same chemically generated life difficulties that he must. The sense of becoming part of a community of previously sick and now recovering people, which the good treatment center creates by group treatment and well-managed residency arrangements, is tremendously therapeutic in helping the addict out of her chemically imposed isolation. She rejoins the human race.

If the treatment program has been an inpatient program, graduating from the program is both a milestone in recovery and a terribly frightening time in recovery. Can I really make it on the outside? Who are going to be my friends now that I don't drink or use drugs? Can I handle my job without drinking? There's so much drug use in my work environment, I don't know if I can continue to work there. How do you have any fun, indeed, how do you live, without drinking or drugging? These and a thousand other questions about normal life torment the person emerging from treatment. And they are real questions, not imaginary fears. If the addict does what he's been told, works a Twelve-Step program, doesn't overstress himself, stays in touch with his counselor, eats and sleeps on schedule, stays away from "slippery" people, places, and things, his recovery will continue. If not, he'll likely relapse.

It takes two or three months of sobriety before the alcoholic or addict begins to see that maybe this recovery business isn't so bad, after all. She feels better, thinks better, works better, sleeps better, eats better, and generally does everything better. There are exceptions, of course. He may not shoot pool better, make friends more easily, be as alcoholically outgoing as before, or do any of the things that depended on alcohol as well as he did them before. These things are called "state-dependent learnings," and fortunately the skills can be fairly easily relearned in time. But in a general way, the alcoholic or addict begins to appreciate that sobriety can be a viable and even enjoyable life-style with substantial benefits attached that go well beyond the fact that he gets to continue living.

As one day of sobriety goes miraculously into the next, the recovering addict begins to experience the dawn of new hope for herself and her life. Through her AA participation, she is exposed to people who have had three years, five years, twenty years, of sobriety. Somehow they've made it, and they seem like regular people like her. Exactly how they have done it isn't yet quite clear, but she begins to have the feeling that if she can just follow, one day at a time, the directions she learned in treatment, maybe a life of permanent recovery could be possible for her, too.

As the recovery progresses, a good deal of the fear about managing normal life begins to dissipate. The addict finds that he can cope, if he takes things a step at a time and does not neglect his recovery. He finds that he can do his job without drinking or drugging, even if he has to approach it a little differently. If he has had to leave an alcohol- or drug-infested work environment to protect his sobriety, he discovers that he can find a new job, often for more money in a more pleasant situation. Little by little, he learns how to have fun without drinking or drugging. He makes friends with other people in the program, and they form the basis for his new social circle.

Not everything is rosy in early sobriety, however. In many cases, the bills are still coming in on the costs of addiction. There may be legal charges to answer, bills to be paid off slowly and patiently, adjustments to a divorce or separation that may have been caused by the addiction, and other assorted difficulties left over from the drinking or drugging days. These tend to come just when the addict would like to put all that behind him and when he needs the stress of coping with these extraordinary difficulties least. They can create a real need for relief, and there is a danger of relapse when the going gets tough. Dealing with "the wreckage of the past" is a trying and stressful process that requires patience and reliance on a solid Twelve-Step program.

To complicate the picture, there may be some surprising and unpredicted marital difficulties. The husband who so desperately wanted his alcoholic wife to receive treatment may resent the time she spends at AA meetings, and may become jealous of her

new AA friends, who may seem to him closer to her in their bond
of addiction than he is to her. While she might have been a sexual
volcano when she was drinking, she may now find sexual inti-
macy awkward, frightening, or uncomfortable, and she may have
difficulty with orgasm. While her husband may never have
shown evidence of having a drinking problem (at least compared
with hers), he may be resentful and uncooperative about the
need for abstinence in the recovering home. He may be unwilling to pursue his own recovery from codependency, continuing
his manipulative, controlling, smothering codependent behaviors and threatening her sobriety with them. The couple may
require marriage counseling with a professional who knows and
understands the difficulties of the recovering couple.

Gradually, things start to get better as the addict gets better.
His functioning in all areas improves, and the benefits begin to
pile up in his marriage, work, finances, and emotional life. He
takes better care of himself, develops new interests, and improves his appearance. It may occur to him that he needs a little
professional coaching with these aspects of his life, and he may
start a counseling relationship with a professional recommended
by his treatment counselor.

The one-year point in sobriety is a momentous and strangely
ambivalent time. There is a high danger of relapse in the elev-
enth through the thirteenth month. The reasons for this are
various and complex. Some addicts feel an inner compulsion to
go back out and try drinking or drugging to "see" if they're
really addicted, or if things just got out of control for a while.
There can be a sudden reappearance of cravings and a reassertion
of addictive denials. For some it dawns on them at the one-year
point that this abstinence thing is really for life, and in a panic
they drink or use just to prove that they still have that option.
A few have given a promise to someone else to stay clean and
sober for one year, and now feel a need to go drink so that they
can get sober for themselves. Some recovering people who

relapsed at the one-year point have told me that they just couldn't deal with the idea that they were going to be successful at achieving sobriety, and had to sabotage their recovery. The reasons for relapse at the one-year point are very complicated, and statistically it is quite a dangerous time.

It is not usually until the second year of sobriety or beyond that the recovering person begins to seriously attend to the issues of emotional and spiritual recovery. The business of taking care of business and doing whatever necessary to maintain abstinence have previously taken up too much time and energy to focus on these deeper and more complex issues. But as sobriety, sanity, and normalcy become a way of life, the recovering person begins to turn to the issues of his dysfunctional thinking, his hurts and resentments, his self-defeating behaviors, his interpersonal and relationship problems, and his relationship to his Higher Power. It is during this period that personal counseling is of the greatest value and greatest reward, if the counseling is undertaken with a therapist who really knows about addiction and recovery. This is a time for exploring how he became the person he is and for understanding the forces that shaped him. He can do the grieving for the childhood that was stolen by his parent's alcoholism, and grieve for the adulthood that was stolen by his own addiction. He can conduct his "fearless and searching moral inventory" with the help of compassionate but professional support. He can identify ideas that are wrong, attitudes that are unhelpful, and behaviors that are destructive. He'll have enough solid recovery and enough contact with the AA program not to let himself fall into the hands of a therapist who will allow him to believe that his addiction was caused by psychological conflict, or of a psychiatrist who will suggest that he take drugs to cure his spiritual pain.

By the fourth or fifth year of recovery, the recovering person is typically catching up with and passing his "normal" (nonaddicted) counterparts in the process of emotional and

The addict is reacting to the changes produced by his use of his substance.

The codependent reacts to changes in her addict.

First use of substance occurs.

Attraction to potential alcoholic/addict. Seems an exciting, romantic, "glittering" person.

Social life begins to change to include substance use.

"Goes along" with social changes. Works to fit in with new friends and aquaintances.

Growing preoccupation with substance.

Accepts substance as part of normal life. May obtain substance for addict..

Increase in tolerance to substance.

Accepts, ignores, even defends, increased use. Puts down her own fears.

Onset of memory blackouts.

Frustration with addict's lapses. Sometimes wonders if it is she who is crazy.

Increased guilt about drinking. Surreptitious drinking.

Is appeased by addict's guilt about drinking. Accepts his promises, feels morally superior at his admissions of remorse.

Refusal to talk about substance use.

Accepts prohibition against acknowledging or talking about drinking. Is intimidated by addict's defensive anger. Begins to "act out" hostility.

Loss of control. Inability to stop when others do, or when intended.

Loss of control. Thoughts, attitudes, decisions, become governed by partner's excesses. Life becomes coping with a series of emergencies.

Rationalizations and excuses.

Rationalizations and excuses for codependent behavior. "Someone's got to take care of things." Buildup of anger and loss of respect toward alcoholic. Punitive, sometimes brutal acting out.

Grandiose, aggressive behavior.

Disgusted by the gradiosity, terrified by the aggressiveness, codependent becomes increasingly withdrawn, silently enraged.

Attempts to control use fail.

Codependent attempts to control addicts use by finding hidden supplies, manipulating activity, withholding sex, extracting meaningless promises, lecturing, haranguing.

Use becomes constant; family and friends avoided. Work, money troubles, build up.

Codependent accepts social isolation. Socializing is not worth the embarrassment. Assumes more responsibility for breadwinning and financial management.

Irrational thinking, buildup of resentments.

Engages in endless, irrational arguments and discussions. Takes partner's resentments personally.

Complete inability to function socially, sexually, occupationally.

Accepts social withdrawal. Secretly grateful for partner's sexual disinterest. Completely takes over breadwinner role.

Physical symptoms of dependence: shakes, unconsciousness, liver disease, withdrawal symptoms. Psychological symptoms resembling mental illness.

Develops stress-related physical problems. Seems crazy to friends. Traumatic medical emergencies occur.

"Hits bottom." Reaches the point where using substance and living becomes an either-or choice Next step is either death or recovery.

Codependent hits bottom. May leave alcoholic, commit suicide, or begin to recover.

Alcoholic or addict reaches a greater-than-normal degree of spiritual and emotional development in recovery.
Codependent develops greater-than-normal spiritual and emotional development in recovery.

Understands self. Eliminates self-defeating behavior. Spiritual growth.
Happiness is based on inner rather than outer factors. Spiritual growth.

Begins to deal with spiritual and emotional issues. Gets counseling.
Passes one year. Feels stable and sane. Healthy self-interest.

Passes one year. High danger of relapse.
Counseling begins to focus on emotional and spiritual issues.

Must deal with "wreckage of the past."
Must deal with "wreckage of the past."

Appreciates advantages of sobriety.
Experiences benefit from healthy behaviors.

New friends, new work, new patterns of activity.
Al-Anon friends. New activities.

Fears diminish. Begins to appreciate sobriety.
Anxiety and depression diminish. Stops enabling and taking responsibility.

Leaves treatment. Fears about new life. Starts AA.
Begins to focus on self rather than partner.

Psychologically improves. Thinking clears, mood improves.
Starts to think more appropriately about situation.

Withdrawal symptoms subside. Feels better. Appearance improves.
Emotional storm subsides. Feels more in control.

Learns addiction is a disease. First hope.
Learns about codependency. Sees others recovering. First hope.

Enters treatment. Implosion of personality. Withdrawal. Depression.
At end of rope, seeks counseling. Enters Al-Anon.

Addict hits bottom. Breakthrough of denial. Admits defeat.
Codependent hits bottom. Chronic depression. Gives up on addict, self.

spiritual development. He has to. The process of facing an addiction and doing what is necessary to recover from it builds spiritual muscle and fiber that most people don't even know they have. Some of the most honest, most humble, most serene, and most mature people I know are recovering alcoholics and addicts with substantial sobriety and recovery. Frequently I feel humble in their presence. Because they have *had* to face their addiction, and to mend their lives slowly and patiently from its devastation, they have acquired a degree of emotional and spiritual development that is comparatively rare among nonrecovering people. In spite of and because of their struggle for recovery, they among all people have found joy and meaning and lasting peace in their lives.

Recovery from addiction is hard, but everyone who's put in the time and the work agrees that it's also joyful. Not a bad trade-off when you consider that practicing an addiction is also very hard, produces a miserable life, and ends in death.

RECOVERY FROM CODEPENDENCY

We saw in chapter 9 how the course of codependency closely parallels that of addiction, that is, the codependent and the alcoholic get sicker and sicker together. When recovery begins, the courses remain quite parallel, as long as each is working on a program of recovery and, of course, as long as they stay together. Typically, a failure to work at recovery on the part of one will result in relapse or slowed recovery in the other, or will precipitate a divorce.

Codependents, more often than alcoholics or addicts, enter recovery by way of counseling. More often than not, they seek counseling, confused, depressed, and terrified as they may be, to try to get their alcoholic or addict to change, rather than to help themselves. Codependents are confusing to therapists who don't know about codependency and recovery, because they are often quite willing and even insistent on spending significant sums of money talking about their spouses rather than about themselves. Most psychologists are trained to be nondirective, that is, to just let their patients talk about whatever they choose. This strategy doesn't work in the early treatment of codependents, because left unchecked, they will focus all their attention in therapy on their alcoholic or addict, just as they do in their lives.

Most codependents are just as stubborn and in as deep denial as their addicts. They don't seek treatment until they have hit bottom. And unlike the addict, few codependents are brought to treatment as the result of intervention. The codependent who has found his bottom is a very sad person. He is confused, unable to organize his thoughts, depressed, tearful, anxious, and frightened. He feels very alone. His self-esteem is at an all-time ebb, in part because he has failed in his efforts to get his addict sober but mainly because he has lost himself. His focus of attention and energy has for so long been on his addict that he has quite literally forgotten or never discovered who he is.

As in addiction, the codependent bottom is the starting point of recovery. Bottom is sometimes more frightening for the codependent than for the addict. The addict is often in a treatment center, where he is protected and attended by trained doctors and counselors. The codependent normally has only his counselor on a once- or twice-weekly basis. (There do exist inpatient treatments for codependents, but they are not yet readily available in most cities.) Codependents may commit suicide at their bottom, or they may act out their despair in frightening and self-destructive ways.

The codependent is actually in a better position to receive appropriate, effective treatment when it is her addict or alcoholic who enters treatment first. In the treatment center, if it is a good one, she will be referred to a counselor or therapist who understands codependency and the issues for recovery. Left to her own devices, she may seek psychiatric therapy, which is in most cases inappropriate, or take her chances with a psychologist who may be both effective and ethical but may not understand codependency.

Once she is in contact with a professional who properly diagnoses her condition, however, the codependent will quickly be introduced to Al-Anon, with the recommendation that she attend from one to five meetings per week. Counseling for codependents in early recovery focuses on education about codependency and on basic issues of self-care and program participation. Early recovery counseling for codependents does not delve into family of origin or childhood issues, because the codependent is normally too sick, depressed, and emotionally exhausted to take on these new psychological challenges.

The first meetings of Al-Anon are real eye-openers for codependents. For years a codependent may have been living in a self-constructed cocoon of isolation and secrecy, believing his situation is shameful and keeping the family secrets. It is amazing to the codependent to hear people at Twelve-Step meetings openly sharing their struggles, sadnesses, and disappointments. When they describe their triumphs, it is often difficult for him to understand what they are talking about. How can *not* interfering with the addict's use be thought of as a triumph? And why is that woman talking about signing up for an aerobics class as some kind of personal victory when she's just said she's afraid to leave her alcoholic alone? While it's usually pretty easy for people to grasp the central idea of addictive recovery (to stop drinking and drugging), it's often very difficult for codependents to understand what recovery from codependency is all about.

Codependent recovery is centered on a few central ideas that the codependent needs to learn, take to heart, and act upon. They are odd ideas to the codependent at first, and it takes time to make them a way of life. The course of codependent recovery is the process of putting these ideas to work.

1. You can't control the behavior of others. The idea that you can is often a holdover from childhood in an alcoholic or otherwise dysfunctional family, where conditions were such that you had to find a way to protect yourself from disappointment, shame, abuse, or desertion. Your manipulations and attempts to control your addict are similar attempts to protect yourself. But these behaviors, even in the rare instances where they succeed, turn you into a not-very-likable person who blames, lectures, manipulates, controls, whines, mopes, pouts, induces guilt, connives, snoops, and generally behaves in obnoxious and inappropriate ways.

2. If you try to control the behavior of others, it will make you sick and crazy. In your misguided efforts to control history and make things come out the way you think they should, you have become depressed, anxious, and ill. You may have developed obesity, ulcers, backache, irritable colon, migraine, high blood pressure, alcoholism, or a host of other medical difficulties. You may have psychological problems such as phobias, obsessions, compulsions, eating disorders, or more serious thought disorders.

3. You need to learn detachment. You have suffered from what the Buddhists call "attachment." You live in a world of "oughta be's." You believe, whether consciously or unconsciously, that you know what is best for others, particularly those who are close to you. You spend your life trying to make your ideas about how things should be come true, instead of spending your time dealing with the way things are. You need to "detach" from ideas about how your addict *should* get sober and your family *should* be happy, and start dealing with how things are, including the fact that you are not happy, and you are not taking care of your main business in life, which is taking care of you.

4. You need to learn to mind your own business. You have spent your time and your energy minding other people's business—making sure they're happy so they'll like you, making sure their responsibilities are taken care of, making sure they are where they're supposed to be and doing what they're supposed to be doing. You may have thought that this activity has made you an efficient manager and the savior of your family. What it's actually accomplished is to enable your alcoholic to drink more, your kids not to grow up, and your own life, which you've failed to make the time and energy for, to become a complete mess.

5. You need to take care of yourself. You have been everybody's caretaker except your own. You cook for, clean for, work for, pay bills for, provide comfort and advice for, and generally try to be a pillar of strength and comfort for everyone in your life except you. You think this makes you some kind of a lovable hero. What it actually does is set you up to be used by every Tom, Dick, or Monica who comes down the pike. You need to learn to say no to other people's requests of you that are not good for you, and yes to your own needs. You need to learn to exercise, to meditate, to take time for yourself, to eat right, to have some fun, and to spend some money on yourself. You need to work your program because it's a good and loving thing to do for yourself. Most of all, you need to learn to love and respect yourself.

It usually comes as a relief, after the shock and outrage wear off, for the codependent to learn that there is something wrong with him, and that his sickness and despair come out of a syndrome of behaviors that are, for once, something he can do something about. As with the addict, the first glimmerings of hope for the codependent come when he hears that he has been sick, and that his trouble has had less to do with the fact that he loves an alcoholic than that, perhaps because of his situation in childhood, he has learned some mistaken and misguided ways of loving, and of living. He learns that whether his addict gets help and recovers or not, he can if he is only sincerely willing to work at it.

In Al-Anon, she discovers that there is indeed a different way to live. She meets people who have set down the burden of their addict's illness and have turned to the joyful responsibility of living their own lives. In classes and lectures, she learns some of the key concepts about codependency, and she identifies some of the mistakes she has been making in her life. In counseling, she begins to define some new ways of going about things, which feel strange and downright scary at first.

Gradually, she begins to experience benefits from this new way of living. She finds that the time and energy she used to spend taking care of others can now be used in new and pleasurable ways on herself. She may feel guilty at first, but soon the reinforcement from her Al-Anon friends and sponsor, and from her therapist, and the benefits themselves from this new way of living begin to cause her to appreciate that it may make sense to change her ways.

From about six months to one year into the codependent recovery, the changes in the codependent become more noticeable and more permanent. The codependent's focus of attention and energy increasingly turn toward himself and his own problems. He seeks medical attention for his health problems, which he has been neglecting "until there's more time." He gets counseling for his anxiety and compulsive symptoms. He starts a program of exercise, and learns to relax by using meditation. He may discover that he has been abusing drugs and alcohol himself, and begin to attend AA in addition to Al-Anon. He begins to feel better, look better, and function better.

The more he pays attention to himself and behaves in self-valuing and self-caring ways, the more his self-esteem is restored. He begins to feel like a member of the human race again. In therapy he works to adopt the idea that he is a dignified and worthwhile human being who is worthy of love and respect.

This new self-esteem shows in her behavior in relationship

to her addict. She will no longer tolerate, excuse, or cooperate in the abuse of her. She begins to spot the "hooks" in her addict's behavior, and starts declining to bite. She learns to let him be responsible for the consequences of his drinking and drugging, and she becomes willing to let him hit bottom, for her sake as well as his.

If her addict entered treatment first, or simultaneously with the codependent, her new behavior not only is more healthy for her, but it also supports and promotes the recovery of the addict in healthy, noncodependent ways. She doesn't check up on him to see if he's been to his meetings, as her nonrecovering counterpart might do. She doesn't sniff his breath when she kisses him hello. When she feels afraid about the possibility of relapse, she tells him, directly and clearly.

The codependent begins to come out of social isolation, and to form real and meaningful friendships, first with other members of the program, and then with some (so-called) normal people. If the couple is recovering, this may be the time when they begin to dare to entertain in their home. If not, the codependent will visit with friends at their home and not hesitate to take part in social activities independent of her drinking or drugging partner.

The using partner may at any point in the codependent's early recovery become attracted to the new quality of his partner's life and be motivated to enter treatment for his addiction without benefit of intervention or of a major crash to bottom. Indeed, I would say that the very best thing a codependent can do to get his addict into recovery, better even than intervention (unless the alcoholic is in very dire condition), is to get healthy herself. It is not possible to overestimate the power of attraction that a healthy recovery generates.

If the using partner cannot or will not enter treatment at some time in the codependent's recovery, the codependent must, inevitably, make the decision to divorce. Put bluntly, it is simply not possible to live indefinitely with a drinking alcoholic or a drug-using addict and mount a stable and healthy program of recovery at the same time. Besides, the codependent's natural growth toward taking good care of himself will lead him to conclude that no matter how much compassion he may feel for his addict, his own health and well-being demand separation or divorce. This point is a sad but important step in recovery. I usually recommend that the recovering codependent defer this decision for at least six months after beginning to participate in an Al-Anon program unless there is physical abuse to the codependent or to the children.

At about the one-year point in recovery, the codependent is ready to seriously take on the emotional and spiritual issues in therapy. Until now, the codependent's counseling has focused on the immediate issues of self-care, education, and changing the grosser forms of dysfunctional behavior. Now the focus of counseling turns to deeper issues. I firmly believe that without some form of group or individual counseling that is growth oriented rather than crisis oriented, the recovery of the codependent is limited. Granted that limited recovery is far, far better than no recovery, the codependent nevertheless needs to engage in personal counseling to deal with the deeper family-of-origin issues of childhood in order to accomplish the inner healing necessary to full health.

In counseling, the codependent deals with the grief and loss she experienced in childhood. She opens her eyes to the fundamental dysfunctionality of her family. Changes occur in the way she relates to her parents, and she may even become an agent of change in that family. Abuse is recognized for what it is, and the inner child, who has been held in a kind of psychological limbo of pain and suffering, begins to heal. The blinders are taken off, the tears are shed, and the entire personality begins to reintegrate into a more healthy configuration.

By the fourth or fifth year of recovery, the codependent has, like her addict counterpart, caught up with and even surpassed the normal level of emotional and spiritual development for "normal" adults of her age. Again, the very process that the codependent must engage in in order to recover forces her to face her past, work on her behavior, learn new ideas, recognize and share her feelings, and develop better communications skills. Most people would benefit from doing all this personal work, but their life circumstances do not force them to do it. The codependent with four or five years or more of recovery is a wonderful person to spend time with. She is serene and content. Her personal boundaries are clear and definite, so that she does not intrude on other people's business and does not impose her personal business on others. She is able to share without enmeshment, communicate without confusion, set limits without being unkind or defensive, to be with herself without loneliness, and to be with others without shame. She takes care of herself well, and it shows in her body, her face, and her eyes.

The addict–codependent couple who have stayed together during these early years of recovery and who have both worked a program with diligence are wonderful to behold. They communicate with clarity and precision. Their priorities are clear to one another, and they do not make demands on each other that compromise each other's abstinence, spirituality, or serenity. They are quite independent of one another, yet they find plenty of time to be together. They are affectionate, sensual, and joyful. They laugh a lot.

I am sorry that my words can convey only the smallest taste of what recovery is like. It's true that it's hard work and takes time and energy, but when you think of how hard you work, and how much time and energy you expend to earn the money to buy material things that rust and decay and fade away, you'll see that the value of recovery far exceeds its cost.

Recovery is God's gift to you. Will you accept it?

16

JOHN AND MARY'S
STORY

John and Mary Williams sat in my living room the other night after dinner, laughing and holding hands as they shared their story. The talk had drifted to the subject of our recoveries.

"I was really a monster after that DWI," John said. "This woman was an absolute saint to stick with me."

"Saint!" Mary snorted. "I was *sick* to stay with you! You can thank your lucky stars for codependency. If I'd been even halfway healthy I would have been out the door months or years before that. But I guess it's a fair trade. If you can be thankful I'm a codependent, I guess I can be thankful you're an alcoholic, because I had a lot of work to do on my life that didn't even concern you, but your alcoholism forced me into my own recovery!"

How strange, I thought, to hear people talk about being grateful that they suffer from a fatal disease, or from depression, traumas, and emotional upheavals. I've heard so many recovering people express this curious feeling of gratitude that it's only when I really think about it that I even feel surprised anymore.

Mary told about making that first phone call to the woman from Al-Anon the day after John's DWI. She and Virginia had met for coffee, and somehow, all of Mary's frustration, disappointment, anxiety, rage, and confusion had come pouring out. "I don't know what it was that helped me open up that day to Virginia," Mary said. "Maybe it was just that she was so patient and caring—she seemed somehow to make it okay. All these things I was so ashamed of just kept coming out, and she wasn't surprised by any of it. I told her about John's drinking, about our fights, about how I was losing control with Jennifer—I even told her about being sexually abused as a girl, and that was something I swore no one would ever find out."

Virginia shared her story with Mary, and to Mary's amazement, it was much worse than anything she had ever experienced. Virginia's husband was an alcoholic who had beaten her on a regular basis, sexually abused one of their daughters, and had taken the family into bankruptcy a short time before he died in a car crash while driving drunk, leaving them penniless. Mary was amazed that this woman, who had suffered so much of the same things she had, only worse, sat before her calmly, apparently happy and at peace with herself. Finally, Mary had asked if Virginia thought there was some way that she could find the peace of heart and mind that Virginia apparently had. Virginia just smiled, and invited Mary to an Al-Anon meeting that evening.

Mary laughed. "That first Al-Anon meeting was so confusing to me! I couldn't understand for the life of me why all these people seemed to be talking as if *they* had a problem. Wasn't this supposed to be a meeting for people who were trying to do something about their alcoholics or drug addicts? They were talking as if they had to do something about themselves, as if they were the problem! It was only toward the end of the meeting, when one poor woman was talking about the things her husband said to her when he was drunk, that I caught myself thinking 'That's sick' and realized it was true. It *was* sick. It was sick that she stood there and took it. I didn't have to think too far beyond that to see that I was sick, too. It was as if it hit me like a bolt out of the blue that the life I was living was twisted, out of focus, and all wrong."

"When I found out that she went to that meeting," John said, "I was madder than hell. Of course, I was madder than hell about everyone and everything in those days." He chuckled and shook his head. "I don't know how it was possible for one person to carry around the load of rage and resentment I had then. I hated the cops for arresting me. I hated my partners for doing better than I. I hated my father, and he wasn't even alive! I hated Mary for being such a self-righteous bitch. The real truth was that I hated myself for what was happening to me, but of course I couldn't let myself see that. So naturally, in my alcoholic state, I took the most effective action I could; when Mary came home, I hollered and screamed for a while about the damage she was doing to my reputation, and then I beat the daylights out of her."

We were all quiet as a tear rolled down John's cheek. I am always caught off guard at the courage of alcoholics when they "admit to God and to another human being the exact nature of their wrongs." We all knew that after five years of sobriety John was still having trouble obtaining his own forgiveness for his violence toward Mary. She reached out and covered his hand with her own.

"I moved out that very night, and took Jennifer to my father's house," Mary said. "That didn't relieve me a whole lot, considering my experience with my father, but I didn't have any money to go to a hotel, and I had fallen so out of touch with any of my friends that I just couldn't call them at midnight needing a place to stay." The next day she called the local bar association because she had heard that they had a program to help alcoholic lawyers. The lawyer who returned her call was a recovering alcoholic who suggested that she might explore the possibilities of intervention. He gave her the name of an intervention specialist and volunteered to be present at the intervention if she thought the story of a brother attorney would help. "I was so thankful that he never asked my name," Mary said. "I don't know what I would have done, because I wanted to get John help, not get him into trouble."

Mary contacted the interventionist, who explained the process to her and helped her get a team of people together, including two of John's partners, Jennifer, the recovering attorney from the bar association, and herself. They decided to leave John's mother out of it, reasoning that if she had put up with John's father for all those years, she probably wasn't going to be of much help with John. After holding a rehearsal session, they all showed up at the Williams home on Saturday morning.

"I was so scared," Mary said. "I called John from my father's house to ask if I could come over to talk about our marriage and what we were going to do now. He was sober and he sounded reasonable, but I was sure that when I showed up with this small army of people, he would go off the launchpad entirely. I had fantasies of his hitting one of his partners, or of his throwing the whole crew out of the home. You could have knocked me over with a feather when he opened the door and said, 'I know why you're all here, and I'll go!' When it sank in that he was agreeing to go to treatment without our even staging the intervention, I was so proud of him and I loved him so much!"

"Well, hell," John said. "I may be an alcoholic, but I'm not stupid. I knew, after having had three days of being sober—and sick with withdrawal—to think about it, what was happening to me. After all, I was the son of an alcoholic, I had had a DWI, I was getting drunk every day, and to top it all off, I'd hit my wife for the second time while I was drunk. Honey, those three days without you were the worst of my life. I was sure I'd lost everything. When you called to talk, I was going to volunteer to go into treatment anyway . . . well, I would have if it took that to get you back, and when I saw all those people coming up the driveway, I knew the jig was up." He flashed an impish grin. "I figured I might as well surrender with some class!"

John told how in treatment he had learned that he had a disease, and what a relief it was, in a curious way. "I'd rather be sick than crazy anytime," he commented. Both John and Mary mentioned how amazed they were at how much better he had looked and felt after just a few weeks of abstinence. "I guess it was the difference in how I felt that convinced me more than anything how seriously alcohol had been affecting me," he said.

"For a while, I was just playing the treatment center's game so that I could get out of there with their stamp of approval and get Mary back," John confessed. "I knew I had a problem, but I just couldn't think of myself as an alcoholic. That would have made me just like my father, and I could hardly stand that idea. I figured I was smarter than my counselor, and I could just make the right noises. After I got out I would figure out a way to drink in a normal and reasonable way.

"It was the other guys in my treatment group who really broke down my denial. They kept bringing me back to the facts. Every time I'd point out that 'the research—which I pretended to know all about—is mixed about what alcoholism really is, and whether people really had to be abstinent to recover,' somebody in the group would say, 'For God's sake, John, come off it. You beat up your wife, and it's because she was concerned about your drinking' or 'John, does the research say anything about why your little girl's afraid of you?' They hit me in the face with the facts until finally I broke down. It was during the third week of treatment that I finally said in the group, 'I see that I'm an alcoholic, that there's nothing I can do to change it, and that my life is a mess because of it.' I've never doubted it since."

John went on to describe how he struggled with the idea of

a Higher Power while he was in treatment. "I couldn't use the word God, because to me it meant some Sunday-school picture of an old man with a white beard sitting on a cloud somewhere, dropping pots of gold on some people and throwing thunderbolts at others. I was an agnostic, and I was proud of it. How could a thinking man believe in God? The counselor who led our group sessions helped me get it, as usual, in a pretty confrontive way. We were talking about a Higher Power, and I was trying to draw the group into a college-bull-session-type discussion about the existence or nonexistence of God. The counselor stopped me and said, 'John, the philosophy's not important. Your definition of God isn't important. He or it doesn't need you to define Him. What is important is that you admit that whoever or whatever makes things happen, it isn't you!' I fired back and told him I believed that I was the captain of my ship, and that I was responsible for everything about my reality. That was when the group just landed on me. 'Great, John, would you make the sun come out? I hate all this rain,' 'Terrific, John, would you change reality just a little so those kids don't starve in Ethiopia?' 'Hey, John, how come you made reality so that your wife gets hit and your kid's afraid of you?' and finally the counselor summed it all up by saying, 'And while you're at it, John, why don't you just change reality and make it so you're not an alcoholic.' Finally, I got the idea. The idea of a Higher Power just naturally followed my admission that I was powerless. If I admitted that I was powerless over many aspects of reality, it followed that someone or something was responsible for them. I started to think of the word *God* as identical with the word *reality*. A couple of years later I was talking with our minister, and he told me that a theologian named Tillich called God 'the ground of all being,' and that made real sense to me."

"The family counselor at the treatment center really pushed me on the issue of my own recovery," Mary said. "Even after I had that flash of insight that I was also sick, I guess I thought that once John went into treatment, the problem was solved. The family counselor was as hard on me as yours was on you, John. She said, 'Mary, you've spent twenty years at least as a depressed person. You were a sexually abused child. You have no life of your own. You have migraines. You are angry and in conflict with your child. By your own admission, a good deal of your behavior has been just crazy. You've spent the last five years paying attention to John's drinking rather than to Mary's needs. You haven't read a book in two years. You've allowed yourself to be beaten and verbally abused. Your self-esteem is at the bottom. Do you really expect all that to go away because John stops drinking? And what if he goes back to it? Where will you be then? The issue is you, Mary. John will take care of John. You need to deal with Mary.' "

The family counselor had referred Mary to a psychologist in the community who worked with many of the treatment center's patients and their families, and who understood the issues involved in both addictive and codependent recovery. "At first, all she seemed interested in was whether I was attending Al-Anon," Mary said. "I couldn't understand why I was paying all this money just to tell someone I had gotten to my three meetings that week, and to receive homework assignments for taking better care of myself. It was nice, I guess, to have doctor's orders to get my hair done, to treat myself to a nice lunch, and to take an afternoon off and take Jennifer to the zoo. But it certainly didn't seem like what I'd always thought counseling was. We didn't really get into talking about my feelings, or the things that had happened when I was a child, until probably six months after John got out of treatment. But I still see Dr. Fran about once a month, just to talk things through and be sure I'm taking care of my own business. I think of her as my recovery coach.

"But the real lifeline to my recovery is my Al-Anon program. I hated it at first, even though every meeting taught me something new. I had been keeping secrets since long before I met John, and the idea of sharing my thoughts and feelings with a group of strangers was repugnant to me. The only reason I did it, at first, was that I thought it would help John get well. . . ." (We all laughed, and Mary blushed. "Well, what do you expect? I *am* a codependent!") "They said that if I didn't get into recovery, either John would go back to drinking or he'd divorce me."

"The first few months out of treatment were really scary for both of us," John said. "We were like two strangers. We didn't know how to talk to each other. It seemed as if we'd forgotten how to make love. Mary was trying so hard to "do recovery right," in the same way she did everything else right, and I was trying to figure out how to do my work, how to talk to my friends and my clients, how to live my life without drinking. Fortunately, I didn't have any problems fitting into AA. The treatment center had gotten me pretty comfortable with groups, and we had a good group of all attorneys who met every day in a conference room at the courthouse, so it was fairly easy to get involved."

"I think I spent the first three months tiptoeing around on eggshells," Mary said, laughing. "I kept thinking that if I said or did the wrong thing, it might 'drive him to drink,' so I would rehearse and critique everything I said before I said it. I worried about his drinking every time he was five minutes late or went out to the store. I think the thing that really started to get us back together was when we discovered the Friday-night meeting that had the AA group in one room and the Al-Anon meeting right down the hall. Fridays became our night. We hired a regular baby-sitter for Jennifer, and just planned on spending the evening together. After the meeting, we'd go out to dinner and just talk. It was wonderful. We hadn't been out together, alone, for several years. I rediscovered all the reasons why I love this alcoholic bum. . . ." Mary's eyes teared up as she turned to John. "And I love him more today than on the day I married him."

"You shouldn't get the impression that I got twenty-eight days of treatment and that everything was great ever after," John went on, after hugging Mary. "It wasn't that I wanted to drink. I'm lucky. I haven't had a drink since the night Mary left me, going on six years ago now, and I haven't really wanted one, except for a moment or two a couple of times. I just wanted to forget the whole lousy chapter in my life, but garbage kept coming up to remind me of it. Our finances were in a mess. We had bills up to our eyeballs. I didn't get the partnership, although my partners did let me know that they wanted me, if I could demonstrate that my recovery was solid over a period of time. We almost lost the house. I'd had to transfer most of my cases when I went into treatment, and new clients were slow in coming in. The only thing that kept us from bankruptcy was the fact that the other attorneys in my home AA group referred some cases to me. And I still had the DWI hanging over my head, although I was on a deferred-prosecution program, so that if I stayed sober and proved I was working my AA program, there would be no prosecution, but it was still a worry, my being an attorney and all."

"And my codependency didn't just go away, either," Mary added. "I had to struggle so much with my tendency to try to work John's program instead of my own. I knew it was stupid, but I kept my own log of how many meetings he'd gone to, when, and where. I still would give him the 'breath check' kiss when he got home," she said, smiling. "I thought he didn't know about that. I think I was just trying to learn not to be codependent by rote for the first eight or ten months. I knew what I was and wasn't supposed to do, but I really didn't, deep down, quite understand, you know? Somewhere around the one-year point was when Dr. Fran and I really began to get into the spiritual issues in my recovery. We talked about my having been sexually abused. I shed so many tears I thought I'd never stop. I saw how little faith or belief I really had in God, and how I'd thought that I had to do his job and manage myself, John, Jennifer, and everybody else in my vicinity. I stopped keeping secrets. I learned to be more assertive (that was hard!) and to communicate with John more effectively. I gave myself permission to meet my own needs, even when it meant not doing what other people wanted me to. We went to Dr. Fran together for a couple of months, to mend some of the hurts and damage to our marriage.

"Even today I still struggle with my codependent stuff, but these days it's more like the exception rather than the rule. I think it was about two years ago that I realized, with amazement, that I was pretty happy. I don't think I'd ever been happy, you know, in the sort of constant way that makes you think of yourself as a happy and contented person." She laughed. "For the longest time I was afraid to say, 'I'm happy' out loud, for fear that God would hear me and correct the situation!"

As I listened to Mary and John, I thought for the thousandth time what a miracle recovery is. Here were two people whose lives had been ravaged by a terminal illness. They had suffered abuse, emotional distortion, medical problems, legal problems, social embarrassment, depression, family disruption, financial hardship, and psychological misery. They had been to the brink of divorce and returned together. And here they sat, talking, laughing, and holding hands like new lovers.

Today, recovery is a life-style for John and Mary. John chairs an AA meeting on Wednesdays and gives a talk at a local treatment center once a month. His practice has become specialized in DWI work, which he appreciates because he is able to help many alcoholics and addicts begin their recovery by way of the deferred-prosecution network. John is still an alcoholic, but he's successful and stable, both professionally and personally. And he doesn't drink. At least not today.

Mary has become a grown-up. She has a life of her own. Two years ago she started her own court-reporting business, and now has four employees. She also chairs an Al-Anon meeting and mentioned that she's currently also going to Codependents Anonymous one night a week. She's learned how to take care of herself, how to identify what she wants and needs, and how to communicate those needs clearly and directly.

I guess the thing that strikes me about John and Mary is not just that they've survived, and not just that their marriage survived, but that they've survived so *joyfully*. I guess I shouldn't be so surprised. I'm pretty happy myself these days.

APPENDICES

I haven't told you everything there is to know about addiction and codependency, but I've told you everything you need to know to begin your recovery. If you've read this far, you probably know more than *anybody* knew as recently as ten years ago. Knowing what you know now won't make you well, but I hope you have some idea of how to get well and what you must do if you are to recover.

On the pages that follow are some addresses and phone numbers of some very useful resources that can help (Appendix A). I haven't included names and addresses of specific treatment resources, of course, but I've left you space to jot down numbers in your area that you'll use (Appendix B).

I've also included a reading list of materials that have been helpful to me as I've worked at recovering, and have been invaluable to me in writing this book (Appendix C). I've taken the liberty of rating them with stars. Three stars mean that I'd recommend that you get hold of this book and read it immediately. Two stars mean that you'll probably want to read it as you get into your recovery but may not need to read it at this point, assuming that things are in a fairly critical state in your life and you need to get into action. One star suggests that this book, which I wouldn't have included if I didn't think it was excellent, is a more scholarly work, and you may or may not ever want to read it, depending on how relatively studious you are.

I wish you the very best of luck as you pursue recovery.

APPENDIX A:
RESOURCES
FOR HELP

HELP FOR THE ADDICT*

Alcoholics Anonymous
General Service Office
468 Park Avenue South
New York, NY 10016
(212) 686-1100

Narcotics Anonymous
P. O. Box 622
Sun Valley, CA 93352
(818) 780-3951

*For information on treatment centers and programs in your area, contact your state's
Office or Department of Alcohol and Drug Abuse.

National Council on Alcoholism
12 W. Twenty-first Street
New York, NY 10010
(212) 206-6770

National Clearinghouse for Alcohol Information
P. O. Box 2345
Rockville, MD 20852
(301) 468-2600

National Clearinghouse for Drug Abuse Information
2600 Fishers Lane
Rockville, MD 20857
(301) 468-2600

HELP FOR THE CODEPENDENT

Al-Anon Group Headquarters
P. O. Box 182
Madison Square Station
New York, NY 10010
(212) 302-7240

Children of Alcoholics Foundation
540 Madison Avenue
New York, NY 10022
(212) 351-2680

National Association for Children of Alcoholics
P. O. Box 421691
San Francisco, CA 94142

APPENDIX B:

YOUR PERSONAL

DIRECTORY

Name	*Contact Person*	*Number*
Alcohol Helpline or Crisis Line	_____	_____
State Office of Alcohol and Drug Abuse	_____	_____
Emergency Medical Service	_____	_____
Local AA Office	_____	_____
Local Al-Anon	_____	_____
Local ACOA	_____	_____
Treatment Center #1	_____	_____
	_____	
	_____	
Treatment Center #2	_____	_____
	_____	
Intervention Specialist	_____	

Name	Contact Person	Number
Counselor	_____	_____
Emergency Shelter (in case of abuse)	_____	_____
AA Friends	_____	_____
	_____	_____
	_____	_____
	_____	_____
Al-Anon Friends	_____	_____
	_____	_____
	_____	_____
	_____	_____
Other	_____	_____
	_____	_____
	_____	_____

APPENDIX C: RECOMMENDED READING

ALCOHOLISM AND ADDICTION

** Ford, Betty. *The Times of My Life.* New York: Ballantine, 1979.

*** Gold, Mark S., M.D. *The Coke Book.* New York: Berkley Books, 1984.

** Gold, Mark S., M.D. *The Facts About Drugs and Alcohol.* New York: Bantam, 1986.

* Goodwin, Donald, M.D. *Is Alcoholism Hereditary?* New York: Oxford University Press, 1976.

* Jellinek, E. M. *The Disease Concept of Alcoholism.* New Haven: Hill House, 1960.

*** Johnson, Vernon E., Ph.D. *I'll Quit Tomorrow.* New York: Harper & Row, 1980.

** Kirkpatrick, Jean, Ph.D. *Turnabout: New Help for the Woman Alcoholic.* New York: Bantam, 1990.

*** Milam, James R., Ph.D., *Under the Influence.* Seattle: Madrona Press, 1981.

*** Mueller, L. Ann, M.D., and Ketcham, Katherine. *Recovering.* New York: Bantam, 1987.
** Pursch, Joseph, M.D. *Dear Doc.* Minneapolis: CompCare Publications, 1985.
** Reilly, Patrick, M.D. *A Private Practice.* New York: Macmillan, 1984.
* Vaillant, George, M.D. *The Natural History of Alcoholism.* Cambridge: Harvard University Press, 1983.
*** Wholey, Dennis. *The Courage to Change.* Boston: Houghton Mifflin, 1884.

CODEPENDENCY

*** Beattie, Melody. *Codependent No More.* New York: Harper & Row, 1987.
*** Beattie, Melody. *Beyond Codependency.* New York: Harper & Row, 1989.
*** Black, Claudia, Ph.D. *It Will Never Happen to Me.* Denver: M.A.C., 1981.
*** Bradshaw, John. *Healing the Shame That Binds You.* Deerfield Beach, Fla.: Health Communications, 1988.
*** Bradshaw, John. *Bradshaw On: The Family.* Deerfield Beach, Fla.: Health Communications, 1988.
** Branden, Nathaniel, Ph.D. *Honoring the Self.* Boston: Houghton Mifflin, 1983.
* Cermak, Timmen L., M.D. *Diagnosing and Treating Codependence.* Minneapolis: Johnson Institute, 1986.
** Drews, Toby Rice. *Getting Them Sober.* Plainfield, N.J.: Bridge, 1980.
** Dyer, Wayne W., Ph.D. *Your Erroneous Zones.* New York: Funk & Wagnalls, 1976.
*** Mellody, Pia, and Miller, Andrea Wells. *Breaking Free.* San Francisco: Harper San Francisco, 1989.
*** Norwood, Robin. *Women Who Love Too Much.* New York: Pocket Books, 1985.

** Rachel V. *Family Secrets: Life Stories of Adult Children of Alcoholics.* New York: Harper & Row, 1987.
** Schaef, Anne Wilson. *Codependence: Misunderstood—Mistreated.* New York: Harper & Row, 1986.
*** Wegscheider-Cruse, Sharon. *Choicemaking: For Codependents, Adult Children, and Spirituality Seekers.* Pompano Beach, Fla.: Health Communications, 1985.
*** Wegscheider-Cruse, Sharon. *Another Chance: Hope and Health for the Alcoholic Family.* Deerfield Beach, Fla.: Health Communications, 1988.
*** Woititz, Janet. *Adult Children of Alcoholics.* Pompano Beach, Fla.: Health Communications, 1983.

GETTING HELP

*** Johnson, Vernon E., Ph.D. *Intervention.* Minneapolis: The Johnson Institute, 1986.
** Moore, Jean, ed. *Roads to Recovery.* New York: Macmillan, 1985.

RECOVERY

*** Anonymous. *Alcoholics Anonymous: The Big Book.* New York: AA World Services, 1955.
*** Larsen, Earnie. *Stage II Recovery.* New York: Harper & Row, 1985.
** Larsen, Earnie. *Stage II Relationships.* New York: Harper & Row, 1987.
* Miller, Alice. *The Drama of the Gifted Child.* New York: Basic Books, 1981.
** Moz, Jane Middleton, and Dwinell, Lorie. *After the Tears.* Pompano Beach, Fla.: Health Communications, 1986.
** Wegscheider-Cruse, Sharon. *The Miracle of Recovery.* Deerfield Beach, Fla.: Health Communications, 1989.

INDEX